D1393866

THE POET'S TIME

POLITICS AND RELIGION IN
THE WORK OF ANDREW MARVELL

THE POET'S TIME

POLITICS AND RELIGION IN
THE WORK OF ANDREW MARVELL

WARREN L. CHERNAIK

LECTURER IN ENGLISH, QUEEN MARY COLLEGE,
UNIVERSITY OF LONDON

CAMBRIDGE UNIVERSITY PRESS

CAMBRIDGE
LONDON NEW YORK NEW ROCHELLE
MELBOURNE SYDNEY

Published by the Press Syndicate of the University of Cambridge
The Pitt Building, Trumpington Street, Cambridge CB2 1RP
32 East 57th Street, New York, NY 10022, USA
296 Beaconsfield Parade, Middle Park, Melbourne 3206, Australia

© Cambridge University Press 1983

First published 1983

Printed in Great Britain by
New Western Printing Limited, Bristol

Library of Congress catalogue card number: 82–4395

British Library Cataloguing in publication data
Chernaik, W.
The poet's time.
1. Marvell, Andrew – Criticism and interpretation
I. Title
821'.4   PR3546
ISBN 0 521 24773 X

TO MY MOTHER
AND IN MEMORY OF MY FATHER

When the Sword glitters ore the Judges head,
And fear has Coward Churchmen silenced,
Then is the Poets time, 'tis then he drawes,
And single fights forsaken Vertues cause.

('Tom May's Death', lines 63–6)

CONTENTS

Contents

ACKNOWLEDGEMENTS

Any scholarly book is a cooperative enterprise, and over the past ten years or so I have acquired many debts of gratitude. Elsie Duncan-Jones, L. A. Davies, and A. J. Smith have read the entire manuscript and made valuable suggestions for its improvement. Judith Chernaik, acting as editor and conscience, has read more drafts than either of us cares to remember. Hilton Kelliher, Thomas Kranidas, Basil Greenslade, Mara Maizitis, Michael Gearin-Tosh, Mark Kishlansky, Donald Friedman, Christine Rees, and Peter Dixon have read and commented on individual chapters or sections in earlier form. Friends who have helped me to clarify my ideas about literature, history, and politics include Charles Peake, Richard Bernstein, Isobel Grundy, Valerie Pearl, Ruth Nevo, Patricia Thomson, Christopher Reid, Michael Bruce, Thomas and Margaret Healy, Meryl Smith, and Howard Zinn. Like all students at Yale twenty-odd years ago, I bear the ineradicable stamp of my teachers, especially Maynard Mack, Talbot Donaldson, and Louis Martz, and I owe an incalculable debt to the writings of Christopher Hill and Rosalie Colie. I am particularly grateful to Caroline Robbins, whose writings on Marvell's political career remain indispensable, and to John Wallace, George de F. Lord, and Annabel Patterson, against whose ideas I have sometimes tested my own, in what I hope is a friendly colloquy and not gladiatorial combat. My work on the book was materially aided by grants-in-aid awarded by the British Academy and by the American Philosophical Society, as well as, in its very last stages, a grant from Queen Mary College. The helpfulness and courtesy of Terence Moore and Maureen Leach of Cambridge University Press have been exemplary, and I have had the expert clerical assistance of Helen Baz and Sherry Zeffert. Portions of this book have appeared, in an earlier form, in *Renaissance and Modern Studies*, 16 (University of Nottingham,

ACKNOWLEDGEMENTS

1972), 25–36; and in *Tercentenary Essays in Honor of Andrew Marvell*, ed. Kenneth Friedenreich (Archon Books, 1977), pp. 268–96: I am grateful for permission to reprint.

London
March 1982

1 · THE TWO WORLDS

The forward Youth that would appear
Must now forsake his *Muses* dear,
  Nor in the Shadows sing
  His Numbers languishing.
'Tis time to leave the Books in dust,
And oyl th'unused Armours rust:
  Removing from the Wall,
  The Corslet of the Hall.[1]

Poets entering the world of politics have always laboured under certain difficulties. The fate of Cinna the poet in *Julius Caesar*, who wandered out on the street and was torn to pieces for the name he bore (or for his bad verses) seems somehow archetypal – the threatened end, all the more painful for its absurdity and utter lack of decorum, lying in wait for all poets who feel impelled to 'leave the Books in dust, / And oyl th'unused Armours rust'. Milton's account of his feelings at taking up his sword is classic:

I trust hereby to make it manifest with what small willingnesse I endure to interrupt the pursuit of no lesse hopes then these, and leave a calme and pleasing solitarynes fed with cherful and confident thoughts, to imbark in a troubled sea of noises and hoars disputes, put from beholding the bright countenance of truth in the quiet and still air of delightful studies to come into the dim reflexion of hollow antiquities sold by the seeming bulk, and there be fain to club quotations with men whose learning and belief lies in marginal stuffings...Let any gentle apprehension that can distinguish learned pains from unlearned drudgery, imagin what pleasure or profoundness can be in this, or what honour to deal against such adversaries.[2]

The worst indignity the poet faces is the likelihood that, having submitted to the onerous command of the 'great task-Master', stifling any feelings of rebellion against 'the meanest under-service, if God by his Secretary conscience injoyn it', he finds that no one will listen to him.³ The blind rage of the mob, even a descent into the fetid morass of political intrigue, are in some ways easier to face than the bland indifference of the practical man of affairs. James Harrington, presenting his elaborate, comprehensive scheme for settling the future of England to Cromwell, who remarked that he had no intention of giving up his power for 'a little paper shot'; Milton, publishing *The Readie and Easie Way to Establish a Free Commonwealth* when the Restoration of Charles II had become a certainty; or, to choose a more recent example described by Norman Mailer in *The Armies of the Night*, the handful of intellectuals outside the Pentagon who thought that the symbolic act of stepping over a police line would overthrow the American military-industrial complex – are all quintessential figures.⁴ A voice crying in the wilderness is, almost by definition, unheard.

Yet the poet-prophet must write; even if the inhabitants of the cave prefer their darkness, the poet cannot cease telling them of the realms of light. Milton's lamentation at the English nation's headlong plunge into the darkness of servility and 'the base necessitie of court flatteries and prostrations' is at once a recognition of man's fear of freedom and an anguished protest, that, even now, it is not too late. In *The Readie and Easie Way*, Milton tries to shame his audience into accepting the responsibility of freedom:

That a nation should be so valorous and courageous to winn thir liberty in the field, and when they have wonn it, should be so heartless and unwise in their counsels, as not to know how to use it, value it, what to do with it or with themselves; but after ten or twelve years prosperous warr and contestation with tyrannie, basely and besottedly to run their necks again into the yoke which they have broken, and prostrate all the fruits of thir victory for naught at the feet of the vanquishd, besides our loss of glorie, and such an example as kings or tyrants never yet had the like to boast of, will be an ignominie if it befall us, that never yet befell any nation possessed of thir libertie. (*CPW*, VII, 428)

The poet's inner necessity is independent of his outer circumstances; indeed, he is driven all the more to sing of light when 'on evil days ... fall'n, and evil tongues; / In darkness, and with dangers compast round, / And solitude' (*Paradise Lost*, VII lines

26–8), asserting his inner freedom when outward freedom appears to have been extinguished.

Marvell's lines in 'Tom May's Death' provide a fine statement of the role and responsibilities of the poet in an ugly and chaotic world:

> When the Sword glitters ore the Judges head,
> And fear has Coward Churchmen silenced,
> Then is the Poets time, 'tis then he drawes,
> And single fights forsaken Vertues cause.
> He, when the wheel of Empire, whirleth back,
> And though the World's disjointed Axel crack,
> Sings still of ancient Rights and better Times,
> Seeks wretched good, arraigns successful Crimes. (lines 63–70)

The ideal stated here serves as explicit standard by which the 'most servil wit, and Mercenary Pen' (line 40) of May, as Marvell presents him in the poem, can be judged. Heroes are rare: most men are ruled by expediency rather than conscience. The Tom Mays of the world aspire to the high office of poet, but are impostors. In many ways, Marvell's attitude toward May resembles Dryden's toward Shadwell. 'Tom May's Death', like *MacFlecknoe*, anathematizes a false claimant to poetic greatness, accusing him of subverting moral and literary standards, prostituting the 'spotless knowledge and the studies chast' (line 72) of poetry to unworthy uses and pretending to a poetic stature he does not possess. Like Dryden, Marvell sets out to refute his opponent's claim to be the true heir of Ben Jonson – in Marvell's case, by bringing Jonson into the poem to serve as his poetic spokesman, banishing May from the Elysian Fields. But the contrast between the ringing denunciations and affirmations of 'Tom May's Death' and the ironic poise of *MacFlecknoe* reflects a fundamental difference in attitude as well as technique. Dryden's terms are more exclusively literary and his stance somehow more secure; he writes as guardian of and spokesman for a tradition, rather than as a lonely, beleaguered voice for right.

The note of heroic defiance in Marvell's lines, with their picture of the one just man armed against adversity by his faith alone, indicates some of the problems a poet may face when he enters into political controversy. Faith requires no food other than the spiritual; but the realm of politics is the actual. The satirist or

3

controversialist needs to prove his case, and the poet enmeshed in circumstances needs somehow to maintain the force of his convictions. The poet's advantage over the ordinary man is that he inhabits two worlds at once. He is not confined to the immediate phenomenal world and its muddled, shifting values, but can preserve a vision of 'better Times' – a paradise lost or the prospect of a paradise regained:

> Hence oft I think, if in some happy Hour
> High Grace should meet in one with highest Pow'r ...
> What we might hope, what wonderful Effect
> From such a wish'd Conjuncture might reflect.
> Sure, the mysterious Work, where none withstand,
> Would forthwith finish under such a Hand:
> Fore-shortned Time its useless Course would stay,
> And soon precipitate the latest Day.
> But a thick Cloud about that Morning lyes,
> And intercepts the Beams of Mortal eyes.[5]

As the lines indicate, though a poet may see reason to hope for the millennium, he can never assume it has occurred. All men are fallible and their vision necessarily limited; poets are not exempt from the taint of mortality, nor from the dangers of error and self-delusion. The two poems by Marvell I have quoted – one, in 1650, bitterly attacking May's apostasy in supporting the Parliamentary side in the Civil War, and the other, written five years later, fixing millennial hopes in Cromwell's government – can indicate how thick the cloud before the eyes even of a poet–seer may be.[6] The poet's daemon may be giving him bad advice; the strongest and most certain convictions may simply be fallacious.

One of Marvell's strengths is his consistent awareness of the dangers of spiritual pride and blind self-assurance. He addresses his insufferable antagonist Samuel Parker to this effect in *The Rehearsal Transpros'd*:

You do hereby seem to imagine, that Providence should have contrived all things according to the utmost perfection, or that which you conceive would have been most to your purpose. Whereas in the shape of Mans body, and in the frame of the world, there are many things indeed lyable to Objection, and which might have been better if we should give ear to proud and curious Spirits. But we must nevertheless be content with such bodies, and to inhabit such an Earth as it has pleased God to allot us.[7]

4

In a sense, the poet is the only realist. His private vision does not blind him to the world around him or disable him from functioning. Instead, it enables him to see more clearly in order to act, to distinguish among alternatives (and to provide guidance for others) in the world he inhabits with all men. As Milton writes in *Areopagitica*:

To sequester out of the world into *Atlantick* and *Eutopian* polities, which never can be drawn into use, will not mend our condition; but to ordain wisely as in this world of evill, in the midd'st whereof God hath plac't us unavoidably. (*CPW*, ii, 526)

Though Marvell and Milton shared many of the same concerns, their careers in the Commonwealth and Restoration years followed different patterns. Where Milton abandoned the world of political action after 1660 in pursuit of a paradise within and dedicated his last years to the construction of a self-contained imaginative universe, Marvell beginning with the mid-1650s deliberately chose action over contemplation, fully aware of what he was sacrificing in doing so. Both Marvell and Milton are in their later poetry committed to a moral vision, but one chose the realm of epic poetry, the other that of satiric and occasional writing, where the imagination, no longer able in entire freedom to create 'Far other Worlds, and other Seas', has to fight a running battle with fact. Perhaps, as several critics have suggested, the delicate and precise equilibrium of Marvell's lyrics, with their elegance, fastidiousness, and worldly unworldliness, represents a precise moment in literary history which could never be extended or repeated.[8] But these lyrics make up a small fraction of Marvell's total œuvre. The debate between withdrawal and involvement was resolved for Marvell (insofar as it can ever be resolved) by the decision to write a literature of commitment, which attempts to preserve the inner vision in the world of action and events. Perhaps the neglect in which Marvell's later writings so long have lain is testimony to how difficult it is for a poet to maintain that vision 'in a troubled sea of noises and hoars disputes'; if the poet himself manages to stay afloat, the reader, surrounded by the flotsam of half-forgotten circumstances, ephemeral quarrels between furious yet shadowy antagonists, is likely to sink or to strike out for shore at the first opportunity, never to venture on these waters again.

Nevertheless, the neglect of the bulk of a major poet's work seems to me unjustified. The stature of the author alone is reason enough to examine Marvell's later writings carefully, and not rest behind phrases like the 'dissociation of sensibility' or the assumption that the past is irrecoverable, a mass of endless, unconnected, ultimately meaningless details, or that involvement in the world means surrender to it.

A satirist, controversialist, or writer on topical subjects presents certain special problems to the critic. A scholar approaching a work by such a writer needs to exercise great tact in maintaining a balance between two perspectives, historical and literary, never allowing one to overwhelm the other. It is equally unsatisfactory to treat a literary work as a neutral historical document or to ignore its historical circumstances entirely. Marvell scholars, when they treat his later works at all, seem to me, with rare exceptions, to have failed to provide an adequate context, literary or historical, by which the works can be understood.

A case in point is John M. Wallace's *Destiny His Choice: The Loyalism of Andrew Marvell*, the most extensive study to date of Marvell's political writings.[9] The general principle which underlies Wallace's study is incontestable: when an author deals with political events and themes, a full understanding of the work requires careful attention to its historical circumstances and to relevant issues of political theory. Yet Wallace's book aids the reader's understanding of Marvell far less than one would hope; indeed, the book seems to me a particularly striking example of learning misapplied, devoting great care, scholarship, and ingenuity to the support of a highly questionable thesis, to which all considerations of literary form or historical context are subordinated. Wallace finds in Marvell a consistent love of 'moderation and agreement', an overriding belief that since the ways of providence are unpredictable, 'loyalism' or nonresistance to *de facto* power becomes a prime moral necessity. 'An Horatian Ode', for all its 'multiple ironies' and 'semblance of impartiality', is to Wallace essentially an argument for accepting the legitimacy of Cromwell's rule; indeed, even Charles I, in his dignified resignation to his fate, is in Wallace's view tacitly abdicating and giving 'permission' to Cromwell's succession. *The First Anniversary* carries the doctrine of acceptance a step further: to Wallace, the poem's unifying factor is a covert argument that Cromwell consent to be crowned as King and inaugurate a new line of English monarchs.[10] Wallace continues to find a consistent 'loyalism' in the anti-government poems and pamphlets Marvell wrote after the Restoration. Poems and prose works which to other readers might appear to be bitter attacks on the court of Charles II (and by implication on Charles himself) are to Wallace adjurations to 'accept what was given and make the best of God's designs... The alternative to loyalty could not be contemplated without the thought of another civil war.' Even *An Account of the Growth of Popery and Arbitrary Government in England* (1677), a Whig pamphlet whose basic attitude is clearly indicated in its title, is somehow transmogrified into a plea for moderation and unity, expressing a 'loyalty ... to Charles II even when there was the least reason to trust him'.[11]

Mr Wallace's book is learned, intelligent, and consistently stimulating, and furthermore he is one of the few critics to treat Marvell's later writings seriously. But the Marvell he presents in his book is simply unrecognizable. The consistent opponent of arbitrary power and champion of man's rational freedom becomes a proponent of 'a strong executive' under all circumstances; the Country Party satirist and pamphleteer, of whom Caroline Robbins can justly say, 'his work became a part of every Whig history, his integrity the text of every diatribe against corruption', is turned into a moderate royalist, not unlike Waller or even Dryden.[12] If a poem like 'The Kings Vowes' or 'The Statue in Stocks-Market' fails to fit into his view of a Marvell consistently respectful of royal authority and dignity, Wallace simply excludes it from the canon, using the argument that 'none of Marvell's indisputable writings can be accused of levity on so important a subject' or shows such 'coarse freedom' or 'the debasement of a low style'.[13] Besides its patent circularity, the statement betrays a radical misunderstanding of the principle governing any author's style and approach, 'the grand master peece to observe' in satire as in any literary work: decorum.[14]

'The debasement of a low style' in Marvell or another satirist is likely to be quite deliberate, since it is one of his major satiric weapons. Style should fit the subject, and when it does not, the satirist argues that the fault lies not with him but with the object of his satire. The inappropriate 'low' terms of *Hudibras*, the inappropriate 'high' terms of *MacFlecknoe*, are designed to reflect and to expose the specious pretences of Presbyterian squire and hack poet. The satirist holds the mirror of truth up to imposture: 'my purpose', Milton writes in one of his anti-prelatical tracts, 'is not ... to looke on my adversary abroad, through the deceaving glasse of other mens great opinion of him, but at home, where I may finde him in the proper light of his owne worth' (*CPW*, I, 869). If he fails to treat Samuel Parker with the dignity becoming a clergyman, Marvell says, it is because Parker has failed to act in a manner befitting his position. Parker has violated reason and decorum, not Marvell:

For it is not impossible that a man by evil arts may have crept into the Church, thorow the Belfry or at the Windows. 'Tis not improbable that having so got in he should foul the Pulpit, and afterwards the Press with opinions destructive to Humane Society and the Christian Religion. That he should illustrate so corrupt Doctrines with as ill a conversation, and adorn the lasciviousness of his life with an equal petulancy of stile and language...In this Case it is that I think a Clergy-man is laid open to the Pen of any one that knows how to manage it; and that every person who has either Wit, Learning or Sobriety is licens'd, if debauch'd to curb him, if erroneous to catechize him, and if foul-mouth'd and biting, to muzzle him. For they do but abuse themselves who shall any longer consider or reverence such an one as a Clergy-man, who as oft as he undresses degrades himself and would never have come into the Church but to take Sanctuary. (*RT*, II, pp. 163–4)[15]

The position Marvell is arguing is commonly upheld by the Augustan satirists in their *apologiae*, as well as by Milton. Like Dryden and Pope, he represents himself as reluctant to unsheathe his sword, even in self-defence: 'not to Write at all is much the safer course of life', and both modesty and Christian charity suggest that it is preferable to 'have sate at home in quiet' than to 'send a Chalenge to all Readers' by entering into controversy (*RT*, II, pp. 159–60). An author ought to be particularly wary, furthermore, of engaging in 'Invective' from reasons of personal pique: 'it is a praedatory course of life, and indeed but a privateering upon reputation' (II, p. 162).[16] Yet when a man (especially one who is 'prosperously unjust') has become, in Dryden's words, 'a public nuisance', it is the poet's responsibility as artist and citizen to speak out:

'Tis an action of virtue to make examples of vicious men. They may and ought to be upbraided with their crimes and follies: both for their own amendment, if they are not yet incorrigible, and for the terror of others, to hinder them from falling into those enormities which they see are so severely punished in the persons of others.[17]

Or, as Marvell puts it, 'wheresoever men shall find the footing of so wanton a Satyr out of his own bounds, the neighbourhood ought, notwithstanding all his pretended capering Divinity, to hunt him thorow the woods with hounds and horn home to his harbour' (*RT*, II, pp. 164–5).

In leading the hue and cry after the vicious man, the poet is acting out of the dictates of his conscience as representative of the community:

He that hath once Printed an ill book has thereby condens'd his words on purpose lest they should be carried away by the wind; he has diffused his poyson so publickly in design that it might be beyond his own recollection; and put himself deliberately past the reach of any private admonition. (*RT*, II, p. 164)

Pope similarly sees the poet as communal voice in those situations where 'private admonition' is no longer sufficient.

> Ask you what Provocation I have had?
> The strong Antipathy of Good to Bad.
> When Truth or Virtue an Affront endures,
> Th'Affront is mine, my Friend, and should be yours...
> Mine, as a Friend to ev'ry worthy mind;
> And mine as Man, who feel for all mankind.[18]

Under ordinary circumstances, a man of the clergy ought to be treated with respect ('the Clergy certainly of all others ought to be kept and preserv'd sacred in their Reputation', *RT*, II, p. 162) and the decencies of public order ought to be observed. But when the times are corrupt, when those in power connive at offences rather than attempt to 'stop the infection ... and chase the blown Deer out of their Heard' (II, p. 164), the poet recognizes a greater obligation than that of expediency, a higher decorum in truth; he 'seeks wretched good, arraigns successful Crimes'. The position which Marvell is arguing here is closely parallel to the liberal contract theory which he defends throughout his political writings. Public order is desirable, but is not an absolute good; when a choice must be made, the commands of conscience take precedence over the commands of the state. Marvell consistently opposes the claim put forth by Parker and other defenders of absolutism that the authority of the state or the requirements of propriety are necessities against which there can be no appeal. The grounds for his defence of individual conscience, as we shall see in later chapters, are both practical and theoretical, secular and religious. But one major element in this defence is an appeal to common sense, in terms which anticipate Locke. When a society is unjust, and those in authority do not 'take care to redress in good season whatsoever corruptions that may indanger and infect the Government', Marvell says in *The Rehearsal Transpros'd*, then the citizens of the state are forced by mere self-preservation, 'Sense and Nature', to exercise their right of revolution and reassume their delegated sovereignty (ii, p. 240). In very similar terms, Locke defends contract theory against accusations that it 'lays a *ferment* for frequent rebellion'. The responsibility for rebellion lies with those who would illegitimately assume arbitrary power, and the exercise of conscientious dissent is not only justified, but inevitable, given the nature of man:

For when the *People* are made *miserable*, and find themselves *exposed to the ill-usage of Arbitrary Power*, cry up their Governours, as much as you will for Sons of *Jupiter*, let them be Sacred and Divine, descended or authorized from Heaven; give them out for whom or what you please, the same will happen. *The People generally ill treated*, and contrary to right, will be ready upon any occasion to ease themselves of a burden that sits heavy upon them.[19]

The view of the artistic and political conscience implicit in Marvell's satires is a militant one, which as we shall see in a later chapter is ultimately religious in origin. 'Tom May's Death' and 'Fleckno, an English Priest in Rome' resemble Marvell's later satires in their essentially Puritan, iconoclastic conception of the function of the artist. In 'Fleckno', the nunnery episode of 'Upon Appleton House', and *The Growth of Popery*, Marvell's strong anti-Catholic bias is not mere xenophobia, but reflects a consistent suspicion of the arts of illusion and 'the Batteries of alluring Sense'. In politics as in art, the poet is 'Sworn Enemy to all that do pretend', exposing the tricks of the enchanters who hold truth prisoner.[20] There can be no compromise with evil and deception:

the figure of Jonson in 'Tom May's Death' and the figure of young William Fairfax in the nunnery episode of 'Upon Appleton House' reflect a militant attitude toward the unending war of truth and falsity which we also find in Milton and Spenser. Any uncertainties which young Fairfax initially feels, when faced with the perfumed 'Art' with which the *'Suttle Nunns'* are enabled to 'cheat' their dupes, are resolved by the Christian hero's clear sense of right and wrong and awareness of moral imperatives: for Fairfax, religion 'dazled not but clear'd his sight' ('Upon Appleton House', lines 94, 204, 228). This is the imagery of Arthur's shield or the stripping of Duessa: Roman Catholicism, typical to Marvell of the illusionists who seek to impose the magical hand of authority over their victims, is defined as a 'bold imposture' masquerading 'under the name of Christianity', depending on the 'credulity of mankind' for the power it holds (*Growth of Popery*, pp. 5–6). Since 'vice infects the very Wall' they inhabit, since they have the ability to 'alter all' around them, turning even the well-meaning waverers 'fraudulent' like them ('Upon Appleton House', lines 215–16), the only recourse is to 'Fly from their Ruine' (line 223) in self-preservation or to oppose them directly.

> But sure those Buildings last not long
> Founded by Folly, kept by Wrong.
> I know what Fruit their Gardens yield,
> When they it think by Night conceal'd.
> Fly from their Vices. (lines 217–21)

The hero-satirist is able to 'set to view' the *'Relicks false'* and 'superstitions vainly fear'd' (lines 260–1) by which the enchanters hoodwink their victims; exposed to the light of day, bereft of his magical arts, the enchanter is stripped bare and revealed in his 'true proportion':[21] 'When th' Inchantment ends / The Castle vanishes or rends' ('Upon Appleton House', lines 269–70). The Parkers of the world and the tyrants they serve hope to avoid discovery by clothing themselves in a borrowed dignity, but the poet, armed with his privileged vision, is able to discover the imposture, to reveal the culprit 'in his own likeness':

This is that man who insists so much and stirrops himself upon the Gravity of his Profession, and the Civility of his Education: which if he had in the least observed in respect either to himself or others…I could never have made so bold with him. And nevertheless, it being so necessary to represent him in his own likeness that it may appear what he is to others, and to himself, if possibly he might at last correct his indecencies, I have not committed any fault of stile ... but in his imitation. (*RT*, II, p. 185)

The 'uncasing of a grand imposture' is a serious business, but seriousness of intent ought not to be equated with unbending dignity of style or lack of humour. Marvell's *The Rehearsal Transpros'd* is, among other things, an attempt to show that it is possible to be 'merry and angry' at once (I, p. 145), to combine what Milton calls 'those two most rationall faculties of humane intellect [,] anger and laughter'.[22] The precise nature of the mixture varies with the satirist and the circumstances; he may choose the stance of Jeremiah or that of the man of the world. But in all cases he seeks to render what is potentially dangerous harmless by ridicule and exposure. *The Rehearsal Transpros'd*, Marvell tells us, in a witty variation on the common Renaissance topic of satirist-as-physician, was designed as 'Physick' for Parker, but proved beneficial to others as well:

But some curious persons would be licking at it, and most Men finding it not distastful to the Palate, it grew in short time to be of common use in the Shops. I perceive that it wrought a sensible alteration in all that took it; but varying in some for the better, in others for the worse, according to the difference of their Complexions. Some were swoln up to the Throat, some their Heads turn'd round, and others it made their Hearts ake; but all these were few in number; most Men found only a little tingling in their Ears, and after its greatest violence, it discharged it self in an innocent fit of uncessant laughter. (*RT*, II, p. 156)

The wit in the passage, as so often in Marvell, lies in its treating an ordinarily submerged or moribund metaphor with an unaccustomed and disconcerting literalness, and thus bringing it to life in unexpected ways. Stylistically and in its approach towards its audience, the passage is far removed from the 'grim laughter' of Milton's 'strong and sinewy' prose. Milton's sense of decorum accommodates 'a vehement vein throwing out indignation, or scorn upon an object that merits it', the holy anger of God's champion smiting his master's enemies (*CPW*, I, 663–4, 889), but Marvell, addressing an audience more likely to recognize a shared bond as wits than as true warfaring Christians, is playful, ironic, flexible in his style. The assumed naïveté with which Marvell lists the extraordinary effects of the dish he has cooked up, the detached neutrality with which the central medical conceit is developed, in language from which any dimension but the purely physical and mechanistic has been deliberately excluded, looks backward to the extended metaphysical conceit and forward to the irony of Swift.

Decorum is necessarily the key to all occasional writing. Decorum of style is only an aspect of a larger decorum; each detail must be appropriate to the occasion and consonant with the work's central purpose. The critic must search for the unifying factor, the fundamental organizing principle of a work – he cannot rest content with providing large and miscellaneous chunks of historical background or a catalogue of metaphors, topoi, or rhetorical devices, but must attempt to ascertain what the author does with his materials, how he organizes them into a coherent whole.

One central distinction in Marvell's writings on political themes is between works which seek to persuade and works which do not. Marvell's two major works upon Cromwell and Fairfax written during the unsettled times of the Commonwealth are among the greatest political poems in the language, but neither 'An Horatian Ode' nor 'Upon Appleton House' can properly be said to be persuasive in intent. Instead, both are works of historical analysis, seeking not to inculcate a particular attitude, but to present a problem in all its complexity, to indicate the choices facing men at a given historical moment. Perhaps the greatness of the two poems lies in part in their refusal to simplify or to assume a straightforward partisan stance, their qualities of 'negative capability'. But after the establishment of the Protectorate in 1654 and, even more definitively, after the collapse of Puritan hopes at the Restoration, Marvell felt less and less able to write poetry and prose which was uncommitted in this sense· The poet is no longer the 'easie Philosopher', passing unscathed through 'busie Companies of Men' in pursuit of his 'delicious Solitude', but a man who has been singled out by 'the same god whoe hath chosen ... out' individual men, however humble and unworthy they may feel themselves to be, 'to beare ... testimony to his truth', and, however great the odds against him may be and however limited the chances of his success, to assume unaided the championship in battle of 'forsaken Vertues cause'.[23] Where earlier his conscience had caused him to hesitate, to see the disadvantages as well as the advantages of involvement in worldly affairs (conscience being a 'Heaven-nursed Plant' which 'shrinks at ev'ry touch', 'Upon Appleton House', lines 355, 358), now he has come to feel that 'God by his Secretary conscience' (Milton, *CPW*, I, 822) has compelled him into action. The most remarkable paradox about Marvell is his being at once a Puritan and a wit, a fastidious ironist and a committed believer. Thus when he enters the arena he brings his full arsenal of wit with him and, with great practicality, deploys it to the maximum persuasive effect. Since the world 'will not be better', it is necessary at all times to 'stand upon [one's] Guard'; 'though I carry always some ill Nature about me,' he writes in *The Rehearsal Transpros'd*, 'yet it is I hope no more than is in this world necessary for a Preservative' (*RT*, II, p. 165):

In this World a good Cause signifys little, unless it be as well defended. A Man may starve at the Feast of good Conscience. My Fencing-master in *Spain*, after he had instructed me all he could, told me, I remember, there was yet one Secret, against which there was no Defence, and that was, to give the first Blow. (*Poems and Letters*, ed. Margoliouth, II, 309)

Marvell's later writings are almost entirely satire and panegyric, genres which can never be neutral, since they aim to persuade, to direct their readers' judgment, often to recommend a particular course of behaviour. In such works, the aesthetic and didactic are inseparable, and the local effects, structural design, and patterns of metaphor and allusion are not only adapted to the particular circumstances from which the work arises, but are intimately connected with, even determined by, its persuasive end.

2 · POWER AND CONSCIENCE: MARVELL AND THE ENGLISH REVOLUTION

I

Though any writer who chooses to write on a political subject seeks to make history coherent, that coherence takes different forms. We can distinguish the approach of the partisan, writing to reinforce the opinions of the converted and win over the uncommitted, from that of the historian, who ideally seeks not to convert but to understand – on the one hand, *Absalom and Achitophel* or John Oldham's *Satyrs against the Jesuits*, presenting the Tory view and the Whig view of the Popish plot; on the other hand, *Julius Caesar*, *Richard II*, the two parts of *Henry IV*. The pattern of Marvell's 'An Horatian Ode', like that of the Shakespearean history play, is dialectical, analysing political events and the moral dilemmas they present in terms of a balance of opposing forces, a dramatic debate between alternatives.

The greatness of the 'Horatian Ode' lies in its ability to rise beyond personal emotion, the natural human need to choose sides, to a level of inevitability where the forces directing choice become visible; the reader is in the position of Milton's God, watching Satan struggle miles below in the toils of illusory freedom. Out of the chaos of individuals and events, the poet finds a controlling dramatic pattern, isolates the historical forces which give the events meaning and coherence. Charles I and Cromwell are seen as actors playing the roles allotted to them. Human events are as inexorably determined as the laws of physics; one cannot escape the inevitable, or expect nature's laws to be suspended in one's favour:

> Nature that hateth emptiness,
> Allows of penetration less:
>> And therefore must make room
>> Where greater Spirits come.   (lines 41–4)

As Joseph Mazzeo has pointed out, Marvell's political realism in the 'Horatian Ode' is akin to that of Machiavelli.[1] The opening section of the poem, with its extended analogy between Cromwell and the overwhelming, amoral force of a lightning bolt, presents a world ruled not by abstract rights or by ethical considerations, but by power. The poet must deal with the world as it is, not the world as we would like it to be:

> .Though Justice against Fate complain,
> And plead the antient Rights in vain:
>> But those do hold or break
>> As Men are strong or weak.   (lines 37–40)

But Marvell differs from Machiavelli in the tribute he pays to the 'antient Rights', and all they represent. To the author of *The Prince*, the criterion of success overrides all other considerations; sentiment, idealism, and ethical scruples are luxuries a ruler cannot usually afford.[2] But to Marvell, ideals retain their validity even in defeat. If the 'antient Rights' and the virtues of 'a greater, a more gracious time', an ordered, aristocratic culture, have been silenced by the incontrovertible demands of historical necessity, this is to Marvell, as it was later to Yeats, a cause for regret.[3] As the roughly contemporaneous 'Upon Appleton House' shows, the poet yearned after the peace, grace, and civility which he felt were no longer able to exist, a world where 'Gardens only had their Towrs, / And all the Garrisons were Flowrs' (lines 331–2). His commendatory poem on Richard Lovelace's *Lucasta* (1649) speaks of Lovelace's poems (most of them written only a short time before) as the product of a departed 'candid Age', already receding into the past, in which a poet's 'sweet Muse' was still able to sing of love and honour. The present 'times', as he portrays them here, are governed by joyless envy, 'much degenerate' from Lovelace's: 'These Vertues are now banisht out of Towne, / Our Civill Wars have lost the Civicke crowne' ('To his Noble Friend Mr. Richard Lovelace, upon his Poems', lines 1–2, 5, 11–12). The best-known lines of the 'Horatian Ode', the portrait of Charles I at the scaffold, represent Marvell's tribute to the doomed civilization, whose values find their clearest expression in defeat. An aristocrat may be defined as one who knows how to die gracefully. Charles I, like Shakespeare's Richard II, acts as a king should only when faced with the prospect of being unkinged. His life is given meaning by its last act:

> *He* nothing common did, or mean,
> Upon the memorable Scene:
>   But with his keener Eye
>   The Axes edge did try:
> Nor call'd the *Gods* with vulgar spight
> To vindicate his helpless Right,
>   But bow'd his comely Head
>   Down, as upon a Bed.   (lines 57–64)

The sympathy in the lines goes hand in hand with dispassionate historical analysis. Given his inner nature and his circumstances, the 'Royal Actor born' (line 53) was irresistibly led to the scaffold, and once there could only behave as he did. The very virtues of Charles and his civilization – taste, good breeding, a strong sense of propriety and restraint, a dignified acceptance of one's fate – go far to explain his defeat.

Man is not able to direct or even to predict his destiny. 'For men may spare their pains where Nature is at work', Marvell writes in looking back upon the events of the Civil War in *The Rehearsal Transpros'd*, 'and the world will not go the faster for our driving' (*RT*, I, p. 135). But man's limited control over his surroundings does not make all action futile. Man's freedom for Marvell is grounded upon his awareness of the limits of his power. We need not, in the terms of 'To his Coy Mistress', languish in time's 'slow-chapt power', but can exercise our wills to control that time allotted us: 'though we cannot make our Sun / Stand still, yet we will make him run' (lines 40, 45–6). In the 'Horatian Ode', Marvell suggests the interplay between what is fated and what is voluntary by speaking of Cromwell as having 'urged his active Star' (line 12). The successful man, in Machiavellian terms, is one who seizes the presented occasion; the time, unfortunately for Charles, was wrong for him, right for Cromwell. Cromwell's iron self-control, expressing itself at the appropriate time as 'industrious Valour' and 'wiser Art' – 'So much one Man can do, / That does both act and know' – enables him to ride the whirlwind, appear for the moment at least to master fortune (lines 33, 48, 75–6).

Virtu, the quality by which men are enabled to master fortune, is in Machiavelli ethically neutral. The question remains whether the *virtu* of Cromwell in the 'Horatian Ode' is similarly neutral, beyond good and evil, and whether the agency the poem describes as controlling men's affairs is an amoral fortune or a Christian providence. Throughout the 'Horatian Ode', Marvell is careful to use terms that are classical rather than explicitly or even covertly Christian; there is none of the transparent pseudo-classical terminology, suggesting a Christian meaning by simple substitution, which we find for example in *Comus*. The one phrase in the poem with strong Christian (or Old Testament) connotations is 'the force of angry Heavens flame' (line 26), and even this phrase is susceptible of a purely classical reading. One cannot assume that palaces and temples, enemies and emulous allies are all being scourged for their sins. To find the heavy hand of judgment and divine election in every line of the poem, consigning Cromwell to a place among the elect and Charles among the damned, is to create an entirely different and quite inferior poem. Indeed, a Marxist or Hegelian reading of the poem, seeing Charles and Cromwell as unwitting agents of the impersonal force of historical necessity (or alternatively, without danger of anachronism, a Harringtonian reading with similar emphases – Marvell was a friend of the author of *Oceana*, published six years later, but begun at about the time of the 'Horatian Ode'), does it far less violence than an overtly Christian reading which would endanger the poem's ironic poise. The classical, secular framework, here as in 'To his Coy Mistress', permits a dramatic tension which the introduction of explicitly Christian terms would subvert: the Roman historical parallels and the classical ethical values implicit in the presentation of Charles and Cromwell are in keeping with the ideas of an amoral Fortune and a Fate indifferent to human ideas of justice and merciless to human weaknesses.

Nevertheless, there is a sense in which the poem's 'Fate' is compatible with Christian providence. An ironic consciousness of human limitations lies at the heart of Marvell's poetry. One of his central themes is education by experience: the contrast between the uninformed, 'unprepar'd' (*First Anniversary*, line 150) and the informed perspective, between naïveté or false expectations and knowledge, unites such disparate poems as 'Clorinda and Damon', 'Young Love', 'The Coronet', *The First Anniversary*, and 'The Picture of little T.C. in a Prospect of Flowers'. But the central awareness that 'Grass withers; and the Flow'rs too fade' ('Clorinda and Damon', line 7), whether stated in Christian or in pagan terms, is only rarely presented as the confrontation of militant truth with error; more often, as in 'The Nymph complaining for the death of her Faun' and 'The Mower's Song', the scrupulousness with which Marvell renders the limited point of view of his puzzled innocent adds to the poem's poignancy. By treating Charles's execution as a dramatic scene enacted on a stage, with the 'armed Bands' (line 55) a callous audience, Marvell achieves a degree of ironic detachment from the painful events described. The scene is explicitly presented as 'Tragick' (line 54), evoking the emotions of pity and fear; yet the death of Charles is seen as an episode in the continuing drama of history, a 'memorable Hour' (line 65) which both separates and links the past and the future. Like the lines in 'Upon Appleton House' on fallen England, the 'dear and happy Isle' (line 321) now laid waste, the lines on the King's execution are informed by a tragic irony based ultimately on a conviction which Marvell shares with Milton: that all human things are controlled by 'the will of Heaven'. We cannot know what lot is assigned to us, but whether it turn out to be 'mean' or 'high', we are compelled to accept it.[4] It is far easier to exult in the moment of victory, to bask in divine approval during periods of good fortune, identifying God's cause with our own, than to recognize a providential pattern in defeat, to contemplate the rubble of our hopes with equanimity: 'History to the defeated / May say alas but cannot help or pardon'.[5]

The final section of 'An Horatian Ode' suggests, more or less conditionally, that there is a higher justice, by which the apparent conflict of impotent right and moral power can be resolved. It may be that the new government which has emerged after the death of Charles I will unite strength and justice, exemplifying not power raging unbounded, destroying all it touches, or powerless civility, but power turned to effective use, held in check by law, reason, and self-control. But if this possibility is envisioned, it is no more than a hope. To think we can anticipate God or fate, or to claim God's imprimatur for our actions, is blind arrogance:

For there is not now any express Revelation, no Inspiration of a Prophet, nor Unction of that Nature as to the declaring of that particular person that is to Govern. Only God hath in general commanded and disposed men to be Governed...but I do not understand that God has thereby imparted and devolved to the Magistrate his Divine Jurisdiction. God that sees into the thoughts of mens hearts, and to whom both Princes and Subjects are accountable, sees not as man sees nor judges as he judges; but is his own Measure and the first Rectitude. (*RT*, II, p. 250)

In speaking of providence, Marvell consistently emphasizes its inscrutability rather than seeking like Milton to demonstrate God's mercy and benevolence: it is hard enough to understand God's ways, much less 'justify' them to man in rational, comprehensible terms. Kings are raised up and pulled down, events follow one another in rapid and confused succession, and we are aware of the providential pattern only in hindsight.

An extended simile comparing Cromwell to a falcon, perching on a tree after his kill and within the falconer's grasp, indicates the seriousness of the problem facing England in 1650, while suggesting a possible solution. The destructive force of the falcon is limitless and irrational in itself, but it can be tamed and made subordinate to the will of the falconer. The arbitrary power men long for, Marvell says again and again in his prose writings, is that of a 'brutal' world, suitable for 'cattle' but not for rational creatures. Those who hold

the Government of Mankind...might have [been] given as large an extent of ground and other kind of cattle for their Subjects: but it had been a melancholy Empire to have been only Supreme Grasiers and Soveraign Shepherds. And therefore, though the laziness of that brutal magistracy might have been more secure, yet the difficulty of this does make it more honourable...Even Law is force, and the execution of that Law is a greater Violence; and therefore upon rational creatures not to be used but upon the utmost extremity. (*RT*, I, p. 111)

The 'Horatian Ode' is at one with Marvell's other political writings in making the renunciation of absolute power the condition upon which the future harmony of the state depends. Cromwell is described as 'Nor yet grown stiffer with Command, / But still in the *Republick*'s hand' (lines 81–2). Several critics have commented on the conditions ('nor yet', 'what he may') hedging round the praise of Cromwell's magnanimity, suggesting a momentary equilibrium which may not last.[6]

He to the *Commons Feet* presents
A Kingdome, for his first years rents:
    And, what he may, forbears
    His Fame to make it theirs:
And has his Sword and Spoyls ungirt,
    To lay them at the *Publick's* skirt.   (lines 85–90)

The lines precisely indicate the form of government which existed at the time of writing: neither a monarchy nor a military dictatorship, but a mixed government, in which the ultimate sovereign power lies, if anywhere, in the '*Publick*', or the legislative. Cromwell, the strong and charismatic military leader, represents the executive or monarchical element in the mixed state, and shares power with the Commons who in turn owe their power to the people of England, whose representatives they are.[7] The strong man, under this system, is in theory at least unable to exercise arbitrary power, since his power is not supreme: he is accountable to Parliament.

The problem, of course, is how to guarantee that Cromwell will continue to lay his sword and spoils at the public's skirt, that he will turn his military might to hunting 'the *Caledonian* Deer' (line 112) and other external enemies, instead of hunting his own countrymen. Marvell is too much of a realist to present the future as other than uncertain. To rely on the voluntary forbearance of one possessed of power is to rely on a slender thread indeed. Though Marvell consistently gives allegiance to the theory of mixed government, he recognizes its intrinsic weaknesses, and does not pretend that any mechanism exists by which the delicate balance of the moment may be perpetuated. The danger inherent in mixed government is that the groups among whom power is divided will engage in a bitter, unending struggle in which each competitor jealously guards the power he has and tries to reduce the power of the others. The history of seventeenth-century England amply bears out Hobbes's dictum:

If any two men desire the same thing, which nevertheless they cannot both enjoy, they become enemies; and in the way to their end, which is principally their own conservation...endeavour to destroy, or subdue one another.[8]

In Marvell's poem, as in historical fact, power was divided not so much between the executive and the legislative, defined by function, as between the military and the parliament, defined as two separate and, as events proved, incompatible interests. In the poem the deliberative arm and the acting arm are in harmony. History tells us the harmony did not last; Marvell can only hope for the best, without disguising the problems and uncertainties that remain.

Indeed, the profoundly disturbing final lines suggest that, under the conditions described in the 'Horatian Ode', power and right cannot be entirely resolved. The man of *virtu*, faced with unsettled times when every man is a potential enemy, can never lay down his sword. Once the poem sets him in motion, bursting out from 'his private Gardens' (line 29) into the public sector, Cromwell is never seen at rest; he must press forward, alert to all possible adversaries, exerting all his energies in maintaining his position, in the hope that he will remain 'the Wars and Fortunes Son'.

> But thou the Wars and Fortunes Son
> March indefatigably on;
> And for the last effect
> Still keep thy Sword erect:
> Beside the force it has to fright
> The Spirits of the shady Night,
> The same *Arts* that did *gain*
> A *Pow'r* must it *maintain*.   (lines 113–20)

Cromwell's right to power lies only in his possession of it. As a result, he is condemned, as it were, to a state of ceaseless vigilance, and the nation can look forward to a future in which opposing forces exist in unresolved tension, extending onward indefinitely like the parallel lines of 'The Definition of Love'. The poem's concluding lines are not so much a warning to Cromwell to use his power well, as a warning to him to realize how tenuous his hold on power, or any man's, in fact is.

II

Marvell's most famous comment on the English revolution, made twenty-odd years after the fact, combines a recognition of the inevitability of historical processes with a sigh of regret that history took the path it did. If only the aggrieved subjects had been content with 'Patience and Petitions', if only the King had carried out the necessary reforms himself. 'An Horatian Ode' and 'Upon Appleton House' view the events of the Civil War from two entirely different perspectives, appropriate to their central figures, Cromwell and Fairfax, but they share with *The Rehearsal Transpros'd* the ironic recognition that what must be – 'such an Earth as it has pleased God to allot us' – takes precedence over what 'might have been better' (*RT*, II, p. 231). The view of human striving in the passage on the Civil War in *The Rehearsal Transpros'd* is akin to the laughter of the grasshoppers at man's pretensions in 'Upon Appleton House', stanza XLVII; the distance imparted by coupling the downfall of Charles I with the return of Charles II gives the events of contemporary history an inevitability that is as much comic as tragic:

Whether it were a War of Religion, or of Liberty, is not worth the labour to enquire. Which-sover was at the top, the other was at the bottom; but upon considering all, I think the Cause was too good to have been fought for...Even as his present Majesties happy Restauration did it self, so all things else happen in their best and proper time, without any need of our officiousness. (*RT*, I, p. 135)

The 'Horatian Ode', written between May and July 1650, celebrates Cromwell's victorious return from his campaign in Ireland and forecasts even more glorious victories in Scotland. Lord Fairfax, with whom Marvell was to be closely associated for the next few years, reacted differently to the projected invasion of Scotland, and on 26 June ended a year and a half in which he had grown more and more unhappy with the course of the English revolution by resigning his commission as commander-in-chief of the army and retiring from public life. The 'Horatian Ode' appears to resolve the debate between action and contemplation in favour of action, presenting a state of affairs where, through necessity rather than choice, the 'Arts of Peace' must give way to those of war, where civilized leisure and the life devoted to study or to artistic creation have become impossible. But where one might expect Marvell to follow the 'Horatian Ode' with a dedication, willing or reluctant, to the public life, in fact Marvell spent the years 1651 and 1652 in retirement with Fairfax upon the former general's estate at Nun Appleton, serving as tutor to Fairfax's daughter and writing poetry. We can never be sure of the dates of Marvell's poems, but we know that 'Upon Appleton House' and 'Upon the Hill and Grove at Bill-borow' were written during this period, and it is likely that most if not all of his poems making use of pastoral conventions, as well as several others, were written at Nun Appleton. Marvell was an inaccurate prophet in the 'Horatian Ode', at least as far as his own life was concerned, since his residence with Fairfax provided him with the 'Sanctuary' ('Upon Appleton House', line 482) against the uncertainties of the outside world he had despaired of finding. The early 1650s, a period Marvell saw as inhospitable to poetry, were in fact the years of his greatest productivity.

And yet if the poems of the Nun Appleton period celebrate the possibility of erecting an impenetrable bastion against the world, a self-sufficient realm of nature and the imagination, 'annihilating all that's made, / To a green Thought in a green Shade', the ultimate lesson of most of these poems is that such a victory over the world is at best temporary or delusive.

> How safe, methinks, and strong, behind
> These Trees have I incamp'd my Mind;
>
> . . .
>
> Bind me ye *Woodbines* in your 'twines,
> Curle me about ye gadding *Vines*,
> And Oh so close your Circles lace,
> That I may never leave this Place.
> ('Upon Appleton House', lines 601–2, 609–12)

The language in both passages suggests that a permanent escape is unattainable, however much we may wish it to be otherwise; the 'Fetters' will necessarily 'prove too weak', the siege of the world's forces too strong to resist. Dryden in the beginning of *Of Dramatic Poesy: An Essay* manages to reduce the guns of war to a musical background for a leisured discussion of poetry; Marvell is either unwilling or unable to perform such a total transformation, and as a result the sounds of battle and disorder are always present in his poems. Any retreat from the world is precariously achieved, and the world rejected is never out of earshot. In the two stanzas quoted above, Marvell exploits the gap between the narrator's limited knowledge and the reader's more fully informed perspective to create an effect of great poignancy. The succession of strong imperative verbs here and in the next stanza

– 'Bind me', 'curle me about', 'chain me', 'nail me through', 'tie my Chain', 'stake me down', – suggest, like similar passages in Donne's *Holy Sonnets*, both the urgency of the poet's desire and his awareness that its fulfilment is literally impossible in man's earthly state.

The heart of 'Upon Appleton House' is the contrast between the ordinary world and the more perfect 'lesser World' (line 765) found in Fairfax's country estate. The poem takes its origin from the hope of finding a spot on the earth as yet unfallen, a microcosm in which one can exist in perfect tranquillity, provided with all the necessities of life without the attendant problems. Where the greater world is a 'rude heap' (line 762), stripped in its fallen state of beauty, harmony, or meaning, the 'yet green, yet growing Ark' (line 484) to which Marvell is able to retreat shows that man and the earth are not utterly corrupted by the 'Traitor-Worm' of sin (line 554), that it is still possible for the earth to be a garden rather than a desert of a 'Camp of Battail' littered with 'Bodies slain' (lines 420, 422).

> 'Tis not, what once it was, the *World*;
> But a rude heap together hurl'd;
> All negligently overthrown,
> Gulfes, Deserts, Precipices, Stone.
> Your lesser *World* contains the same.
> But in more decent Order tame;
> *You Heaven's Center, Nature's Lap.*
> *And Paradice's only Map.* (lines 761–8)

One difference between 'An Horatian Ode' and 'Upon Appleton House' is the pervasive Christian imagery of the latter poem: here Marvell sees contemporary political events and incidents drawn from the day-to-day life on Fairfax's estate in a fundamentally religious perspective as emblems of man's fall and his search for a possible redemption. And yet the hope of recapturing paradise, of finding an impregnable retreat 'where the World no certain Shot / Can make, or me it toucheth not' (lines 605–6) is balanced against the awareness that what is irremediably lost cannot be recaptured, that certain fruits do not grow in 'our Earthly Gardens' but only in realms 'eternal, and divine' (lines 356, 359). The dialogue between soul and body, with their mutually exclusive demands, can never be resolved: the two are indissolubly bound together, incapable of either divorce or separation, condemned to an unending struggle which neither can win.

Though Marvell's poetry is enormously varied, in a sense he has only one subject: the fall of man. As in Aristophanes' myth in the *Symposium*, fallen man is incomplete, cut in two, and yearns after a lost, unattainable wholeness. In one situation after another, man is placed in a position where he must choose, knowing that neither of the alternatives before him is satisfactory. Implicit in all the debates in Marvell's poetry – that between the soul and the body, between the simplicity of green nature and the complexities of civilization, between participation in the world of affairs and a contemplative withdrawal, between the hope of exercising power over time and fate and the fear of total powerlessness – is the overwhelming consciousness of man's fallen state and the necessity of adjusting to it or seeking somehow to overcome it.[9]

Many of his poems deal directly with the perception of the loss of innocence. The mower, whose 'Mind was once the true survey / Of all these Medows fresh and gay', finds himself suddenly cast adrift in a universe devoid of inner harmony; all is infected by the taint of death he carries within him: 'For She my Mind hath so displac'd / That I shall never find my home.' Obsessed by consciousness of his own unhappiness and enraged at nature's 'gawdy May-games', its blithe indifference to his plight, he is led to a frenzy of destruction, in which, like Milton's Satan, he hopes to blot out the tormenting memory of a happier state by 'depopulating all the Ground', involving nature with him 'in one common Ruine'. In the mower poems as in 'The Garden', the principle of destructiveness is identified with sexuality, as well as with the nuisance of having to cope with other people: 'Two Paradises 'twere in one / To live in Paradise alone.'[10]

Pastoral poetry ordinarily contrasts the 'fragrant Innocence' of 'plain and pure' rural nature with the 'polish'd' yet corrupt world of sophisticated urban man:

> The Pink grew then as double as his Mind;
> > The nutriment did change the kind.
> With strange perfumes he did the Roses taint.
> > And Flow'rs themselves were taught to paint.
> > > ('The Mower against Gardens', lines 4, 9–12, 34, 37)

But in Marvell's poems the innocent world of nature is not free from invasion, since the principal of corruption lies within. The fall is re-enacted every day; the human condition guarantees that the tempter will find a receptive echo in the mind:

> For *Juliana* comes, and She
> What I do to the Grass, does to my Thoughts and Me.
> ('The Mower's Song', lines 29–30)

The heroine of 'The Nymph complaining for the death of her Faun' desires above all else to remain in a world of white, uncomplicated innocence, but the 'false and cruel men' (line 54) who control events – 'unconstant Sylvio' (line 25), 'the wanton Troopers' (line 1) – refuse to allow it to exist. The only recourse of Diana's nymph is to die, and hope that in 'fair *Elizium*' (line 107) she can find the state of perfect whiteness she cannot find on earth. It is impossible for her to achieve her end in this world, since what she desires is a state of infinitely prolonged childhood, a total instinctual absorption into nature, free from the canker of thought. The mower, longing to recapture a lost harmony with nature, remembering the days before 'Love here his Thistles sow'd' ('Damon the Mower', line 66), similarly yearns after the unattainable.

'Bermudas' is perhaps the one poem in which Marvell allows the polarities to be reconciled. Here the possibility of a recovered paradise on earth is not a distant flickering hope, but an immediate, present reality. Other religious poems by Marvell, in contrast, are grimly or ruefully ascetic, presenting the natural creation as irremediably corrupted as a result of the fall. Life on earth, in such a view, is a series of snares cast in the path of the resolved soul: 'Ah, foolish Man, that would debase with them, / And mortal Glory, Heavens Diadem!' ('The Coronet', lines 17–18). But in 'Bermudas' the natural world is entirely unfallen, and soul and body live in complete harmony. God has provided not only relief 'from the Storms, and Prelat's rage' (line 12) but a second paradise fully equal to the first. God and man remain, as in the prelapsarian state, in constant communion through nature. Man's everyday activities sing the creator's praises, and the birds of the air play the role of angelic messengers, testifying to God's unceasing 'care' of his children: '[He] sends the Fowl's to us in care, / In daily Visits through the Air' (lines 15–16). Yet we are not allowed to forget that such a state of affairs is not the norm; the 'Isle ... far kinder than our own' (lines 7–8) is only a single island in a vast sea, resting 'remote' and 'unespy'd' (lines 1–2) by all but the fortunate few. The poem makes the ideal seem attainable, but it is still essentially a prospect, a vision, something to steer towards. 'An holy and a chearful note' (line 38), the poem is directed in part at encouraging those English Puritans who have not received such tangible evidence of God's grace.

'Upon Appleton House' contains no such confident affirmations; the hope of perfection, of finding a 'Sanctuary' (line 482) free from the power of time and destructive human passions, plays a major role in the poem, but hope is set against the prevailing fact of uncertainty. The poem's polarities are not resolved, perhaps because the poet did not see them as resolvable at that time and under those particular conditions. In the poem's best-known lines, the loss of Eden is specifically identified with the Civil War. The lines are especially moving because they see the loss as both absolute and incomprehensible; God's judgment is final, beyond cavil, and fallen man's vivid memory of the world he has lost serves only to intensify his pain and bewilderment:

> Oh Thou, that dear and happy Isle
> The Garden of the World ere while,
> Thou *Paradise* of four Seas,
> Which *Heaven* planted us to please,
> But, to exclude the World, did guard
> With watry if not flaming Sword;
> What luckless Apple did we tast,
> To make us Mortal, and Thee Wast?
>   ('Upon Appleton House' lines 321–8)

In this passage there is none of the grudging respect shown in the 'Horatian Ode' toward amoral *virtu*, sheer energy sufficient to 'ruine the great Work of Time' (line 34). The war in 'Upon Appleton House' is seen as an unmitigated catastrophe, destroying utterly and irrevocably the simple, placid existence of pre-war England.

> Unhappy! shall we never more
> That sweet *Militia* restore,

When Gardens only had their Towrs,
And all the Garrisons were Flowrs,
When Roses only Arms might bear,
And Men did rosie Garlands wear?   (lines 329–34)

Both of these stanzas raise questions to which there can be no answer: however much we may regret this loss, we have no choice other than to accept it. A passage in *The Rehearsal Transpros'd*, where Marvell comments at length on the fall and its consequences, bears directly on this section of 'Upon Appleton House'. The dream of living in a state of 'perpetual Peace' and prelapsarian tranquillity, he tells us, is futile:

Ever since the first Brother Sacrificed the other to Revenge, because his Offering was better accepted, Slaughter and War has made up half the business in the World, and often upon the same quarrel, and with like success. So that as God has hitherto, instead of an Eternal Spring, a standing Serenity, and perpetual Sun-shine, subjected Mankind to the dismal influence of Comets from above, to Thunder, and Lightning, and Tempests from the middle Region, and from the lower Surface, to the raging of the Seas, and the tottering of Earth Quakes, beside all other the innumerable calamities to which humane life is exposed, he has in like manner distinguish'd the Government of the World by the intermitting seasons of Discord, War, and publick Disturbance. (*RT*, II, pp. 231–2)

Not only does God 'permit' evils, He actively ordains them: 'Neither has he so order'd it only (as men endeavour to express it) by meer permission, but sometimes out of Complacency' (*ibid.*) – i.e., by active approval, by 'contented acquiescence or consent' (*OED*). The term 'Complacency' in such a context seems shocking to a modern reader; yet to Marvell as to Milton, God takes pleasure in the working out of his own justice, even though men, aware only of their own suffering, are unable to recognize the divine pattern.

The political position reflected in 'Upon Appleton House' is a complex and delicate one. Fairfax, who in the late 1640s had been, together with his fellow general Cromwell, one of the two most powerful men in England, had abandoned public life entirely in 1650 at the age of thirty-eight. Fairfax had supported the revolution in its initial stages, but like some other presbyterian moderates had opposed the trial and execution of the King. His sense of scruples had caused him to absent himself from the trial proceedings, refusing as a personal act of conscience to take part in an action of which he disapproved, though his loyalty to his former associates had kept him from speaking out in public against the trial or against the Commonwealth regime. His retirement was to be permanent, but neither Fairfax nor Marvell knew at the time that it would be. A second, probably earlier poem to Fairfax, 'Upon the Hill and Grove at Bill-borow', states the choice between the active and contemplative life in different terms, honouring the man who is able to inhabit both worlds, each at its proper time:

> Much other Groves, say they, than these
> And other Hills him once did please.
> Through Groves of Pikes he thunder'd then,
> And Mountains rais'd of dying Men.
> For all the *Civick Garlands* due
> To him our Branches are but few.
> Nor did our Trunks enow to bear
> The Trophees of one fertile Year.   (lines 65–72)

The implication is clear that Fairfax is free to re-enter the world where 'Civick Garlands' are won whenever he wishes to do so – like the Roman heroes Cincinnatus or Scipio, or like the Cromwell of the 'Horatian Ode', leaving the 'reserved and austere' life of his 'private Gardens' as his 'active Star' led him (lines 14, 29–30). Fairfax's 'retreat' to his country estate is seen in 'Upon the Hill and Grove at Bill-borow' as a stage in his career, not as its culmination.

> Therefore to your obscurer Seats
> From his own Brightness he retreats:
> Nor he the Hills without the Groves,
> Nor Height but with Retirement loves.   (lines 77–80)

No such easy reconciliation is proposed in 'Upon Appleton House'; here the problem of choice is set out in fundamentally Christian (and Platonic) terms as a posing of two incompatible alternatives, neither of which can be considered satisfactory.

For a man like Fairfax, the decision to give up entirely on the state was an acutely painful one, an admission of defeat, abandoning the hope, central to his career, that public and private virtue could be reconciled. Like Milton, Marvell in his political writings constantly raises the question of whether man is worthy of the gift of freedom: if God has rendered the just state no longer capable of achievement, then the virtuous man must turn his attention to the state of his own soul. In dark times, 'one just Man', withdrawing from physical contact with a corrupt society, should seek 'to save himself and household from amidst / A World devote to universal rack'. The Stoic version of the dilemma of the man of conscience in the degenerate state, as Seneca presents it, is phrased in prudential terms rather than those of strenuous physical combat, but the conduct recommended is essentially the same:

If the state is too corrupt to be helped, if it is wholly dominated by evils, the wise man will not struggle to no purpose, nor spend himself when nothing is to be gained.[11]

Yet several questions immediately suggest themselves. How can one know that the state has passed the point beyond which political action becomes futile? Can a man be sure that by abandoning the political arena entirely, he is not purchasing a freedom from pain at the cost of any moral principles in which he may believe, and possibly at the cost of suffering to others? Inaction may bring about those things most feared; a disclaimer of personal responsibility may not be sufficient to still the pangs of conscience, and passive obedience and non-resistance may serve to strengthen the unjust state and confirm it in its injustice.

'Upon Appleton House' then takes as its starting point a decision by Fairfax (and by implication by Marvell) which is possibly reversible, possibly unwise, and incalculable in its consequences, yet felt in its immediate circumstances to be necessary. The poem looks on much of the past and present with pained distaste, and any hope with which it views the future is tempered by the knowledge that earlier hopes have proved fruitless. Though the poem deals with serious matters, its prevailing tone is comic – the comedy which includes a tragic awareness and yet goes beyond it. The wit in the poem qualifies the feeling, the feeling gives added poignancy to the wit. Marvell's characteristic poise enables him at once to celebrate the possibility of a green world exempt from earthly decay and to suggest, with unblinking ironic awareness, that the fortress we built may be less secure than we think.

The problematical side of Fairfax's withdrawal is largely absent from the first two of the poem's six sections, which wittily describe the house itself and narrate its history. Though the manner here is light and amusing, the content is serious: defining by negatives (contrasting Fairfax in the first section with proud men swollen with a sense of their wordly greatness and William Fairfax, founder of the line, with the sinister temptresses who were the earlier owners of the property, the 'suttle Nunns' (line 94) of Appleton Priory), Marvell is writing about the nature of virtue and of temptation, suggesting that neither action nor contemplation is necessarily good or bad, but that moral choice is always an individual matter, dependent on circumstances and on an ability to look beyond surface appearances. The emotional and thematic centre of the poem is its third section, a description of and a meditation upon the gardens of Appleton House. The tradition in which Marvell is working here and in the sections that follow – the meadow, the forest, and the final address to young Maria Fairfax (and through her, to the future) – is 'occasional meditation' on the book of the creatures, readings in 'Natures mystick Book' (line 584). Nature's lessons are available to anyone who will look: throughout the poem, man serves as audience for and occasional participant in the masque nature performs in his presence. The poet's role is to serve as interpreter and guide, appealing to the senses, the imagination, and ultimately the understanding of the reader.[12]

Marvell's psychology, derived from Renaissance Platonism, has much in common with the characteristic idealism of the Romantic poets: the conduit between man and nature is the imagination, which is intermediate between sense perception and rational understanding. The phenomena of nature make their initial appeal to the senses. As Joseph Hall writes, in language curiously anticipating Wordsworth, meditations can take their origin from any natural objects which we happen to observe: 'Our active Soule can no more forbeare to thinke, then the eye can choose but see, when it is open... No object should passe us without use.'[13] Throughout 'Upon Appleton House' Marvell places a similar emphasis on physical sense-data and on the role of chance in bringing 'these scatter'd *Sibyls* Leaves' before the eye and ultimately before the mind: 'And see how Chance's better Wit /

Could with a Mask my studies hit!' (lines 577, 585–6). But the process of understanding as he presents it in the poem is far from automatic: the imagination, which can feed off the materials of sense but is free to make of them what it will, is to Marvell as to a number of Renaissance Platonists a necessary transforming agent which can mediate between the realms of sense and spirit. As his contemporary Ralph Cudworth writes:

Sense is but the offering or presenting of some object to the mind, to give it an occasion to exercise its own inward activity upon . . . For knowledge is not a knock or a thrust from without, but it consisteth in the awakening and exciting of the inward active powers of the mind.[14]

In his emphasis on the active role of the mind in perception and on the difficulty of distinguishing between inner and outer reality, the 'phantasms' of the imagination and the objects of sense – the world available to the senses is compared in 'Upon Appleton House' (lines 637–8) to a river 'Where all things gaze themselves, and doubt / If they be in it or without' – Marvell shares the epistemological concerns of the Cambridge Platonists and anticipates Romantic idealism. This conception of the imagination as the eye of the mind and on its evocative powers as a means of awakening the dormant soul in potential readers finds parallel in the theory of meditation during the Renaissance, with its exhortations 'to see with the eyes of the imagination the corporeal place where the thing I wish to contemplate is found'.[15] The image-making faculty by which a poet can create or recreate 'other Worlds' on the page and in the minds of his readers is to Marvell the poet's distinctive province. Though the materials of the imagination are drawn from nature, the imagination (Marvell does not generally use the word, but in Renaissance fashion speaks of 'Phancy', 'Wit', or 'the Mind'), far from being passive or constrained, exults in its freedom: its world is limitless.

> Mean while, the Mind, from pleasure less,
> Withdraws into its happiness:
> The Mind, that Ocean where each kind
> Does streight its own resemblance find;
> Yet it creates, transcending these,
> Far other Worlds, and other Seas;
> Annihilating all that's made
> To a green Thought in a green Shade.
>
> ('The Garden', lines 41–8)

The complex interchange between the outward world of sense experience and the inward world of imagination is illustrated throughout the poem. In the garden, meadow, and forest episodes, the subject of the imagination's transforming flights is always a literal scene unfolding before the reader's eyes. What the mind does with the materials it receives is unpredictable. The very apartness of the natural world makes man want to possess it, enter it, either submerge himself in it or assimilate it to himself, interpreting natural phenomena in anthropomorphic terms. In the open meadow, the observing mind is free to create whatever fleeting combinations of images it will; the external world is reduced here to a stage in which a series of 'pleasant Acts' (line 465) can be presented for the mind's entertainment. The poet, as in *L'Allegro*, is a looker-on at rural scenes, the more reflective for being uninvolved. But the parade of images turns out to be less pleasant than one might expect. The sight of the new-mowed plain calls forth an image of the prelapsarian world and then a telling correction:

> The World when first created sure
> Was such a Table rase and pure.
> Or rather such is the *Toril*
> Ere the Bulls enter at Madril.   (lines 445–8)

No one and nothing in the fallen world can be a *tabula rasa*; the world we inhabit resembles an arena, and moments of apparent purity and innocence are mere *trompe-l'oeil*. The pictures that flash before the mind's eye in the meadow section of the poem are emblems of mortality, emphasizing the instability of all earthly things and the ubiquity of violence and pain. 'Death Trumpets creak' (line 415) in the call of a bird, the ordinary activity of mowers prompts one to 'wonder how they rise alive' (line 377) from the sea of grass in which they are submerged, hay-making becomes a masque of war, and the familiar contours of the landscape are transmuted into something far more threatening. With 'Precipices' (line 375) on one side, an 'Abbyss' (line 369) on the other, man cannot presume on the solid, comforting reality of his surroundings.

The powers and limits of the imagination are further illustrated in the poem's fifth section, in which the narrator retreats from the flooded meadow into the woods. Here the poet-persona, who has appeared fleetingly earlier as a modest, peripheral observer, is suddenly propelled into the centre of the picture: Marvell uses the first person singular forty times in the forest episode, as against only three times in the rest of the poem.[16] The hope that by the power of the imagination man can be redeemed from the debris of his life is presented here in intensely personal terms. Searching for a refuge, the narrator envisages the forest's 'huge Bulk' (line 501) as providing an impenetrable barrier, stern in excluding the hostile world 'without' yet hospitable to its friends 'within':

> [It] stretches still so closely wedg'd
> As if the Night within were hedg'd.
>
> Dark all without it knits; within
> It opens passable and thin.   (lines 503–6)

In the heart of the forest, the ordinary separation between man and nature is lessened; his normal human restlessness stilled, the narrator imagines himself entirely at one with nature:

> Thus I, *easie Philosopher*,
> Among the *Birds* and *Trees* confer:
> And little now to make me, wants
> Or of the *Fowles*, or of the Plants.
> Give me but Wings as they, and I
> Streight floting on the Air shall fly:
> Or turn me but, and you shall see
> I was but an inverted Tree.   (lines 561–8)

Other seventeenth-century poets (Vaughan, for example: 'I would I were a stone, or tree, / Or flowre by pedigree...') attribute to the natural creation a wholeness and simplicity which divided, unstable man, with his nagging self-consciousness, is unable to attain.[17] One difference between Marvell's lines and characteristic passages in Herbert and Vaughan is that the narrator in 'Upon Appleton House' does not long for absorption into the natural world and loss of his human identity, but imagines himself to have achieved such a state – or in this stanza, to be on the verge of achieving it. But though the experience described is that of ecstasy, the language and tone in stanza LXXI are witty, dis-passionate, uninvolved; as in many of the conceits of 'Upon

Appleton House' (the antipodes in shoes, the house swelling to a
sphere to admit its owner, the mowers diving through the grass),
the poet appears to be savouring their comic grotesqueness, their
violation of the norms of the ordinary world.

Stanza LXXII, on the other hand, presents the experience of
ecstatic communion directly, without the ironic distancing of the
preceding stanza (though the modulation in tone is subtle, and the
opening couplet recognizes the comic aspects of the spectacle of
the poet-linguist conversing with the birds in their 'most learn'd
Original'). In imagery and tone this stanza resembles stanza VII
of 'The Garden', the emotional climax of that poem. Both
passages offer glimpses of a state of timeless perfection in which
man, no longer conscious of his self-division and alienation, can
enter worlds ordinarily denied him:

> Already I begin to call
> In their most learn'd Original:
> And where I Language want, my Signs
> The Bird upon the Bough divines;
> And more attentive there doth sit
> Than if She were with Lime-twigs knit.
> No Leaf does tremble in the Wind
> Which I returning cannot find.   (lines 569–76)

As in the casting aside of the body's vest in 'The Garden', and as
in mystical experience generally, the ecstatic state is characterized
by a simultaneous heightening and calming of the senses.
Ordinary means of communication, the reflection of man's confused, dualistic existence, becomes unnecessary; instead, the
observer feels every motion of the leaf and immediately, intuitively
knows its meaning. Rather than being constrained to rely on the
slow, inaccurate gathering and sifting of information by untrust-
worthy senses and a faulty memory, man can know with in-
stantaneous certainty, as angels do. Removed from the ordinary
flux of time, the poet is able to hold past, present, and future in
a single perspective. In stanza LXXIII, the leaves of the forest are
'Sibyls Leaves' from which the poet's 'Phancy' can weave 'Strange
Prophecies' (lines 577–8), and his gift of divination is accompanied by equal comprehension of events past: 'What *Rome*,
Greece, *Palestine* ere said / I in this light Mosaick read' (lines
581–2). The lines bear directly on Marvell's conception of the

imagination or 'Phancy' as the link between man and nature. Where in the previous stanza, the identification between man and the world of bird and leaf is seen as absolute, with no possibility of misunderstanding (or so the narrator claims), here the role of man as interpreter is stressed: the phenomena of nature need to be 'read'. By developing the metaphor of nature as book with pages to be turned, as material for a historical narrative (line 579), as painting to be viewed (line 580), Marvell stresses the separateness of the observer from the thing observed. The problem with imaginative or emotional empathy is that it is likely to be deceived: 'Thrice happy he who, not mistook, / Hath read in *Natures mystick Book*' (lines 583–4). Though the Book of Nature serves as both a repository of wisdom and a source of contentment for the man fortunate enough to be able to read it, the qualification 'not mistook' adds a touch of realism, a reservation, even at the moment of ecstasy. There is always the possibility of self-hypnosis, seeing what one wants to see, convincing oneself that what one desires is actually happening.

The garden, meadow, and forest sections of 'Upon Appleton House' enact a dialect of gradual withdrawal, similar in some ways to the central stanzas of 'The Garden'. In both poems the reader is led through a number of stages, each of which appears for a moment to be a final resting place but none of which proves fully satisfying, toward a climactic experience of imaginative ecstasy, involving a sense of oneness with nature and a loss of consciousness of self. But the moments of greatest emotional intensity in 'Upon Appleton House', unlike the mimesis of ecstasy at the heart of 'The Garden', are devoted to uncertainty, loss, or hope in defiance of any rational expectation, 'begotten by despair / Upon Impossibility' ('Definition of Love', lines 3–4). The hope that by the transforming and enkindling power of the imagination the forces of destruction can be held at bay receives its most memorable expression in the garden section.

The wide-ranging conceits of stanzas XXXVI–XLV all take their origin from descriptive fact: all the Fairfaxes were military men, so it was quite appropriate for the gardens of Nun Appleton to be laid out 'in the just Figure of a Fort' (line 286), serving their owner as a constant reminder of his earlier life. To the prosaic eye, flowers are flowers, worth a casual glance in passing; to the imagination, they come to life, waking in the morning in order to pay tribute and to stand guard.

> The Flow'rs their drowsie Eyelids raise,
> Their Silken Ensigns each displayes,
> And dries its Pan yet dank with Dew,
> And fills its Flask with Odours new.   (lines 293–6)

> Well shot ye Firemen! Oh how sweet
> And round your equal Fires do meet;
> Whose shrill report no Ear can tell,
> But Echoes to the Eye and smell.   (lines 305–8)

War here has lost its potential destructiveness and become wholly a game, an opportunity for colourful pageantry (as well as for the poet's wit and precise miniaturist's observation). Real bullets kill, but the 'fragrant Volleyes' (line 298) of the flower-troops are harmless and aesthetically pleasing.

Here and in the next stanza the tenderness of feeling and expression reminds one of Blake's *Songs of Innocence*, and the sense of a secret life within the closest recesses of nature, which may reflect the Hermetic tradition with which Marvell and Fairfax were familiar, anticipates the ecstatic communion with bird and leaf later in the poem.[18] In the garden section, man is observer more than participant, and nature, anthropomorphized, is seen as his servant – indeed, as in Blake, the angelic guardians of paradise take on a natural form.

> But when the vigilant *Patroul*
> Of Stars walks round about the *Pole*,
> Their Leaves, that to the stalks are curl'd,
> Seem to their Staves the *Ensigns* furl'd.
> Then in some Flow'rs beloved Hut
> Each Bee as Sentinel is shut;
> And sleeps so too: but, if once stir'd,
> She runs you through, or askes *the Word*.   (lines 313–20)

The tone remains playful; as with many metaphysical conceits, the wit lies in the surprising yet apposite nature of the comparisons. We are amused by the author's ingenuity and applaud the skill with which he extends the central metaphor in ways we do not anticipate. The lines contain a quality which is even more unexpected and is a major source of their power – a sudden charge of emotion, making one aware that the need for protection is genuine. In a sudden widening of perspective in the stanzas that follow, the garden of Nun Appleton is subsumed under the garden-state of pre-war England, whose loss lies at the heart of all human pain. As Hopkins writes, 'Now no matter, child, the name: / Sorrow's springs are the same'.[19] As the tone darkens, Nun Appleton comes to be seen as an anachronism, reasserting earlier values of gentleness, civility, and human sympathy which appear to have been obliterated from the world outside Fairfax's private gardens – an oasis in a desert of war, somehow managing to embody the principle of life in a universe of death, magically exempt for the moment at least from the raging destructiveness surrounding it:

> The *Gardiner* had the *Souldiers* place,
> And his more gentle Forts did trace.
> The Nursery of all things green
> Was then the only *Magazeen.*
> The *Winter Quarters* were the Stoves,
> Where he the tender Plants removes.
> But War all this doth overgrow:
> We Ord'nance Plant and Powder sow.   (lines 337–44)

In the broader context of fallen men and ruined England, the fanciful conceits of the earlier stanzas and of the Nun Appleton garden's design appear mere games, attempts to assert the will's sovereignty where in fact it bears only a temporary and limited sway. The imagination is not after all autonomous; the nature of freedom makes it inevitable that the mind in meditation, not limited only to pleasant thoughts, will eventually recall or recreate out of 'that Ocean, where each kind / Does streight its own resemblance find' ('The Garden', lines 43–4), the very conditions which it is seeking to escape.

What we have in this passage – and it is characteristic of the poem – is a constant revaluation of perspective, an illustration of both the power of imagination and the countervailing power of stubborn reality. To choose necessarily entails loss; a commitment to a single course means a closing of possibilities. Yet rejected alternatives, memories of the past, old loyalties, abandoned hopes, cannot simply be blotted out. The human condition makes it impossible to escape what 'Knowledge forces [us] to know; / And

Memory will not forego' ('A Dialogue between the Soul and Body', lines 39–40). Within the sanctuary of Appleton House, one cannot escape the shadow of the ravaged garden outside; each sight is able to awaken remembered pain. Stanza XLIV, which deals directly with Fairfax's decision to retire from active life, leaves the reader with a sense not of powers kept under control by self-discipline or turned to better use, but of powers wasted, possibilities thwarted:

> And yet there walks one on the Sod
> Who, had it pleased him and *God*,
> Might once have made our Gardens spring
> Fresh as his own and flourishing.
> But he preferr'd to the *Cinque Ports*
> These five imaginary Forts:
> And, in those half-dry Trenches, spann'd
> Pow'r which the Ocean might command.   (lines 345–52)

These moving lines combine a profound regret for the dead hopes of the past with a resigned submission to the will of God. 'Had it pleased ... God', the garden-state might still be flourishing. But our own desires cannot deflect God's immutable judgments: we cannot understand the past and we cannot predict the future.

Ultimately, the claims of the conscience are uncompromising; faced with a choice between ordinary human values or feelings and 'Flowrs eternal, and divine' (line 359), we must turn our allegiances entirely to the latter. To retreat within the garden is to abandon the world outside to eternal perdition. In human terms, such a decision can never be easy to make; the tolerant humanist side of Marvell would inevitably find a source for sorrow and regret in a conclusion the Puritan in him found inevitable. In the rigid either/or calculus of Calvinist morality, a man of conscience must still any sympathy he may feel for the unhappy legions of the damned, who may include among them infants, innocent pagans, and men of good will; his only concern is his own salvation. The weeds must be separated from the flowers:

> For he did, with his utmost Skill,
> *Ambition* weed, but *Conscience* till.
> *Conscience*, that Heaven-nursed Plant,
> Which most our Earthly Gardens want.

A prickling leaf it bears, and such
As that which shrinks at ev'ry touch;
But Flowrs eternal, and divine,
That in the Crowns of Saints do shine.   (lines 353–60)

When in *Comus* Milton uses similar imagery ('The leaf was darkish, and had prickles on it, / But in another Countrey, as he said, / Bore a bright golden flowre, but not in this soyl', lines 631–3), it is with entirely different implications. The action of *Comus* continually reminds us that though most men do not recognize the priority of heavenly values, some men do: Milton's masque is dedicated to showing that it is possible to lead a virtuous life, that earth and heaven are not discrete, mutually exclusive realms, but harmonious, reconcilable. Marvell on the other hand in stanza XLV as in 'The Coronet' and 'On a Drop of Dew' emphasizes the exclusiveness of the conscience's demands, suggesting that involvement in the affairs of the world, even with the best of intentions, necessarily ensnares one in 'wreaths of Fame and Interest' ('The Coronet', line 16).

The unresolved debate in 'Upon Appleton House', appropriately for its setting of rural England in time of civil war, sets the fear that nature is irremediably fallen against the hope that nature can be redeemed. Within the mortal state the soul cannot exist apart from the body, or free from the shackles of time and the undeniable contingent presence of a world beyond the self. In our imaginations we are able to accomplish all our desires, but iron necessity does not readily allow challenges against its power:

And yet I quickly might arrive
Where my extended Soul is fixt,
But Fate does Iron wedges drive,
And alwaies crouds it self betwixt.
('The Definition of Love', lines 9–12)

The soul proclaims its own reality as sovereign, but it necessarily lives in a world of extension. The attempt to erect an impregnable citadel where the soul may enjoy its own society alone is thus as likely to prove disappointing as the attempt to reshape the world around us to make it fit our heroic conceptions. It is the ironic tension between the hope of triumphing over the world's destructive forces and the recognition of man's limited power over events which gives such poignancy to the garden section of 'Upon

Appleton House'. Its central images of garden and fortress, fruitful paradise and wasteland, reverberate throughout the poem.

III

By the time of *The First Anniversary of the Government under His Highness the Lord Protector* (1655), the political situation in England had changed considerably. In 1650–2 the poet was unable to give a final commitment to any one man or cause. An old order had died and it was unclear what was to take its place: 'the forced Pow'r' had been 'assur'd' by Charles I's execution ('Horatian Ode', line 66), since one of the rival claimants to sovereignty had been wiped out. In both the 'Horatian Ode' and 'Upon Appleton House', the future exists only as potential, a subject for fervent hope and clouded prophecy – political in one poem, domestic in the other – while the past is dead beyond recall; a single, ever-fading moment marks the limits of man's certainty. The elegiac note is more pronounced in 'Upon Appleton House', which holds forth little or no prospect of exercising mastery over events:

> Unhappy Birds! what does it boot
> To build below the Grasses Root;
> When Lowness is unsafe as Hight,
> And Chance o'retakes what scapeth spight?　(lines 409–12)

But Cromwell rising from his 'private Gardens' to the public stage ('Horatian Ode', line 29) and Fairfax retreating from fame and glory to the 'dwarfish Confines' of his house and the 'imaginary Forts' of his garden ('Upon Appleton House', lines 38, 350) are complementary figures, representing two possible responses to revolutionary upheaval.

The difference between *The First Anniversary* and the two earlier poems is in part a matter of genre, in part a reflection of new circumstances and the poet's developing political views. *The First Anniversary* is a panegyric in praise of Cromwell and of the Protectorate government, which finds in that leader and in that government a possible resolution of the problem of power and right, left unresolved in both the 'Horatian Ode' and 'Upon Appleton House'. The poem contains none of the reservations and qualifications of the 'Horatian Ode', but is entirely committed to Cromwell's continued rule. Indeed, the poem's aim is to convince others of the legitimacy of the Protectorate government. In *The First Anniversary* and in 'A Poem upon the Death of His late Highnesse the Lord Protector' (1658), Marvell argues, in contrast to his position in the earlier poems, that the Christian conscience and the life of action, 'Justice' ('Horatian Ode', line 37) and *de facto* power, are fully reconcilable – as, for instance, in this tribute to Cromwell and the New Model Army:

> He first put Armes into *Religion's* hand,
> And tim'rous *Conscience* unto *Courage* mann'd;
> The soldier taught that inward Maile to weare,
> And *fearing God* how they should *nothing feare.*
> Those strokes, he said, will pierce through all below
> Where those that strike from *Heaven* fetch their Blow.
>
> ('Poem upon the Death', lines 179–84)

Here conscience, rather than shrinking from any earthly touch, makes action seem imperative.

The characteristic imagery of the 'Horatian Ode' and *The First Anniversary* is drawn from two different spheres: the earlier poem is consistently classical, full of analogies from the history and literature of Rome, where *The First Anniversary* draws on the millenarian Protestant thought of the time and emphasizes Marvell's Puritan side, his desire like Milton to unite the classical and Christian traditions. A vision of empire, potentially of 'wonderful Effect' (*First Anniversary*, line 135), informs each poem. But in the 'Horatian Ode', the imperial vision ('A *Caesar* he ere long to *Gaul*', line 101) is entirely secular, and the prophecy is cast in classical, Roman terms rather than those of typology and apocalypse. The fervour of the religious imagery of the later poem, its careful marshalling of the resources of language in support of its persuasive end, differentiate it sharply from the spare, dry classicism of the earlier poem. In the one case we have the language of ironic detachment, etched precision, astringent realism, in the other language intended to convey or bring about the conviction of faith.

Cromwell is seen in the one poem primarily as destroyer, in the other as architect, as creative and ordering force. In the 'Horatian Ode', the hero's quality of *virtu* is presented as amoral. His greatness is manifest by events, and he has amply demonstrated his possession of the military virtues of strength, shrewdness, and self-discipline. But his moral qualities ('goodness' rather than 'greatness', in Fielding's terms), his ability and inclination to turn his gifts in some direction other than to 'ruine', 'blast', lay waste, can only be taken on trust. The poem's extended metaphors – the lightning bolt, the hunter, the bird of prey – reflect the political situation in 1650, a state of continued war, in which ordinary men and poets, caught up in events, search eagerly for favourable portents for the future even in the most unpromising circumstances, thus confessing their powerlessness before the forces directing events.[20] In *The First Anniversary*, on the other hand, Cromwell is explicitly presented as a Christian hero. Cromwell's Puritanism, as illustrated by his habitual use of the vocabulary of Calvinist self-examination and his conviction that through all the uncertainties of the Civil War period God had directed his hand, is as omnipresent in the characterization of Cromwell in *The First Anniversary* as it is excluded from his portrait in 'An Horatian Ode'. In a later poem we find not a half-reluctant, ironic recognition of historical or providential pattern in events in some ways painful or unpleasant ('A bleeding Head where they begun, / Did fright the Architects to run; / And yet in that the *State* / Foresaw it's happy Fate', 'Horatian Ode', lines 69–72), but a triumphant assertion of divine justice. The poem is written from the secure perspective of the true believer: Cromwell, the assumed audience, and (by implication) the author himself are all raised above the unregenerate and ignorant multitude by their awareness of and responsiveness to the will of God:

> What since he did, an higher Force him push'd
> Still from behind, and it before him rush'd,
> Though undiscern'd among the tumult blind,
> Who think these high Decrees by Man design'd.   (lines 239–42)

A passage in *The First Anniversary* which presents Cromwell explicitly as a Christian hero is strikingly similar in its imagery to the closing lines of the 'Horatian Ode', with significant differences which typify the approaches of the two poems:

> And well he therefore does, and well has guest,
> Who in his Age has always forward prest:

And knowing not where Heavens choice may light,
Girds yet his Sword, and ready stands to fight.
                              (*First Anniversary*, lines 145–8)

Both poems treat conscious and vigilant action as the only satisfactory moral response to uncertainty; in a sense, our inability to
know the future frees us to act in the present, without being dis-
tracted by the 'Tinsel Wing' of 'feeble Hope' ('The Definition of
Love', lines 7–8). But if the view of uncertainty as a spur to
action is characteristic of Marvell, the force directing human
affairs is in some of his poems presented as entirely amoral, and
human action as equally so:

Come little Infant, Love me now,
    While thine unsuspected years
Clear thine aged Fathers brow
    From cold Jealousie and Fears...

So we win of doubtful Fate;
    And, if good she to us meant,
We that Good shall antedate,
    Or, if ill, that Ill prevent.   ('Young Love', lines 1–4, 21–4)

The authority of Time and Fate here as in 'The Definition of
Love' and 'To his Coy Mistress' is quite literally 'Tyrannick' ('The
Definition of Love', line 16), a matter of physical force alone and
in no sense a moral authority; like Odysseus in the cave of Polyphemus, we are justified in using any means at our disposal to
escape if we can. The perspective of the last lines of the 'Horatian
Ode' is similarly secular rather than Christian: the erect sword is
a practical weapon, rather than the symbolic sword of the soldier
of Christ, the constant pressing forward is not the stance of the
true warfaring Christian, but a necessary consequence of the
fragility of Cromwell's political power. In 'Horatian Ode', lines
113–20, Cromwell is given sound advice out of *Il Principe*, to keep
his wits about him and exercise the same 'Arts' (line 119) and
force of character that brought his power in ceaseless care to
maintain it against the discontented intriguers who watch for any
slackening of the reins. In *The First Anniversary*, Cromwell uses
his sword not to overawe potential political opponents, but to
fight the Lord's fight against Satan and his minions on whatever
battlefield the Lord chooses. His sword and 'immortal Shield' are
no more than any Christian carries – righteousness, conscience, a

regenerate and 'resolved Heart' ('Resolved Soul', lines 2, 10). If Cromwell's opportunities are greater than those of ordinary men, if Marvell is able to hold out the possibility that millenarian prophecies may be realized through him, the credit lies not so much with Cromwell himself as with the 'High Grace' of God (*First Anniversary*, line 132).

The religious dimension of *The First Anniversary* sets it apart both from the 'Horatian Ode' and from the many contemporary tracts arguing for the legitimacy of Cromwell's rule on prudential grounds alone, claiming that 'he who spits against the wind, spits but in his own face'.[21] Isabel Rivers, in her excellent commentary on the poem, sees the apocalyptical imagery in *The First Anniversary* as primarily persuasive in intent: the poet, in this view, chooses the language which is most suitable for its intended audience and 'turns millenarianism against the millenarians'. But in fact the treatment of the theme of biblical prophecy is entirely characteristic of Marvell, in juxtaposing great hopes against the human limitations which make their fulfilment doubtful.[22] Milton, whose *Second Defence of the English People* (1654) is extremely close to Marvell's poem both in its general assumptions and in its political stance, similarly argues that however promising the auspices may be, freedom and glory can come only to those who are worthy of these gifts:

It will be a source of grief that to such great undertakings, such great virtues, perseverance was lacking. It will seem to posterity that a mighty harvest of glory was at hand, together with the opportunity for doing the greatest deeds, but that to this opportunity men were wanting...You, therefore, who wish to remain free, either be wise at the outset, or regain your senses as soon as possible. If to be a slave is hard, and you do not wish it, learn to obey right reason, to master yourselves.[23]

The reign of Cromwell, as Marvell presents it in *The First Anniversary*, shows promise not only of patriotic triumphs, but of a far greater glory: the 'blest Day' (line 155) of millenarian hopes, when the course of time, 'fore-shortned' (line 139), will draw to an end and prophecies of a New Jerusalem will come to fruition. Yet even the greatest heroes are subject to the instability of fortune and to human sin and error – as illustrated in the poem by a lengthy (and, one must add, poetically inert) episode devoted to a coaching accident which threatened Cromwell's life: 'Thee proof beyond all other Force or Skill, / Our Sins endanger, and shall one day kill' (lines 173–4). The painful descent from vision to gray reality is a legacy of the fall:

> For the great Justice that did first suspend
> The World by Sin, does by the same extend.
> Hence that blest Day still counterpoysed wastes,
> The Ill delaying, what th'Elected hastes;
> Hence landing Nature to new Seas is tost,
> And good Designes still with their Authors lost.   (lines 153–8)

The metaphor of unexpected shipwreck in sight of port, here as in 'A Dialogue between the Soul and Body', suggests the suddenness with which human hopes can come to grief. 'The great Designes kept for the latter Dayes' (line 110) can be accomplished only if men are worthy of their task and are aware of their opportunity; if they are 'unconcern'd or unprepar'd' (line 150), beset by jealousies and factionalism so that they 'know them not, and what they know not hate' (line 112), 'headstrong' (line 224), 'brutish' (line 177), unaware, then the great task will pass them by.

For all the apparent signs of Cromwell's election as one designed for great deeds, then, the future, as Marvell sees it in *The First Anniversary*, is cloudy:

> That 'tis the most which we determine can,
> If these the Times, then this must be the Man.   (lines 143–4)

The dangers are as clear as are the opportunities, and the poem is quite explicit about what these dangers have been and will continue to be. Even those passages which praise Cromwell as a being superior to ordinary men do not exempt him from the taint of mortality. The sombre extended conceit with which the poem begins defines Cromwell's greatness ('Cromwell alone . . .') by distinguishing him from other men and other rulers:

> Like the vain Curlings of the Watry maze,
> Which in smooth Streams a sinking Weight does raise;
> So Man, declining alwayes, disappears
> In the weak Circles of increasing Years;
> And his short Tumults of themselves Compose
> While flowing Time above his Head does close.   (lines 1–6)

But the lines suggest that in certain unavoidable ways all men are one: we never cease to be aware that, for all Cromwell's great gifts, the river of time will ultimately close over his head as it has for everyone else.

The primary dangers to the future stability of the state in 1655 were the legacy of the recent past. The 'Times' that had produced Cromwell were chaotic, and the potential still remained for a discord great enough to bring about the dissolution of the state. At the time Marvell wrote, opposition to Cromwell was widespread; indeed, perhaps the main problem the Cromwell regime faced was that it never enjoyed the support of more than a minority of the English people. One of the aims of the poem is to discredit the motives of the opponents of Cromwell within the state, who are characterized as 'stubborn men' (line 78), deaf to reason and the need for cooperation, each demanding 'the highest Place' (line 82) in the state for himself. In associating the domestic opposition to Cromwell with the forces of disorder and unreason, the poet provides a series of powerful arguments for accepting the legitimacy of the Protectorate government. The poem seeks to show both that the Cromwellian settlement, with its concentration of power in the hands of a single man, is compatible with the principles under which the revolution has been fought and that the republican diehards who refuse to acknowledge Cromwell's rule fundamentally misunderstand the nature of liberty.

> That sober Liberty which men may have,
> That they enjoy, but more they vainly crave:
> And such as to their Parents Tents do press,
> May shew their own, not see his Nakedness. (lines 289–92)

The allusions to the biblical story of Noah throughout lines 283–94 subserve Marvell's persuasive end, in attributing to Cromwell the virtues of sobriety, benevolence, and foresight, while associating his opponents with drunkenness, 'the Wars Flood' (line 284), the 'Chammish issue' (line 293) raging through the land, and, in the lines quoted above, the uncovering of the patriarch's nakedness by his disrespectful sons.

Marvell attacks three groups explicitly in the poem: the members of the Rump Parliament, who had attempted to preserve themselves eternally in office under claims of parliamentary supremacy; the Levellers, radical democrats; and the extreme sectaries, who claimed an absolute liberty of the spirit. For each, as Marvell presents them here, the desire for untrammelled liberty masks a lust for power or an urge for mere destructiveness. To some extent, these attacks on political and religious radicals, which closely parallel Cromwell's own remarks on the Fifth Monarchists in his speech to the Protectorate Parliament, display the same kind of instinctive conservatism exhibited by Cromwell and Ireton in the Putney debates, the fear of the man of property directed at the irrational mob who would level all distinctions.[24] No man's motives are absolutely pure, especially when the man in question is defending his own exercise of power or seeking to persuade others that power is being exercised justly. But the explicit partisanship of *The First Anniversary* ought not to lead us to dismiss the political position argued there as a mere ratification of power and privilege. Though the poet's immediate allegiances may have differed at other times (so that, for example, his writings after the Restoration show far more sympathy for radical sectaries and his earlier writings are more reserved in their attitude toward Cromwell), he remains constant throughout his career to the ideal of rational, Christian liberty expressed in this poem. Like Milton, Marvell is committed to a belief in 'the cause of true and substantial liberty, which must be sought, not without, but within', and like Milton he distinguishes rational liberty from licence:

> But this is got by casting Pearl to Hogs,
> That bawl for freedom in their senseless mood,
> And still revolt when truth would set them free.
> License they mean when they cry liberty;
> But who loves that, must first be wise and good.[25]

The events of the year and a half before Marvell's poem indicate how close England was to a state of anarchy where power alone ruled, and provided ample support for Marvell's belief that liberty was only possible under the rule of law. In April 1653 Cromwell had marched into the House of Commons with his troops and dissolved the Long Parliament, which under the Commonwealth government supposedly held sovereign authority. From April to July, in the words of J. P. Kenyon, 'England was simply ruled by Cromwell by virtue of his post as commander-in-chief, and nothing else.'[26] The experiment of a Nominated

Parliament to exercise legislative responsibility, sharing power with the Lord General and the army, lasted six months; it abolished itself in December, at which time the Protectorate was proclaimed. The Protectorate government was not a seizure of power but an attempt to put an end to the naked rule of the sword. Cromwell's speech to the Protectorate Parliament indicates how urgently he desired a 'settlement', to avoid the twin dangers of anarchy and tyranny:

My power again by this resignation was as boundless and unlimited as before; all things being subject to arbitrariness, and [myself] a person having power over the three nations boundlessly and unlimited, and upon the matter, all government dissolved, all civil administrations at an end.[27]

The essence of the new government was the division of power. A written constitution, the Instrument of Government, rested the supreme legislative authority jointly in 'one person [the Lord Protector], and the people assembled in Parliament'.[28] The Lord Protector had wide powers, but bounds and limits were provided by Parliament, with control of finances and the power to pass laws which the Lord Protector could not veto, and a Council of fourteen members, whose advice and consent were required for all major foreign and domestic matters, including the power of declaring war and the disposition of military forces (acting in the last case in lieu of Parliament when it was not in session). Under the Protectorate government, as Cromwell's own account described it, no one man or one group could exert arbitrary power:

I did not receive anything that put me in a higher capacity than I was in before, but...it limited me and bound my hands to act nothing to the prejudice of the nations without the consent of a Council until the Parliament [met], and then limited [me] by the Parliament.[29]

But the mixed government proposed in the Instrument of Government failed, as other attempts at mixed government had failed in the Civil War period. When the Protectorate Parliament met in September 1654, its members immediately set to work revising the constitution to give themselves a preponderance of power. After several months in which Parliament seemingly fought the old battles with Charles I once again, passing no supply or other bills, demanding for themselves a total power over the army, even a legal sovereignty, and further offending Cromwell by attempting to limit freedom of worship, Cromwell dissolved the Parliament – the third parliament to be dissolved in less than two years. For the next few years, England was run by Cromwell with the aid of ten military governors, each assigned to a province. The Protectorate, against Cromwell's wishes, now rested entirely upon the implied threat of physical force.

In December 1654, when Marvell wrote the poem, Parliament was still in session and the hope for a lasting settlement had not evaporated. The poem reflects essentially the same situation and the same hopes as Milton's *Second Defence*, written about six months earlier, before the scheduled sitting of the Protectorate Parliament:

Cromwell, we are deserted! You alone remain. On you has fallen the whole burden of our affairs. On you alone they depend. In unison we acknowledge your unexcelled virtue. No one protests save such as seek equal honors, though inferior themselves, or begrudge the honors assigned to one more worthy, or do not understand that there is nothing in human society more pleasing to God, or more agreeable to reason, nothing in the state more just, nothing more expedient, than the rule of the man most fit to rule.[30]

Marvell like Milton is writing in defence of the well-ordered state, to show that the exercise of power by those most worthy to rule is compatible with, even necessary for, the preservation of liberty. Both *The First Anniversary* and the *Second Defence* are, in part at least, pleas to those of republican principles to support Cromwell's Protectorate. Like Milton and like the author of *A True State of the Case of the Commonwealth*, issued on behalf of the government in 1654 to rally support for its constitutional settlement, Marvell seeks to show that the Protectorate has not betrayed the principles of the revolution, to refute 'divers Doubts' which 'may be seen to arise in the minds of some sober Men concerning the present Change . . . as if we had turned our backs upon our former Principles, and introduced that very Thing, which was the great Bone of contention' (i.e., monarchy).[31] John Wallace's commentary on the poem recognizes its persuasive intent, but seems to me to misstate its fundamental argument by turning the poem into an appeal to Cromwell to accept the crown. The reestablishment of monarchy under Cromwell was certainly one possible remedy for the difficulties facing the state in 1655; it would provide for the succession after Cromwell's death and would help to legitimize his authority. The proposal that he become king had been made to Cromwell before, and would be made again. But the inauguration of a new line of kings was not the only possible solution to the problem of power and justice in the state: it was not the solution favoured by Cromwell, who refused the crown each time it was offered; by his closest advisers, who loathed the very name of king; and, most important, by the constitution of the Protectorate, about which Marvell is writing in the poem. The very title of the poem, *The First Anniversary of the Government under His Highness the Lord Protector*, indicates that Marvell is not writing about a form of government which might be established at some point in the future, but about a government which had been functioning for one year at the time the poem was written.[32] Under the Instrument of Government, the Lord Protector was a powerful executive but, quite explicitly, not a king either in name or in function. Much of the poem is devoted to attacks on the institution of kingship: the 'heavy Monarchs' (line 15) of the earth, Marvell argues in the opening forty-eight lines, are both ineffective and tyrannical, 'only... against their Subjects strong' (line 28). Monarchy, as Marvell presents it throughout the poem, is part of the discredited old order, the realm of 'Malice', 'Errour', and ignorance (lines 117–18); like Milton in the *Second Defence*, he presents the Lord Protector as actuated by the recognition that the only true king is God.[33] The failure of the 'earthy Projects' (line 19) of monarchs is inevitable because of their commitment to false sublunary values, as the tribute paid to Cromwell by a representative of Europe's petty monarchs at the end of the poem suggests: 'O could I once him with our Title see, / So should I hope yet he might Dye as wee' (lines 391–2).

The ideal state, in the words of *A True State of the Case of the Commonwealth*, avoids 'Division, Faction, and Confusion' on the one hand and 'the Inconveniences of absolute Lordly power on the other', but instead 'appears so well bounded on both sides, against Anarchie and Tyranny' that it may 'be of a durable continuance to succeeding ages' (pp. 51–2). Or, in Marvell's words:

> 'Tis not a Freedome, that where All command;
> Or Tyrannie, where One does them withstand:

But who of both the Bounders knows to lay
Him as their Father must the State obey.
(*First Anniversary*, lines 279–82)

The Protector here is seen not as patriarchal monarch, but as law-giver: he seeks not to hold on to his power or to command unquestioning obedience, but to create a lasting state. In *The First Anniversary*, Marvell does not go as far as his friend James Harrington, who depicts the Lord Archon of Oceana (an idealized version of Cromwell) as resigning up his power to the state after the constitutional settlement had been achieved.[34] But though his version of the 'well ordered Common-wealth' differs from Harrington's in many details, he similarly portrays Cromwell as benevolent legislator, desiring to impose limits on his power and to construct an edifice that will endure through all vicissitudes:

Choosing each Stone, and poysing every weight,
Trying the Measures of the Bredth and Height;
Here pulling down, and there erecting New,
Founding a firm State by Proportions true. (lines 245–8)

A series of witty, elaborate musical and architectural conceits show Cromwell as striving to bring earthly cacophony in tune with the 'Musique' (line 47) of the heavenly spheres. Just as the divinely inspired musician Amphion had charmed the rocks of Thebes by the power of his lute, causing the stones to '[dance] up in order' from their quarries (line 52) and form themselves into graceful and harmonious structures, so the legislator Cromwell would, by a seeming miracle, create order in the state:

All other Matter yields, and may be rul'd;
But who the Minds of stubborn Men can build?
No Quarry bears a Stone so hardly wrought,
Nor with such labour from its Center brought;
None to be sunk in the Foundation bends,
Each in the House the highest Place contends,
And each the Hand that lays him will direct,
And some fall back upon the Architect. (lines 77–84)

The advantage of the mixed state, as Marvell presents it here, is that it recognizes how recalcitrant its human materials are. Aware of the potential for disharmony, the factionalism, ambition, jealousy, and destructiveness natural to man in society, Cromwell the architect seeks to turn these things to his advantage.

'Compos'd by his attractive Song' (line 85), drawn by the magnetism of musical harmony and momentarily tamed by it, the people of England enter into the Commonwealth he has constructed.

> Such was that wondrous Order and Consent,
> When *Cromwell* tun'd the ruling Instrument.   (lines 67–8)

The pun on 'Instrument' is central to the passage: Marvell is talking, in quite specific terms, about the Instrument of Government, the constitution of the new state. In lines which are a brilliant metaphorical *tour de force*, the poet shows how the principle of *concordia discors* works in the mixed state, how the constitution of the Protectorate creates an overall harmony out of the opposing interests of discordant groups.

> The Common-wealth does through their Centers all
> Draw the Circumf'rence of the publique Wall;
> The crossest Spirits here do take their part,
> Fastn'ning the Contignation which they thwart;
> And they, whose Nature leads them to divide,
> Uphold, this one, and that the other Side.
> But the most Equal still sustein the Height,
> And they as Pillars keep the Work upright;
> While the resistance of opposed Minds,
> The Fabrick as with Arches stronger binds,
> Which on the Basis of a Senate free,
> Knit by the Roofs Protecting weight agree.   (lines 87–98)

Each group has its necessary place in the structure. The 'publique', the people *en masse*, democratic element in the mixed state, serves as the building's outer wall. Those elements which potentially endanger the state are by Cromwell's architectural skill and foresight so disposed that they contribute to the solidity of the edifice. Just as an arch 'stronger binds' by resolving two opposing pressures, vertical and horizontal, the 'opposed Minds' and conflicting interests within the state would keep one another in check. The 'crossest' and most contentious of the citizens, however much they might wish to 'thwart' a settlement, find that they 'thwart' it in another sense, helping fasten the wooden framework into which they fit, cross-wise. The most quarrelsome and divisive men in the state find themselves metamorphosed into walls facing one another, in eternal opposition; again energies which could be destructive are made to serve the good of the state. Marvell continues the architectural conceit in describing the role of the aristocratic element in the state: 'a Senate free' provides the base or foundation of the state, and the 'most Equal' and deserving of citizens (in terms of the constitution, probably comprising the Council of State) serve as 'Pillars' to 'sustein' the building and keep it 'upright'. Finally, the capstone of the building, the state's supreme executive, the Lord Protector, serves to 'knit' the structure together by 'the Roofs Protecting weight'. Hope for the future stability of the state, Marvell is arguing, lies not only in the personal greatness of Cromwell, God's warrior, but in his wisdom in providing a constitution that might endure, based on the liberal principle of division of power.

IV

Other political poems by Marvell with elements of panegyric written between 1653 and 1655 display attitudes similar to those in *The First Anniversary*. Where 'An Horatian Ode' and 'Upon Appleton House' measure ideals by uncompromising and tragic reality, these poems attempt to show the ideal as realizable. The earth, the poet suggests, can be a barren wilderness or a fertile garden, depending upon God's grace and upon man's ability to take advantage of the present occasion.

'A Letter to Doctor Ingelo', a Latin poem addressed to a member of an embassy sent by Cromwell to Queen Christina in 1653, elegantly praises the civilizing function of good government, which can transform the frozen landscape of Sweden into a flourishing paradise:

> Incolit, ut fertur, saevam Gens mitior Oram,
> Pace vigil, Bello strenua, justa Foro...
> Illic Lacte ruant illic et flumina Melle.
> ('A Letter to Doctor Ingelo', lines 11–12, 81)

> [A milder race, it is said, inhabits the harsh region,
> Vigilant in peace, vigorous in war, just in public affairs...
> There the rivers may run with milk and honey.][35]

Queen Christina and Cromwell are presented as models for other princes and warriors to follow: they are aware they rule by

God's sufferance, and they dedicate themselves to the service of God, unlike most monarchs, who are greedy, childish, and pre-occupied with trifles ('Ingelo', lines 93–6). The political intent of the poem, which presumably underlies all the praise addressed to Queen Christina, is to urge an alliance between the two Protestant powers, England and Sweden. In praising the active foreign policy Cromwell favoured, the poem continues the imperial imagery of the 'Horatian Ode' and *The First Anniversary*. As in *The First Anniversary*, where Marvell calls on the Protestant princes of Europe to rise out of their 'Regal sloth' (line 122) and join against the common enemy, the poet envisages a resounding victory over the forces of tyranny, in which Cromwell and his allies pursue 'the Monster thorough every Throne' back to her '*Roman Den*' (lines 128–9). Such a victory for the united armies of Protestant freedom over German eagle and Roman wolf ('Ingelo', lines 99–100) is presented as a more immediate prospect in 'A Letter to Doctor Ingelo':

> Vos etiam latos in praedam jungite *Campos*,
> Impiaque arctatis cingite Lustra Plagis.
> *Victor Oliverus* nudum Caput exerit Armis,
> Ducere sive sequi nobile laetus Iter.   (lines 101–4)

> [You two should join your camps in search of spoil,
> And surround the dens of iniquity with tightened nets.
> Victorious Oliver exposes his bare head in battle,
> Glad to lead or to follow a noble course.]

A similar patriotic imperialism and a similar confidence in the rightness of Cromwell's rule informs 'The Character of Holland', written in the same year. Holland, as presented in the poem, is Carthage to England's Rome (lines 141–2). The British fleet is the arm of Britain's rising empire; under Cromwell, England is able to enjoy its rightful place in the world.

> For now of nothing may our *State* despair,
> Darling of Heaven, and of Men the Care;
> Provided that they be what they have been,
> Watchful abroad, and honest still within.
> For while our *Neptune* doth a *Trident* shake,
> Steel'd with those piercing Heads, *Dean, Monk*, and *Blake*,
> And while *Jove* governs in the highest Sphere,
> Vainly in *Hell* let *Pluto* domineer.   (lines 145–52)

The ideal of government implicit in the concluding lines of 'The Character of Holland' is similar to that in 'An Horatian Ode' and in the lines in *The First Anniversary* praising the proposed constitution of the Protectorate: a balance between action and counsel, executive power and parliamentary judgment. In all these poems and in 'A Letter to Doctor Ingelo' as well, good government depends in large degree upon the wisdom and restraint of those in power: kings who serve God, military leaders who refuse to prey on the weak or measure their stature by the amount of blood they can spill, statesmen and senators who are 'watchful' and 'honest', conscious of their responsibilities. But there are significant differences in the form of government, the specific division of power within the state, suggested in each poem. In the 'Horatian Ode', hope for the future lies in the perpetuation of the uneasy balance of power between the conquering general and the legislature. 'The Kingdome old' has been cast 'into another Mold' (lines 35–6), but it is not yet clear what form of government will emerge or what its chances of survival are, though many of the auguries are good. 'The Character of Holland' is largely devoted to the consequences of Cromwell's aggressive foreign policy; having successfully hunted the Caledonian deer, he then turns to the Dutch. The Parliament's role, presented here, is distinctly subordinate, consisting largely of giving sound and honest counsel and not interfering with the navy or with Cromwell's foreign policy. Lines 145–8 suggest that the Parliament is decidedly the weak link in the government; where the navy is the object of praise, the agent of Britain's destined domination of the civilized world, the legislators need to be cautioned about their responsibilities.[36] Cromwell's position in the state, as presented in 'The Character of Holland', is clearly that of supreme executive (Jove governing in the highest sphere), rather than, as in the 'Horatian Ode', military conqueror, in some degree subordinate to parliamentary authority. In April 1653, somewhat less than two months after the probable date of the poem, Cromwell dissolved the Long Parliament.

There is no mention of Parliament in 'A Letter to Doctor Ingelo'; the Nominated Parliament may already have ended its brief existence when Marvell wrote, and in any case he had little sympathy with the assembly of saints. Cromwell is praised for his responsible use of power, his natural sense of justice, uniting strength and forbearance, but, though his virtues are regal ones and the poem praises the stability of monarchical government under Queen Christina of Sweden, Cromwell figures in the poem as military leader rather than as ruler of a state. He can both command and obey, and awaits a sign from heaven to indicate the direction of future events. By the time of *The First Anniversary*, slightly more than a year later, the signs were still unclear, but the form of government had evolved further. As we have seen, Marvell's poem is an explicit argument for acceptance of the Protectorate constitution, which attempts to solve the problem of the instability of power by 'founding a firm State by Proportions true' (line 248), seeking by the mechanisms of mixed government to hedge in the power of the executive without impairing its efficiency, and to guarantee individual liberties without promoting anarchic divisiveness.

The First Anniversary failed in its intended purpose. Between the composition of the poem in December 1654 and its publication in 1655, the settlement Marvell urged had become impossible; what was of immediate, vital concern in December had been made irrelevant a few months later by the inexorable pressure of events. The obduracy of the Protectorate Parliament in rejecting the terms of the constitutional settlement had caused Cromwell to exercise the absolute power he claimed not to want, dissolving the Parliament and along with it any pretence that he ruled by constitutional means. The problem of power remained insoluble. Poets and constitution-makers can present their dreams of perfection, but reality exacts its revenges.

In some ways the failure of *The First Anniversary* to influence events illuminates a difficulty endemic to the genre of panegyric. The panegyrist is wedded to his interpretation of events, is forced to make the best of whatever material he is offered. He may never dedicate himself entirely to the realm of imagination or that of fact, but must mediate between them, in a constant effort to show that the world as it is conforms, despite contrary appearances, to the world as it should be. A satirist is equally committed to the dual existence of hard fact and the unchanging ideal, but it is easier and more rewarding to show the divergence of reality from the ideal than to argue for their convergence. And a poem like the 'Horatian Ode', committed to nothing except the impersonal solidity of fact and not surrendering its clear-sighted independence even to that, owes much of its extraordinary, disturbing power to its refusal to simplify and resolve the complex and irresolvable. Its historical analysis remains valid, its balance of emotions convincing, even when the historical circumstances that produced it have ceased to exert any hold over the reader.

Panegyric and satire argue a case, and there is always at least as strong a case to be made for the opposition. Even though Marvell in *The First Anniversary* argues eloquently for the co-existence of order and liberty, of power and justice, other men, with equal conviction, could see in Cromwell's government an excessively strong concentration of executive power and found the limits on that power in the proposed constitution to be nominal rather than real. The Council of State, playing the role of the aristocracy in the tripartite division of power, consisted entirely of generals and civilians who gave full support to Cromwell's regime, appointed by name in the Instrument of Government. Vacancies were to be filled by indirect election, with a veto on all nominees in the hands both of the sitting Council and of the Protector. 'There was no procedure for removal except by death; so, though Parliament was to meet every three years, it was effectively deprived of control over the executive ... The Common's financial control was greatly limited by writing an Army of 30,000 men into the constitution, as a first charge which must be met.'[37] Though power was divided under Cromwell's 'ruling Instrument', there is no question that a preponderance of power lay with the executive. Indeed, Marvell's poem is largely dedicated to showing how the subordination of lesser to greater is compatible with Christian liberty and equality, how individual freedom is not injured but secured by the exercise of strong, benevolent executive power. It is in a sense the argument of *Paradise Lost*, transferred to the secular sphere. One can easily find arguments for the other side in a pamphlet like *The Tenure of Kings and Magistrates* or in one of Marvell's later anti-government satires: man's birthright of freedom should not be given away for a promise of benevolence; the insecurities of liberty are to be preferred before the specious certainties of order and obedience.

Perhaps Cromwell's attempt to bring about a stable mixed government failed because it was based on a series of fictions which only he and a minority of supporters were willing to accept. The rule of the sword, even with constitutional trappings (a constitution written by the army which the Parliament was not allowed to amend), remained the rule of the sword. The theory of consent was applied to a government which in fact had never received and did not enjoy the consent of those governed by it, ruling by simple right of conquest. Cromwell in 1655 had both too much power and too little power. No one was able effectively to challenge his authority, but a large number of Englishmen, perhaps even a majority, disliked and opposed his rule. Royalists who remained loyal to the monarchy, Presbyterians who had initially favoured the revolution but bitterly opposed the execution of Charles I, republicans who felt that Cromwell's dictatorship was a betrayal of the cause of liberty, never granted Cromwell's Protectorate any more than a passive and sullen acquiescence. For all the power concentrated in his office, Cromwell had no power over events, nor was he able to move men to a voluntary acceptance of his authority. The rational, lasting settlement he desired remained out of reach. His mastery did not extend beyond the present moment, and was precarious even there; he was unable to find any way to assure the future of the revolution or of his own government, and within a year after his death the Protectorate government collapsed entirely.

Marvell's 'Poem upon the Death of His late Highnesse the Lord Protector' (1658) grasps at straws in the hope of finding favourable auguries attending Richard Cromwell's succession. The new Protector had lived a retired life bare of accomplishments, but then so had his father until the crisis of the Civil War had impelled him on the public scene:

> He, as his Father, long was kept from sight,
> In private to be view'd by better light;
> But open'd once, what splendour does he throw:
> A *Cromwell* in an houre a Prince will grow!   (lines 309–12)[38]

He did not have his father's strength of character or his military skills, but perhaps 'his milder beams' (line 307) would assure a reign of peace and stability. The 'pearly rainbow' (line 317) seen at Richard's accession, after the fierce storms that had accompanied Oliver Cromwell's death, is presented as a sign of heaven's favour, the typological equivalent of the rainbow which God sent after the deluge as a symbol of his covenant with Noah never again to send the waters as 'a flood to destroy all flesh' (Genesis 9: 15). A time of peace had succeeded that of war, and a new kind of leadership was necessary:

> We find already what those Omens mean,
> Earth nere more glad, nor *Heaven* more serene:
> Cease now our griefs, Calme Peace succeeds a War;
> Rainbows to storms, *Richard* to *Oliver*.
> Tempt not his Clemency to try his pow'r
> He threats no Deluge, yet foretells a Showre.   (lines 319–24)

The compliment is elegantly turned, but Marvell has to search hard to find favourable omens. Richard Cromwell's peaceable nature led him indeed not to 'try his pow'r', since that power was virtually non-existent. Opposition by both army and newly assembled Parliament led to his abdication within seven months. A year later, the monarchy was restored under Charles II.

In none of his later political writings does Marvell give his wholehearted allegiance to a single man or government. The ideal no longer seems on the verge of fulfilment, but instead, in the verse and prose satires Marvell wrote in the years following the Restoration, serves to point up the inadequacies of the ugly reality men are forced to live with, and suggests a direction for needed reforms. Marvell became a satirist because of his conviction that the forces of darkness in post-Restoration England were stronger than the forces of light.

But it is here as in Gaming, where, tho the Cheat may lose for a while, to the Skill or good fortune of a fairer Player, and sometimes on purpose to draw him in deeper, yet the false Dice must at the long run Carry it, unless discovered, and when it comes once to a great Stake, will Infallibly Sweep the Table. (*Growth of Popery*, p. 155)

The poet's responsibility is to discover the cheat; fortified by his vision of the unchanging realm of truth, he seeks to open the eyes of those around him who are blinded by appearances.

Wit in a poet such as Marvell is an act of legerdemain, producing light out of darkness, yet at the same time admitting that the darkness still remains. The idealist (and the partisan) in Marvell sees the hope of a luminous order, where the realist in him sees the evident disorder that surrounds him. *The First Anniversary*, in proposing a possible solution for the problem of authority and liberty, a possible way of reconciling the conflicts of discordant groups and bringing about a stable commonwealth based on the principles of justice and reason, pays tribute to the forces of disorder in man and his universe which make such a perfect existence so unlikely. We are simultaneously aware of the vision of the ideal and of the dangers threatening it; neither is allowed to overshadow the other. In Marvell's satires, the ideal is powerfully invoked by evidence of its repeated violation. The satires present a 'disorder'd' world of 'Drunkards, Pimps, and Fools' ('Last Instructions to a Painter', lines 12, 209), a world where standards are topsy-turvy, where an inept statue which seems 'to change' the King 'into a Jack-pudding', reflects reality better than it intends: 'For 'tis such a king as no chisel can mend' ('The Statue in Stocks-Market', lines 42, 56). Such works seek to arouse in the reader a dissatisfaction that can lead to reform, by reminding him of the existence of a better world, standards to live up to. *An Account of the Growth of Popery, and Arbitrary Government in England* (1677), the most bitter of Marvell's polemical works, begins with a tribute to the British limited monarchy as closer than any other form of government 'to the Divine Perfection' (p. 5), and then proceeds to document the many ways in which reality has fallen short of the ideal. Throughout Marvell's works, the hope of bringing about a state of existence more comfortable with the ideal is balanced against an ironic awareness that the gap between the world we inhabit and the world we long for is enormous. In their differing ways all these works maintain that though man cannot control his destiny, he can act in defence of his beliefs, surrendering neither to complacency nor to despair.

3 · IN THE ARENA

I

The debate between action and retirement illustrated by the
'Horatian Ode' and 'Upon Appleton House' was resolved for
Marvell in a quite different way in the years following the
Restoration. Marvell had entered public service as Latin Secretary
in 1657, and served for nearly twenty years in Parliament, beginning with Richard Cromwell's Parliament in 1659. Until 1666,
the poet appears to have been relatively inactive in parliamentary
politics, speaking rarely and spending most of the years 1662–5
abroad on diplomatic and political missions to Holland, Russia,
Sweden, and Denmark. Then and later his parliamentary service
was marked by the scrupulousness with which he looked after the
interests of his constituency and the frequency with which he
reported to the corporation of Hull, in newsletter fashion, about
the business transacted in Parliament. He was one of the few
members of Parliament to receive a regular salary from his con-
stituents (6s. 8d. a day while Parliament was in session), and he
evidently attempted to live on this modest income. His poverty
was scorned by his detractors and celebrated by his friends and
political allies.

It is difficult for the twentieth-century reader, accustomed to
thinking of Marvell as a major figure in the canon of English
poetry, to see Marvell as his contemporaries saw him. Marvell's
lyric poetry was virtually unknown during his lifetime, and it is
likely that his *Miscellaneous Poems* were published in 1681, after
his death, largely because of his reputation as satirist and political
figure.[1] The early editions of Marvell's poems, up to and including Grosart's edition in 1872, all emphasize the patriot and
statesman. The life of Marvell prefixed to Thomas Cooke's edition in 1726 scarcely mentions his non-satiric poems and presents

Marvell as actuated by 'publick Spirit', by 'Love, and Hatred, of Right, and Wrong':

My Design in this is to draw a Pattern for all free-born *English-men*, in the Life of a worthy Patriot, whose every Action has truely merited to him, with *Aristides*, the Sirname of the *Just*. And my Intention, in the frequent Quotations from his Works, is to shew the Principles of the Man; and to make this, not only the Life of a Person, but a compleat System of sound and wholesome Doctrines.[2]

Marvell is a major figure in the collections of political satire published under the general title of *Poems on Affairs of State* in 1689, 1697, and thereafter.[3] A publisher's preface to the 1697 volume speaks of the authors represented as 'no less inspir'd by the injur'd Genius of their Country, than by the Muses ... The following poems, writ by Mr. *Milton*, Mr. *Marvell*, &c ... will shew us, that there is no where a greater Spirit of Liberty to be found, than in those who are Poets.' The poems, according to the Preface, were written against 'the selfish evil Designs of a corrupt Court' in an attempt 'to remove those pernicious Principles which lead us directly to Slavery'.[4] The author of 'On his Excellent Friend Mr. Andrew Marvell' (1678) similarly sees Marvell as 'this island's watchful sentinel', sounding the alarum against 'the grim monster, arbitrary power' and by his weapons of 'truth, wit, and eloquence' winning a victory for the forces of liberty.[5]

Marvell's transformation into satirist, polemicist, and scourge of the court begins in 1666, together with the first appearance of an organized opposition in Parliament.[6] Though Marvell wrote satiric poems before the Restoration, these were not political satires of the sort that won him praise over the next century as the resolute opponent of tyrannical power. The first of the works which form the basis of Marvell's later reputation is 'The Last Instructions to a Painter' (1667), an attack on the venality of the court at the time of the Second Dutch War. The chief villain of 'Last Instructions' is the Earl of Clarendon, and other poems attributed to Marvell in 1666–7 similarly accuse Clarendon of overweening pride and ambition.[7] Marvell was in the forefront of the Parliamentary attack on Clarendon and his administration, and after Clarendon's downfall in 1667, the poet, unlike some of his former allies whose concern for reform ceased when they had gained office, remained steadfast in opposition to the Cabal government which succeeded Clarendon:

> It is also my Opinion that the King was never since his coming in, nay, all Things considered, no King since the Conquest, so absolutely powerful at Home, as he is at present.
>
> . . .
>
> In this Session the Lords sent down to Us a Proviso for the King, that would have restored Him to all civil or ecclesiastical Prerogatives which his Ancestors had enjoyed at any Time since the Conquest. There was never so compendious a Piece of absolute universal Tyranny...We are all venal Cowards, except some few.[8]

His next major satiric work, *The Rehearsal Transpros'd* (Part I, 1672; Part II, 1673), once more attacks the would-be statesmen who in pursuit of their own advancement seek to impose upon England a government in which the rulers exercise 'uncontroulable and unlimited universal Authority' over the subjects: 'They are Men of a fiery nature, that must always be uppermost, and, so they may increase their own Splendor, care not though they set all on flame about them' (*RT*, I, pp. 65, 106). In *The Rehearsal Transpros'd*, as in the later pamphlet *Mr. Smirke; Or, The Divine in Mode* (1676), Marvell's main object of attack is the political clergy, 'so ambitious of a fortune, that [they] cannot be content with the Spirituals of *Simon Magus* and the Temporalls of *Caligula*' (*RT*, II, p. 219), whom Marvell sees as the chief proponents of arbitrary power.

> For whether it be or no, that the Clergy are not so well fitted by Education, as others for Political Affairs, I know not ... yet it is generally observed that things miscarry under their Government. If there be any Counsel more precipitate, more violent, more rigorous, more extreme than other, that is theirs. (*RT*, I, pp. 133–4)

Though in *The Rehearsal Transpros'd* and 'Last Instructions' he exempts the King himself from his attacks on those courtiers who seek 'to change the Lawfull Government of *England* into an Absolute Tyranny' (*Growth of Popery*, p.3), in several verse satires written during the 1670s he aims his shafts directly at Charles II and his brother and heir the Duke of York.

> As cities that to the fierce conquerors yield
> Do at their own charges their citadels build,

So Sir Robert advanced the King's statue, in token
Of bankers defeated and Lombard-street broken.
　　　　　　　('Statue in Stocks-Market', lines 1–4)

But though the whole world cannot shew such another,
Yet we'd better by far have him than his brother.　(lines 59–60)

'The Kings Vowes' (c. 1670), more good-humoured and less bitter than several satires by Marvell, treats Charles II as contemptuous of constitutional restrictions, committed only to the pursuit of his own pleasure, indifferent to the welfare of his subjects, tyrannous because of love of ease rather than love of power:

I will have a fine Tunick, a shash and a Vest
Though not rule like the *Turk* yet I will be so drest
And who knows but the mode may soon bring in the rest?

I will have a fine pond and a pretty Decoy
Where the Ducks and the Drakes may their freedoms enjoy
And quack in their language still, *Vive le Roy.*

Marvell's authentic poems stop short of calling for revolution, though several poems falsely attributed to Marvell are openly republican ('But canst thou Divine when things shall be mended? / When the Reign of the Line of the Stuarts is ended').[9] Nevertheless, most of Marvell's writings in the last three years of his life are clarion calls, warning that the nation is in grave danger. Charles's rule had been a disaster ('O what fools were you to receive him!') and James was likely to prove even worse ('But if ever he get / For himself up to set, / The whole Nation may live to repent it'). Only the vigilance of Parliament had kept the King and his courtiers from having 'burglar'd all our Propriety'; while the court continues at what Marvell calls in one of his letters 'the highest Pitch of Want and Luxury', the nation suffers: 'their Churches unbuilt / And their houses undwelt / And their Orphans want bread to feed 'm.' No amount of power or wealth can satisfy the insatiable appetites of Charles and his courtiers:

I see, whoe'er's freed,
　　You for Slaves are decreed
Untill you all burne againe, burne again.[10]

Throughout this period, Marvell was generally recognized as a leading figure in the Country Party. Pro-government writers frequently attacked him as an unrelenting member of the Parliamentary opposition and as the leading pamphleteer against the government.[11] Most of Marvell's later writings, indeed, are specifically designed to stir up sentiment against those in power – from the call for Clarendon's impeachment or removal from office that concludes 'Clarindon's House-Warming' and (if the poem is Marvell's) 'The Second Advice to a Painter' to the attempt, in his last important work, *An Account of the Growth of Popery, and Arbitrary Government in England*, to expose a plot, extending over several years, 'to introduce a *French* slavery, and ... to establish the *Roman* Idolatry' (p. 14). The function of *The Growth of Popery*, as of Marvell's other satiric and polemical works, is to reveal, to make public what has been concealed, to force on the reader's notice what he might otherwise prefer not to see: 'Thus far hath the Conspiracy against our Religion and Government been laid open, which if true, it was more than time that it should be discovered' (p. 153).

The satirist's responsibility is to speak the truth even when it is painful. As Marvell writes in his last work, *Remarks upon a late Disingenuous Discourse*, 'It is not what this or that man, but what Truth saith that is to be regarded.' Similar statements of the poet's moral obligation to speak out, eschewing flattery, echo throughout Marvell's works and find parallels in the writings of many other satirists. The envoi of 'Third Advice', sometimes attributed to Marvell, states the position clearly: 'What Servants will conceale, and Couns'lors spare / To tell, the Painter and the Poet dare.'[12] In Dryden's words, 'the true end of *Satyre*, is the amendment of Vices by correction. And he who writes Honestly, is no more an Enemy to the Offendour, than the Physician to the Patient, when he prescribes harsh Remedies to an inveterate Disease.' It is possible, though unlikely, that the 'Offendour' himself is educable and that the sight of himself in the satirist's mirror will help bring about his reform. 'I have not, so much as an uncharitable Wish against *Achitophel*', Dryden tells us, 'but, am content to be Accus'd of a good natur'd Errour; and, to hope with *Origen*, that the Devil himself may, at last, be sav'd.'[13] Marvell's anatomy of abuses leading to revolution in *The Rehearsal Transpros'd* posits an initial stage in which the 'Society it self' is given the opportunity to correct its own faults.

For all Governments and Societies of men...do in process of long time gather an irregularity, and wear away much of their primitive institution. And therefore the true wisdom of all Ages hath been to review at fit periods those errours, defects, or excesses, that have insensibly crept on into the Publick Administration; to brush the dust off the Wheels, and oyl them again, or if it be found advisable to chuse a set of new ones. And this Reformation is most easily and with least disturbance to be effected by the Society it self...all Societies having the liberty to bring themselves within compass. (*RT*, ii, p. 239)

But though self-amendment is possible, it is not very common. A body of men or an individual under accusation, more often than not, 'shall be so far from correcting its own exorbitances, as to defend them even to the offence and invasion of the Universality' (*RT*, ii, p. 240). Only in rare men is the appeal of private interest less strong than that of the common good. Therefore, in the case of political abuses, the hope for reform devolves on a person or body possessing jurisdiction over the offender, able to overrule him, strip him of his power, or otherwise prevent him from doing further damage. 'Last Instructions', the 'Second Advice' and 'Third Advice', and *The Growth of Popery* all end with addresses to Charles II, urging him to restore the state to health, countering the malign influence of the 'scratching *Courtiers*' who 'undermine a *Realm*', gnawing like rodents through 'the Palace's Foundations', 'burr'wing themselves to hoard their guilty Store' ('Last Instructions', lines 978–80):

This Book...however it may be calumniated by interested persons, was written with no other intent than of meer Fidelity and Service to his *Majesty*...that his *Majesty* having discerned the Disease, may with his Healing Touch apply the Remedy. (*Growth of Popery*, p. 156)

In addressing the King in such a manner, Marvell exercises the right of a virtuous citizen in advising his prince, praising certain kinds of behaviour and dispraising others, warning against counsels he considers pernicious: 'Kings in the Country oft have gone astray, / Nor of a Peasant scorn'd to learn the Way' ('Last Instructions', lines 959–60). He has of course ample literary precedent in the Renaissance; Sir Thomas Hoby, for example, writes in the 'Breef Rehersall of the Chiefe Conditions and Qualities in a Courtier' appended to his translation of Castiglione's *The Courtier*:

The final end of a Courtier, wher to al his good condicions and honest qualities tende, is to beecome An Instructer and Teacher of his Prince or Lorde, inclininge him to vertuous practises: And to be francke and free with him...in matters touching his honour and estimation, alwayes putting him in minde to folow vertue and to flee vice, opening unto him the commodities of the one and inconveniences of the other: And to shut his eares against flatterers, which are the first beeginninge of self seekinge and all ignorance.[14]

Marvell does not see the King's direct intervention as the only cure for the evils of the state – especially since the King himself is often a major cause of these evils. The poet and his political allies were firm believers in Parliament's responsibility to act as guardian of the interests of the nation; though the King's person is in theory considered 'most sacred and inviolable', 'his Ministers ... are accountable for all and must answer it at their perills' (*The Growth of Popery*, p.4). The principle of ministerial accountability, now and for many years a mainstay of the British system of government, was by no means universally accepted in Marvell's day, and indeed the bitter constitutional conflicts of the seventeenth century turned largely on questions of how far the power of Parliament on the one hand, and the King and his ministers on the other, extended.[15] 'Last Instructions' presents Parliament as the main check on the desire for arbitrary power which motivates Clarendon, the Earl of Arlington, and other great lords of the court. The plea to Charles II at the end of the poem to remove from power the palace guard 'who the *Court* restrain, / And where all *England* serves, themselves would reigne' (lines 965–6) does not assume Charles's dedication to principles of good government, but warns him that kings too may be called into account. In a dream vision reminiscent of Richard III's vision the night before his climactic battle at Bosworth Field, the King is represented as the unwilling object of a ghostly visitation. The vivid physical details are meant to bring the warning home, to the reader as to the reluctant monarch:

> Shake then the room, and all his Curtains tear,
> And with blue streaks infect the Taper clear:
> While, the pale Ghosts, his Eye does fixt admire
> Of Gransire *Harry*, and of *Charles* his Sire.
> *Harry* sits down, and in his open side
> The grizly Wound reveals, of which he dy'd.

And ghastly *Charles*, turning his Collar low,
The purple thread about his Neck does show...
The wondrous Night the pensive *King* revolves,
And rising, straight on *Hyde*'s Disgrace resolves.   (lines 915–26)

In 'Clarindon's House-Warming', written several months earlier in anticipation of the Parliamentary session beginning on St James's Day, 25 July 1667, Clarendon's downfall is also predicted, but in this poem the King is scarcely mentioned. The responsibility for bringing an end to the Chancellor's misrule is here placed in the hands of Parliament, acting as representatives of the people of England: 'When like the whole Ox, for publick good cheare / He comes to be roasted next St James's Faire.'[16]

In attacking the King's chosen ministers or the corruption of court society, Marvell is treading on dangerous ground, since the King was the leading figure in that society, closely associated with those ministers (who indeed may simply have been acting to carry out royal policies). The advice he offers the King in these works cannot often have been welcomed. Indeed, many of Marvell's satiric writings in verse and prose were considered seditious by the government, and attempts were made to suppress their circulation. Several of the poet's political associates were executed for treason, and when he died there were rumours that he had been poisoned. The element of personal risk involved in the career of a satirist may be witnessed in the sub-title of *The Rehearsal Transpros'd; The Second Part*: 'Occasioned by Two Letters: The first Printed, by a nameless Author ... The Second Letter left for me at a Friends House, Dated Nov. 3, 1673. Subscribed J.G. and concluding with these words; If thou darest to Print or Publish any Lie or Libel against Doctor Parker, By the Eternal God I will cut thy Throat. Answered by Andrew Marvell' (*RT*, ii, p. 147).[17] His most direct challenge to royal power is his witty and audacious 'Mock Speech' of April 1675, a parody of the royal speech from the throne at the beginning of a parliamentary session, which is said to have been smuggled into the House of Commons and distributed to every member. 'His Majesty's most Gracious Speech to both Houses of Parliament' is an appeal to Parliament against the King, urging the Parliament by implication to exercise its responsibility and deny the irresponsible, dissembling monarch any supply.

It seems a good part of my Revenue will faile in two or three Yeares, except You will be pleas'd to continue it. Now I have this to say for it, Pray why did you give me so much except you resolv'd to go on? The Nation hates you already, for giving so much, and I will hate you now if you doe not give me more.[18]

The blame for corruption and mismanagement in the government of England, according to the 'Mock Speech', rests not with the King's ministers alone, but with the King himself. In similar fashion, 'The Kings Vowes', 'The Statue at Charing Cross', and other verse satires of the 1670s find the court and the King inseparable. Perhaps the King rules the Lord Treasurer, perhaps the Lord Treasurer rules the King ('Though the *King* be of Copper and *Danby* of Gold'); in either case the spectacle of the court of Charles II is enough to make his father's statue weep:

> Though of Brasse yet with greif it would melt him away
> To behold ev'ry day such a *Court*, such a *Son*.[19]

The ultimate appeal in Marvell's satiric writings is to a wider audience. A ruling cabal is able to maintain its power by secrecy; as with the nuns in 'Upon Appleton House', once the 'super-stitions vainly fear'd' and '*Relicks false*' are 'set to view' (lines 260–1), the power of the enchantment is broken. Roman Catholicism is able to maintain its hold over its deluded followers, according to *The Growth of Popery*, by keeping hidden what God has revealed to all men, 'sequestring' the Word of God in its exclusive possession:

For having thus a book which is universally avowed to be of Divine Authority, but sequestring it only into such hands as were intrusted in the cheat, they had the opportunity to vitiate, suppresse, or interpret to their own profit those Records by which the poor People hold their salvation. (p. 6).

Truth and justice can be served by stripping the veil of secrecy from the arcana of government. To inform the reader of what he might otherwise not know will serve the satirist's cause more effectively than insistent moralizing. Much of *The Growth of Popery* is taken up with a straightforward historical narrative, and many documents are printed verbatim.

But my intention is onely to write a naked Narrative of some of the most considerable passages in the meeting of *Parliament* the 15 of *Febr.* 1676.

Such as have come to my choice which may serve for matter to some stronger Pen and to such as have more leisure and further opportunity to discover and communicate to the Publick. This in the mean time will by the Progresse made in so few weeks, demonstrate at what rate these men drive over the necks of King and People, of Religion and Government. (pp. 16–17)

The Growth of Popery, like 'Last Instructions' and others of Marvell's satires, is valuable to modern historians for the amount of information it contains, and its detailed reports on the proceedings in Parliament and the manoeuvres of the court party during the years 1672–7 served for contemporary readers an even more significant function in making public what might otherwise not have come to light.[20]

II

Marvell's later writings generally seek to award blame or praise – in the words of Ruth Nevo, they 'present the deformed image of vice and the fair face of virtue at one and the same time'.[22] On the one hand, such works 'represent / In quick *Effigy*, others Faults, and feign / By making them ridiculous to restrain' ('Last Instructions', lines 390–2); on the other, they encourage those the author considers worthy of praise in hopes of increasing their number and strengthening their resolution. Most men are blinded by their folly: in their 'brutish fury' (*First Anniversary*, line 177), their greed, their swollen self-conceit, they are sunk in a 'Lethargy' or boil in 'a Feaver' (*RT*, II, p. 152), unable to distinguish objective reality from their diseased imaginings. Marvell's extended ironic diagnosis of Parker as incurably maddened by pride is characteristic both in its wit and in its evocation of standards of rationality, humility, and self-knowledge:

This thing alone elevated him exceedingly in his own conceit, and raised his *Hypocondria* into the Region of the Brain: that his head swell'd like any Bladder with wind and vapour...He was stretch'd to such an height in his own fancy, that he could not look down from top to toe but his Eyes dazled at the Precipice of his Stature. (*RT*, I, p. 30)

The 'addle-brain'd Citts' who abase themselves before Charles II and the Duke of York and 'in chaines offer up [their] Freedome' ('Upon his Majesties being made free of the Citty', lines

12–13) the ambitious statesmen maddened by 'overweening Presumption and preposterous Ambition' (*RT*, I, p. 29) all walk in a self-imposed darkness. The power of self-interest makes it difficult to follow the narrow path of righteousness, but man is under a moral obligation to strive to distinguish between good and evil and not be ruled by mere expediency, not blind himself to a reality higher than his own comfort, his own flattering self-image. 'The world in all', Marvell says in 'The Loyal Scot', contains 'but two nations', namely 'the Good' and 'the Bad', capable of 'worth heroic' or 'heroic crimes': 'Under each Pole place either of the two, / The Bad will basely, Good will bravely do.'[23]

This clear-cut division of mankind into 'the Good' and 'the Bad' characterizes all of Marvell's satiric writings, and often takes the form of a contrast between the unregenerate multitude and a saving remnant. From 'Last Instructions to a Painter' to *The Growth of Popery* he singles out for praise a handful of men who 'stood up . . . for the *English* Liberties' though 'under all the disadvantages imaginable', being 'overlaid by Numbers' in Parliament (*Growth of Popery*, pp. 60–1) and at all times conscious of the weight of power exerted against them.

> But notwithstanding these, there is a hanfull of *Salt*, a sparkle of *Soul*, that hath hitherto preserved this grosse Body from Putrefaction, some *Gentlemen* that are constant, invariable, indeed *English*-men; such as are above *hopes*, or *fears*, or *dissimulation*, that can neither flatter, nor betray their King, or Country: But being conscious of their own Loyalty, and Integrity, proceed throw good and bad report, to acquit themselves in their Duty to God, their Prince, and their Nation; Although so small a Scantling in number, that men can scarce reckon of them more than a *Quorum*. (p. 79)

In speaking of this small group of resolute patriots, Marvell frequently uses military metaphors, calling forth the traditions of unselfish heroism associated with epic poetry and with republican Rome. Thus in 'Last Instructions' an outnumbered Country Party M.P., faced with a surprise attack in a thinly populated house, is described as 'fighting it single till the rest might arm', holding off the foe like Horatius at the bridge: 'Such *Roman Cocles* strid: before the Foe, / The falling Bridge behind, the Stream below' (lines 248–50). Confident because they stand up for the interest of the people of England, these brave men are able to counteract the superior force of their opponents:

These and some more with single Valour stay
The adverse Troops, and hold them all at Bay.
Each thinks his Person represents the whole,
And with that thought does multiply his Soul:
Believes himself an Army.   (lines 267–71)

Marvell's consistent emphasis on the small number of true patriots and the difficulty of remaining steadfast in the face of the designs of those in power no doubt reflects his Puritan conviction that man and nature are deeply infected by original sin and that the regenerate elect are at any time few in number. A belief in the innate sinfulness of man runs through his works: 'Men,' he says in *Mr. Smirke*, 'are all infirm and indisposed in their spiritual condition.'[24] Marvell's essential Puritanism shows itself in his consistent adherence to the doctrine of justification by faith: to assume that we can merit salvation by our own unaided virtue, that the superlative merit we see in ourselves will be recognized in heaven, is in his view mere pride.

To render men capable of Salvation there is a more extraordinary influence of Gods Spirit required and promised...For mine own part I have, I confess, some reason, perhaps particular to my self, to be diffident of mine own *Moral Accomplishments*, & therefore may be the more inclinable to think I have a necessity of some extraordinary assistance to sway the weakness of my belief, and to strengthen me in good duties. (*RT*, II, pp. 267–8)

The truly virtuous men – those whom Marvell calls 'the little invisible *Catholick Church*', a 'Congregation of the Faithful' (*Short Historical Essay*, p. 23) who resist the external pressures, in religion as in politics, to follow the lure of power 'as nimbly as the Needle to the Load stone' (*Mr. Smirke*, Sig. g2), but instead have 'always searched and believed the Scriptures' and 'made a stand by their Testimonies and sufferings' – are always in a minority (*Short Historical Essay*, p. 23). Like other Puritans of the libertarian left, Marvell questioned the rigidity of the orthodox Calvinist view of predestination, but no less than Milton he held that few men are found worthy of salvation.

The recurrent image of the 'small ... Scantling' of honourable men also reflects the belief, particularly characteristic of Restoration satire and comedy, that the fools make up an overwhelming majority in any company, and that the true wits, to whom the artist addresses himself, are no more numerous than the truly virtuous. The prose satires *The Rehearsal Transpros'd* and *Mr. Smirke* are explicitly addressed to an elite of true wits (as their titles, derived from Buckingham's *The Rehearsal* and Etherege's *The Man of Mode*, suggest) and owe much of their effectiveness to Marvell's skill in manipulating the responses of a court audience, each member of whom is eager to be enrolled in the ranks of the elect in the war against folly. Dryden, whose political allegiances were entirely opposed to those of Marvell, similarly singles out in *Absalom and Achitophel* a loyal few who 'ev'n in the worst of days' remained true to their principles. In Dryden's satire as in 'Last Instructions' and *The Rehearsal Transpros'd*, literary convention is ultimately inseparable from moral, aesthetic, and political convictions.

The emphasis throughout Marvell's works on the 'hanfull of Salt' within the 'grosse Body', moreover, reflects political realities as Marvell saw them. The court had many weapons at its disposal, not the least of which was the distribution of honours and offices, and Clifford before 1674 and Danby afterwards succeeded by wholesale bribery in converting opponents to supporters of the court. As Marvell writes in a letter of 1671:

Nevertheless such was the Number of the constant Courtiers, increased by the Apostate Patriots, who were bought off, for that Turn, some at six, others at ten, one at fifteen, thousand Pounds in Mony, besides what offices, Lands, and Reversions, to others, that it is a Mercy they gave away not the whole Land, and Liberty, of *England*.[25]

For the Country Party opposition to muster a majority in Parliament on a particular issue, it was necessary for the small band of steadfast opponents of the court to gain allies. In 'Last Instructions', Marvell attributes the defeat of the court's excise bill to the votes of an 'unknown Reserve' of country gentlemen, financially independent and grown critical of the abuses of the court: 'A *Gross* of *English Gentry*, nobly born, / Of clear *Estates*, and to no *Faction* sworn' (lines 286–8). By the time he wrote *The Growth of Popery*, ten further years of experience with the same House of Commons had made him more sceptical about the motivation of his temporary allies, and he speaks of 'the assimilation of ambitious, factious, and disappointed Members, to the little, but solid, and unbyassed Party' (p. 79).

The contrast between the 'two nations', the unregenerate many and the virtuous few, helps give unity to the otherwise diffuse and anecdotal 'Last Instructions to a Painter'. Though no one figure dominates the poem, the Earl of Clarendon is presented both as the leader of the court forces and as the embodiment of the principles of ambition, greed, and disorder. Here as in 'Clarindon's House-Warming', the Chancellor is depicted as swollen with pride, insatiable in his craving for power: 'See how he reigns in his new Palace *culminant*, / And sits in State Divine like *Jove* the *fulminant!*' (lines 355–6). The 'painter' motif serves both to provide rhetorical patterning and to call the reader's attention to the painful discrepancy between reality and ideal: look here upon this picture, and on this. The deliberately grotesque and ugly details in the extended portraits of the Earl of St Albans, the Countess of Castlemaine, and the Duchess of York ('Paint her with Oyster Lip, and breath of Fame', line 61) supplant conventional ideas of artistic decorum with an iconoclastic aesthetic suitable to a 'race of Drunkards, Pimps, and Fools' (line 12), while they suggest the emptiness and futility of a life devoted solely to the headlong pursuit of power and pleasure:

> Paint *Castlemaine* in Colours that will hold,
> Her, not her Picture, for she now grows old.
> She through her Lacquies Drawers as he ran,
> Discern'd Love's Cause, and a new Flame began.
> Her wonted joys thenceforth and *Court* she shuns,
> And still within her mind the Footman runs.   (lines 79–84)

All the courtiers in 'Last Instructions' live by a Hobbesian calculus, in which motivations are devalued to the merely physical – 'Love's Cause' is a penis, the 'mind' can express itself only in bodily terms (as with the Speaker of the House of Commons, Sir Edward Turner: 'When *Grievance* urg'd, he swells like squatted Toad', line 87).

Because Clarendon's confederates are led entirely by self-interest, there are no feelings of loyalty among them, as there is no fidelity to principle. Thus when Clarendon loses the King's favour, his former associates are quick to abandon him and make him a scapegoat for the failures of the policies they had supported:

To her own Husband, *Castlemain*, untrue,
False to his Master *Bristol, Arlington*,
And *Coventry*, falser than any one,
Who to the Brother, Brother would betray;
Nor therefore trusts himself to such as they.   (lines 932–6)

The lesser troops of the court party are equally ruled by the desire for personal aggrandizement. The lengthy mock-heroic account of the battle of the excise, in which debtors, procurers, drinkers, martyrs to the pox, and the bloated 'Troop of Clarendon, all full' (line 177) pass in review, once again presents the institution of Parliament as having been debased by men who are ruled by physical appetite alone. Though a disorderly mob, 'whose Horses each with other interferes' (line 196), each seeking his own benefit and indifferent to any other concerns, they are united and given a semblance of military discipline by their awareness that their interest can best be served by selling their votes to the court: 'For always he commands that pays' (line 172).

To them succeeds a despicable Rout,
But knew the Word and well could face about;
Expectants pale, with hopes of spoil allur'd.   (lines 157–9)

Opposed to the corrupt many in 'Last Instructions' are the upright few, who maintain their principles in spite of the utter darkness that surrounds them. Though they inhabit a world 'rul'd by cheating' where all values appear to be inverted, yet a few men are able somehow to persevere in a course of honour and integrity.[26] In such a world, heroic and virtuous action is necessarily its own reward, since it is not likely to meet with any earthly success. Any victories are likely to be temporary, the result of momentary good fortune, defying all ordinary expectations:

It is lesse difficult to conceive, how Fire was first brought to light in the World then how any good thing could ever be produced out of a House of Commons so constituted, unless as that is imagined to have come from the rushing of Trees, or battering of Rocks together, by accident. (*Growth of Popery*, p. 79)

At times, all one can do is to die bravely in defence of one's beliefs. The death of Archibald Douglas, described in an extended episode, is thus a paradigm of how one should behave when faced with disaster, and the gallantry of Douglas points up the in-

77

adequacy of the models of behaviour provided by those around him, with no sanctions to call on other than self-interest. The 'feather'd *Gallants*', hoping to find entertainment in the spectacle of a battle, run away 'when first they hear the Gun' (lines 597–9); the sailors 'refuse to mount our Ships' or desert to the Dutch in anger over not having been paid (lines 600–1). The lines on 'brave *Douglas*' are immediately preceded by a complementary portrait of Sir Thomas Daniel, 'of Person tall, and big of bone', whose deceptive martial appearance hides 'a vain Terror', so that when faced by the Dutch fireships '*Daniel* then thought he was in *Lyons* Den' and deserted his ship (lines 633, 637, 642). Douglas behaves differently:

> Fix'd on his Ship, he fac'd that horrid Day,
> And wondred much at those that run away...
> That precious life he yet disdains to save,
> Or with known Art to try the gentle Wave.
> Much him the Honours of his ancient Race
> Inspire, nor would he his own deeds deface.   (lines 661–2, 671–4)

Like the outnumbered band of parliamentary warriors who are able to 'recall to mind' their 'former Trophees' (line 253) before going into battle, secure in their knowledge that they fight not for themselves but as representatives of an honourable tradition, Douglas is incapable of fear. He faces death with aristocratic calm, in lines reminiscent of Marvell's account of Charles I on the scaffold; as with Charles I, his entire life has been preparation for this climactic moment:

> Down on the Deck he laid himself, and dy'd,
> With his dear Sword reposing by his Side.
> And, on the flaming Plank, so rests his Head,
> As one that's warm'd himself and gone to Bed.   (lines 687–90)

The Douglas episode seems in some ways anomalous, since it is an extended set piece, stylistically and tonally at variance with most of the poem, and Marvell in fact used the episode a second time in an entirely different context, as the nucleus of 'The Loyal Scot' (c. 1670). But the function of the episode in 'Last Instructions' is clear: it provides, after a manner familiar in satire, an explicit statement of the ideal against which the deviations from that ideal can be measured. As in Marvell's non-satiric works, the reality of nature fallen, pressing in on our consciousness from all sides, is contrasted with the hope of nature redeemed. Art, like life, can provide patterns for imitation, both positive and negative:

As Mr. *How*'s Letter may serve for a Pattern of what is to be imitated, so *The Discourse* may remain as a Mark (the best use it can be put to) of what ought to be avoided in all writing of Controversies, especially by Divines, in those that concern Religion. (*Remarks upon a late Disingenuous Discourse,* p. 16)

Despite the apparent helplessness of poetry before the massed forces of earthly might, the poet's power, like that of beleaguered virtue, is infinite, since he bears the gift of immortality.

> Fortunate Boy! If either Pencil's Fame,
> Of if my Verse can propagate thy Name,
> When *Oeta* and *Alcides* are forgot,
> Our *English* youth shall sing the Valiant *Scot.*
> ('Last Instructions', lines 693–6)

In a world where values are topsy-turvy, the poet is the voice of unchanging truth, seeking to right the balance and bring others to their senses. When other potential champions have run away or bowed down before the altar of triumphant injustice, 'then is the Poets time, 'Tis then he drawes, / And single fights forsaken Vertues cause' ('Tom May's Death', lines 65–6). Though the political circumstances of individual works differ, Marvell's political writings share the same fundamental attitude: the body politic is diseased, and the necessary first step towards a cure is to face the truth.

In a variant on the familiar satirist-as-physician metaphor, Marvell likens the poet in the envoi concluding 'Last Instructions' to an astronomer, discovering spots which obscure the light of royal sun:

> So his bold Tube, Man, to the Sun apply'd,
> And Spots unknown to the bright Star descry'd;
> Show'd they obscure him, while too near they prease,
> And seem his Courtiers, are but his disease...
> Blame not the *Muse* that brought those spots to sight,
> Which, in your Splendour hid, Corrode your Light.   (lines 949–58)

The lines attempt, as by a surgical operation, to divide the King from the corruption of his court. The ministers may try to shelter themselves behind the royal prerogative, attempting by flattery to convince the King that their interests and his are one, but by legal definition a monarch who 'can do no wrong, nor can he receive wrong' must be distinguished from his appointed ministers, 'accountable for all ... at their perills' (*The Growth of Popery*, p. 4). The King is represented here as the principle of health and continuity in the state, where the intriguing courtiers are represented as ephemeral, diseased, the enemies both to his power and to his justice, in spite of their pretensions to the contrary. Throughout the envoi, a blind commitment to self-interest and its consequence, the Hobbesian universal war of each against each, are contrasted with the harmonious state, a flourishing organism whose members recognize the reciprocal ties that link them together. The ruler's interest is not separate from the public interest, because 'the Country is the *King*' ('Last Instructions', line 974). Disease is thus presented as a conspiracy against health, an attempt to overturn a natural, established system of government in which the King, rather than acting according to his private desires or whims, is ruled by law. The conspirators, as Marvell presents them, would blindly destroy all around them in their obsessive pursuit of gain:

> Bold and accurs'd are they, that all this while
> Have strove to Isle the *Monarch* from his *Isle*:
> And to improve themselves, on false pretence,
> About the Common *Prince* have rais'd a Fence;
> The *Kingdom* from the *Crown* distinct would see,
> And peele the Bark to burn at last the Tree. (lines 967–72)

Satirists notoriously find it harder to express convincing positives directly than to adumbrate an ideal realm, often associated with an unreachable transcendent sphere or an irrecoverable past, which fitfully illuminates sordid and ludicrous reality. Even in lines like those just quoted, where the principles of natural harmony and reason evoked are given as self-evident, not open to disagreement, the effectiveness of the passage comes from the gap disclosed between the ideal commonwealth and the distorted actuality. At the end of 'Last Instructions' Marvell seeks to translate the idea of a saving remnant into concrete, practical form, suggesting the kind of men the King ought to appoint as his advisers. Such men, the poem states, comprise a natural aristo-

cracy – one primarily of character rather than birth, though
Marvell like other liberal theorists of the period seemed at times
to make landed wealth a prerequisite to virtue.[27] The lines carry
less poetic conviction than the previous attack on 'scratching
Courtiers', yet they hold open the hope that not all men are
greedy and vicious, that there are potential counsellors who seek
nothing for themselves and desire only the public good, that the
ideal is perhaps not entirely beyond reach:

> But they whom born to Virtue and to Wealth,
> Nor Guilt to flatt'ry binds, nor want to stealth;
> Whose gen'rous Conscience and whose Courage high
> Does with clear Counsels their large Souls supply...
> (Where few the number, choice is there less hard)
> Give us this *Court*, and rule without a *Guard*.   (lines 983–90)

Marvell does not delude himself about the character of the
king he is addressing, or about the likelihood of bringing about
such far-reaching reform. To speak of *The Rehearsal Transpros'd*,
as its editor D. I. B. Smith does, as illustrating a courtier's skills
in presenting 'a picture of the King, as he might well have visualized himself at a moment of complacency', is entirely to mistake
the nature of the work and of Marvell's rhetorical techniques in
such satires as *The Rehearsal Transpros'd* and 'Last Instructions'.[28] The praise of King and constitution in Marvell's satires
is normative: he is holding up a standard against which shameful
reality can be measured, reminding his audience that there
are alternative standards for behaviour other than self-interest.
Though the passages devoted to Charles II in 'Last Instructions'
and Marvell's other satires show him to be 'a man, with as little
mixture of the seraphic part as ever man had', nevertheless the
poet treats him here as capable of recognizing the truth when it is
shown him and of acting in a manner suitable to a prince.[29]
   As Marvell's satires constantly point out, the temptations of
power are exceedingly difficult to resist. Such poems as 'The
Kings Vowes' and 'Upon his Majesties being made free of the
Citty' portray Charles II as a man whose love of ease inclined
him toward the belief that he could rule by consulting only his
immediate pleasure. A similar view of Charles II, as governed by
'this principle of making the love of ease exercise an entire

sovereignty in his thoughts', finds expression in Halifax's 'Character' and in Rochester's notorious 'scepter' lampoon, and, more militantly stated, in such anti-monarchist satires as 'Britannia and Raleigh' and 'The History of Insipids': 'They [kings] know no law but their own lust' or, as Rochester puts it tersely, 'his scepter and his prick are of a length'.[30] The portrayal of Charles II in 'Upon his Majesties being made free of the Citty', the two 'statue' poems, and the mock speech from the throne is no less unflattering and coldly realistic. Charles as presented here is more an embodiment of disorder than of order – irresponsible, selfish, contemptuous of the restrictions of reason and of law (much like the courtiers in 'Last Instructions'). Appeals to nature, reason, and the good of the nation, as 'Last Instructions' and Marvell's other satires make abundantly clear, may well fall on deaf ears. Nevertheless, the poet must speak out. Here as elsewhere in Marvell, an unblinking awareness of man's boundless capacity for vice, folly, and self-deception is balanced against the hope that truth may at last prevail.

III

Throughout his satires in verse and prose, Marvell's muse, like Swift's, is Truth. His many statements expressing scorn for hypocrites and timeservers who flee from 'forsaken Vertues cause', 'Apostatizing' from the 'spotless' truth of the artist whenever subjected to the slightest pressure, reflect his independence of character, while they also express a deliberately chosen artistic stance ('Tom May's Death', lines 66, 72–3). Considered rhetorically rather than autobiographically, such statements serve as 'ethical proof', intended to show the author to be a man of integrity, whom readers can trust.[31] A great number of poets, from Skelton to Yeats, have proclaimed 'walking naked' as their artistic credo, and the suspicion of rhetorical ornamentation is as common among satirists as the suspicion of wordly wealth and power. The pretence of objectivity, the claim of eschewing all artifice, is of course itself an artistic device, potentially one of the most powerful weapons in the artist's arsenal; 'naked Narrative', furthermore, is an especially demanding form of art, and one particularly suited to satire. The works of Swift illustrate the effectiveness in persuasive writing of a calm, seemingly objective and unemotional tone in gaining the confidence of readers.

Yet the belief that truth is naked, single, and absolute raises problems for the artist. The commitment to dry factuality which we find in *The Growth of Popery* may be seen as the logical culmination of Marvell's career, and yet in some ways it represents a position inimical to art, the origins of which we can trace in Marvell's earlier writings. 'Tom May's Death', Marvell's most explicit statement of the responsibilities of the artist, is more or less royalist in its politics, but it is rigidly Puritan in its aesthetic attitudes. A similar attitude finds expression in his verse satires of the 1670s, in *The Growth of Popery*, and in such lyrics as 'The Mower against Gardens': metaphors are likely to be lies, and true art is 'sworn Enemy to all that do pretend' ('Tom May's Death', line 30), forswearing the fraudulent and corrupt inventions by which 'Luxurious Man' seeks to transform 'plain and pure' nature into his own 'double' and fallen image ('The Mower against Gardens', lines 1, 4, 9). The uncompromising severity of his attacks upon May, presented in 'Tom May's Death' as a sycophant willing to sell his services to the highest bidder, or upon the courtiers of Charles II, presented in his later verse satires as bloated, greedy men who allow the body politic to become more and more diseased as they erect palaces and statues of a specious grandeur, reflects a suspicion of art similar to that in 'The Mower against Gardens' and 'The Coronet'.

Marvell's satires are all essentially iconoclastic, directed at illegitimate assumptions of heroism, dignity, and grandeur, the impressive but specious 'Pageantry' and 'Chimaeras' with which men deceive others and themselves. In organizing many of his satiric poems around an address to a painter, sculptor, or architect, he makes his iconoclasm quite explicit: such poems as 'Last Instructions to a Painter', 'The Statue at Charing Cross', and 'Clarindon's House-Warming' seek to establish an aesthetic of realism in opposition to the idealizing tendencies characteristic of 'historical' painting, statuary, and grand public buildings as of heroic panegyric.[32] Here as elsewhere, Marvell sees his role as the servant of truth, however unpalatable the truth may be in contrast with comforting illusion. Each victim, whether he be hack poet, ambitious clergyman, Lord Chancellor, or occupant of a throne, is left 'scarce ... a rag to his breech' ('Statue in Stocks-Market', line 52), stripped of the false dignity with which he clothes himself, revealed in all his deformities by the harsh and ungenerous light of wit: 'Where ought is extolled beyond reason ...it is necessary to depreciate it by true proportion' (*Short Historical Essay*, p. 19).

'Tom May's Death' and Marvell's 'painter' and 'statue' poems direct their attack at false art, art which deliberately sets out to mislead. Yet implicit in all these works is the Platonic and Puritan charge that all art lies. 'The Coronet' suggests that even if the artist has not, like May, consciously 'prostituted' his art ('Tom May's Death', line 71), he must inevitably succumb to the pursuit of a compromising 'mortal Glory'. The most subtle temptation facing the artist, according to 'The Coronet', is the belief that his own art is not contaminated by the fall, and the hardest test for the Christian is to give up what is most beloved to him when his master demands it:

> But thou who only could'st the Serpent tame,
> Either his slipp'ry knots at once untie,
> And disintangle all his winding Snare:
> Or shatter too with him my curious frame:
> And let these wither, so that he may die,
> Though set with Skill and chosen out with Care.   (lines 18–24)

'The Coronet' owes much of its poignancy to the paradox it embodies, as a plea to resolve a conflict which it knows can never be resolved, invoking an ideal simplicity by means of a complex and carefully woven wreath of language. Like Herbert in 'Jordan' I and II, Marvell proclaims that truth must be single, in the ironic awareness that every line of the poem shows it to be multiple. Marvell's satires at their best show a similar recognition of the doubleness of truth. In them, as in effective satire generally, the impulse toward action and the impulse toward the aesthetic are held in equipoise. Yet in the course of Marvell's later career, we can trace a gradual movement away from ironic equipoise, away from art.

For an artist to dedicate himself entirely to action, to reject art as inevitably fraudulent, incompatible with the singleness of truth, is self-defeating. In the beginning of 'Last Instructions', Marvell cites the traditional story of the painter Protogenes, who, in a rage at being unable to draw the flecks of foam around a dog's mouth, threw his pencil at the canvas:

> The Painter so, long having vext his cloth,
> Of his Hound's Mouth to feign the raging froth,
> His desperate Pencil at the work did dart,
> His Anger reacht that rage which past his Art;
> Chance finisht that which Art could but begin,
> And he sat smiling how his Dog did grinn.   (lines 21–6)

The parable can be read as illustrating that anger and art are perhaps after all compatible, that it is possible to be 'merry and angry' at once.[33] Yet in another interpretation of the parable, the implications are despairing and ultimately destructive of art. When reality is sufficiently ugly, the parable suggests, art becomes impossible; the muses are silenced. Under such circumstances the choices left for the conscientious artist are limited: he can seethe in impotent rage or he can seek to draw truthfully the ugliness of reality, to make the intolerable appear intolerable in hopes of awakening an audience who blandly accepts any ignominy as a matter of course. The danger is that the swamp of reality will engulf the artist, causing him to succumb to despair:

> For the graver's at work to reform him thus long.
> But alas! he will never arrive at his end,
> For 'tis such a king as no chisel can mend.
> ('Statue in Stocks-Market', lines 54–6)

No art, Marvell tells his painter in 'Last Instructions', can 'match our crimes' (line 13): reality requires not marmoreal precision and weight, but the art of the caricaturist, who can capture the momentary appearance of ugliness. The artist must draw grotesques, forgetting about the ideals of beauty and permanence except as implicit standards of measurement by which one can measure what has been lost. An artist brought up to believe in the normal Renaissance canons of art may find reality 'too slight grown or too hard' to imitate. Paradoxically, the most suitable artist to 'serve this race of Drunkards, Pimps, and Fools' (lines 4, 12) is a bad artist, like the inept sculptor who designed the statue of Charles II in Stocks-Market, 'a thing / That shews him a monster more like than a king' ('Statue in Stocks-Market', lines 11–12).

> Canst thou paint without Colours? Then 'tis right:
> For so we too without a Fleet can fight.
> Or canst thou dawb a Sign-post, and that ill?
> 'Twill suit our great debauch and little skill.
>
> ('Last Instructions', lines 5–8)

The dry factuality of *The Growth of Popery* represents a further stage in the rejection of art. It is not a satire, but an 'account', a 'naked Narrative'. Rather than employing the art of the satiric caricaturist, who seeks to heighten reality for comic and persuasive effect, following the dictates of traditional theorists who define satire and comedy as showing men as worse than they are (where panegyric and the heroic forms show them as better than they are), here Marvell strives for unembellished truth, simple fact.[34] He aims to persuade, of course, but he no longer seeks to amuse. In the opening sentence, we find no aesthetic indirectness; he chooses his words carefully for effect, but is no longer concerned 'to make a malefactor die sweetly'. The artist has been submerged into the revolutionary agitator:

There has now for diverse Years, a design been carried on, to change the Lawfull Government of *England* into an Absolute Tyranny, and to convert the established Protestant Religion into down-right Popery. (*Growth of Popery*, p. 3)

The distance between such a statement and 'Upon Appleton House' is immense. Meditative retirement, the free flow of the imagination, the life of the *'easie Philosopher'* able to 'securely play' ('Upon Appleton House', lines 561, 607) on the world, drawing on the riches of nature and the even greater riches of the mind, are no longer possible. The artist's role has been reduced to documentation, demonstration, even to providing raw factual materials, texts of speeches and bills brought before Parliament, statistics. Such a work, indeed, with its raw data, minimally selected and arranged, 'which may serve as matter to some stronger Pen and to such as have more leisure' (*Growth of Popery*, p. 17), represents a total, desperate renunciation of art.

The Growth of Popery expresses in the clearest and most uncompromising form the diminishing of aesthetic disinterestedness, of the free play of wit, which characterizes many of Marvell's later writings. As in some of the bleaker passages in *Paradise*

Regained, the pressure of the ugly times impinging on the poet's consciousness has led to an increasing pessimism and a narrowing of the range of choice:

> He who receives
> Light from above, from the fountain of light,
> No other doctrine needs, though granted true;
> But these are false, or little else but dreams.
>   (*Paradise Regained*, IV, lines 288–91)

At the end of his life, Marvell felt that conscience required that a final choice be made between art and action; the debate between soul and body, withdrawal and involvement, whose unresolved tension had been the source of Marvell's characteristic wit and poignancy, now at last found a resolution, if at considerable cost. As with the Milton of *Paradise Regained*, the final choice of uncompromising bareness is more satisfying doctrinally than artistically. Marvell does not share the late Milton's rejection of politics, and thus for him moral choice continues to take a specifically political form, an activist's desire to 'change' the world rather than simply 'interpret' it. For the artist of conscience living in a society he finds diseased beyond hope of immediate remedy, the only alternatives remaining, Marvell came to believe, were lonely, silent despair or the discipline of cooperative political action toward a revolutionary end.[35]

IV

In the decade between 'Last Instructions' and *The Growth of Popery*, Marvell turned more and more from the indirectness of art toward direct action. With the exception of *The Rehearsal Transpros'd* and *Mr. Smirke*, his satiric and polemical writings during this period tend to be corporate rather than individual productions, aimed at the widest possible audience, written in a simple popular style for maximum effectiveness ('When each one that passes finds fault with the horse, / Yet all do affirm that the king is much worse', 'Statue in Stocks-Market', lines 13–14).[36] One can detect in such poems as 'The Statue in Stocks-Market' and 'Upon his Majesties being made free of the Citty', as in the prose pamphlets *The Growth of Popery* and *A Seasonable Argument*, an increasing bitterness and pessimism, together with

the assumption that since neither King nor Parliament has ful-
filled their responsibility 'to redress in good season whatsoever
corruptions that may indanger and infect the Government', a
further appeal is necessary. By implication, these works invoke
the Lockean right of revolution, which Marvell cites in more
abstract terms in *The Rehearsal Transpros'd*:

If the Society it self shall be so far from correcting its own exorbitances...
this work, being on both sides neglected, falls to the Peoples share. (*RT*, II,
p. 240)

The revolutionary implications of Marvell's writings of the middle
and later 1670s further suggest a certain organizational discipline
not detectable in his earlier writings: they reflect not only his own
political beliefs, but a party line. Though such recent scholars as
John M. Wallace and Donal Smith have treated Marvell as
essentially a moderate trimmer, 'a curiously detached spectator
in the House of Commons', unaffiliated to any party, Marvell in
fact worked closely with the other leaders of the Country Party
to organize a coherent parliamentary opposition. Caroline Robbins
has pointed out that the poet was not only a mainstay of the
Country Party, but helped make up 'that small section of the
party which was consistently in opposition throughout the
reign'.[37]

Though the voice of the parliamentary opposition was to some
extent stilled by the downfall of Clarendon, Marvell was not
appeased by a change of faces in the court guard. The court
described in 'The Kings Vowes' in 1670 is essentially the court
described three years earlier in 'Last Instructions': nothing had
changed but accidental externals of style. Indeed, the state of the
kingdom is seen as worse in 'The Kings Vowes' than in the earlier
poem, since the corruption, as presented here, extends throughout
the court and Parliament without relief, finding its ultimate
source in the King himself:

> I will have a fine *Parliament* always to freind
> That shall furnish me Treasure as fast as I spend,
> But when they will not they shall be at an end.

> I will have as fine Bishops as were e'er made with hands
> With consciences flexible to my commands,
> But if they displease me I will have all their lands. (lines 10–15)

The assumption inherent in 'Last Instructions' and *The Rehearsal Transpros'd* that the King is educable, that Charles's advisers rather than Charles himself are responsible for the drift toward absolutism, is less realistic than the assumption, made explicit in these lines, that the King is directly responsible for the evils of the state, but the former assumption is politically more useful. To see the King as a tyrant, unprincipled, manipulative, with no checks on his power, can ultimately lead only to despair or to a call for revolution, and indeed Marvell's letters at this time see little hope for reform. No English King, he says in a letter of 1670 quoted earlier, has ever been 'so absolutely powerful':

Nor any Parliament, or Places, so certainly and constantly supplied with Men of the same Temper. In such a Conjuncture, dear *Will*, what Probability is there of my doing any Thing to the Purpose? (*Poems and Letters*, ed. Margoliouth, II, 315)

The Rehearsal Transpros'd attempts like 'Last Instructions' to separate the King from his advisers, enlisting the King on the side of limited government, toleration of dissent, and prudent moderation, as against the absolutist courses urged by false counsellors.

Kings...are fain to condescend to many things for peace-sake, and the quiet of Mankind, that your proud heart would break before it would bend to...Will your Clergy only be the men, who, in an affair of Conscience, and where perhaps 'tis you are in the wrong, be the only hard-hearted and inflexible Tyrants; and not only so, but instigate and provoke Princes to be the ministers of your cruelty? But, I say, Princes, so far as I can take the height of things so far above me, must needs have other thoughts...They do not think fit to command things unnecessary, and where the profit cannot countervail the hazard. (*RT*, I, pp. 108, 111)

The politics of *The Rehearsal Transpros'd* are complex, and the poet's balancing act is a delicate one. Charles II had always favoured religious toleration, and against the advice of the high Anglican party whose adherents had been among his chief supporters, 'having at last rid himself of a great Minister of State [Clarendon] who had headed this Interest', he issued in 1672 a Declaration of Indulgence, suspending the execution of laws prohibiting the public worship of dissenting Protestants. Charles's ministers supported the Declaration of Indulgence for widely varying reasons – Buckingham and Shaftesbury, later to become Marvell's close political allies, consistently supported toleration for dissenters, where Arlington, Clifford, and Lauderdale favoured the Declaration insofar as it strengthened the royal prerogative.[38] But though Marvell and other members of Parliament with similar views believed strongly in religious toleration, they could not approve the King's method of bringing it about. When Parliament met several months later, a majority in the House of Commons demanded that the King withdraw the Declaration as an unwarranted invasion of the rights of Parliament, an illegitimate attempt to make law by royal fiat. The constitutional issue scarcely entered into *The Rehearsal Transpros'd*, but afterwards both Marvell and Shaftesbury, along with their allies in the Country Party, came to see it as all-important. Though the end was desirable, the means proposed for achieving that end were extremely dangerous. Rather than an example of moderation and forbearance, Marvell and his political allies came to see in the Declaration a large step toward absolutism, part of a conspiracy against the freedom of the English peoples:

It was the Master-peice therefore of boldnesse and contrivance in these Conspirators to issue this Declaration...gaining by this a President to suspend as well all other Laws that respect the Subject's Propriety, and by the same power to abrogate and at last inact what they pleased, till there should be no further use for the Consent of the *People in Parliament*. (*Growth of Popery*, p. 35)

One reason the Country Party demanded the cancellation of Declaration of Indulgence in 1673 is that it became associated with a foreign policy they hated and feared. In 1670, Parliament had voted a generous supply on the basis of a Triple Alliance with the Protestant powers Holland and Sweden against France, not knowing that several months before Charles and his pro-Catholic ministers had negotiated a secret alliance with France against Holland. Assured of the money voted him by Parliament and the further promises of an annual subsidy to be paid secretly by Louis XIV, Charles prorogued Parliament and did not allow it to meet again for nearly two years. The policies he carried out in the interim bore out Marvell's charges of a conspiracy to impose absolutist government on England, and greatly embittered the opposition. Though the secret provisions of the Treaty of

Dover were not known until some time later, especially that provision in which Charles II agreed to declare his allegiance to Roman Catholicism 'as soon as the state of his country's affairs permit', nevertheless there was widespread fear of Catholic influence in the government. The passage in 1673 of the Test Act, incapacitating Catholics from holding office, indicates how strongly Parliament felt about the dangers of Popery, and the public revelation that the Duke of York, heir to the throne, was a Catholic made the imminent threat of a Popish succession the most important political issue in England for the rest of Charles II's reign. The forced resignation from office of Lord Clifford and other prominent Catholics increased rather than allayed fears of Catholicism; though the Duke of York had to resign his position as Lord High Admiral, he remained a potent influence, and *The Growth of Popery* suggests that many crypto-Catholics had 'the art to continue in Offices' even though some of their co-conspirators had 'quitted their present imployments ... rather than falsify their opinion'. Catholic influence for the Country Party also implied French dominance: 'we truckle to *France* in all Things,' Marvell writes in a letter of August 1671, 'to the Prejudice of our Alliance and Honour'. *The Growth of Popery* and other anti-government pamphlets regularly make the charge that the conspirators seeking to turn England into an absolute monarchy 'were acting in the interest, and perhaps in the pay of Louis XIV, the greatest Roman Catholic despot in Europe'.[39]

Perhaps the most arbitrary of Charles II's acts during this period was the declaration of war against Holland on 17 March 1672, a war declared on the most transparent of pretexts, with virtually no popular support. 'It was now high time to Declare the War, after they had begun it,' Marvell writes scornfully, 'and therefore ... the pretended Causes were made public' – causes which included the failure of the Dutch fleet to strike sail as a sign of respect to 'a sorry Yatch' bearing the English flag, and a number of 'Pillars, Medalls, and Pictures' alleged to be insulting to England.[40] When Parliament finally met in February 1673, they were faced with a war started a year earlier without their consent, in alliance with the great Catholic power many Englishmen feared, with the announced aim of the extirpation of the Dutch. The problems Marvell and other men in public life faced in opposing the actions of their government in time of war are likely to strike a responsive chord for contemporary Americans to whom the war in Indo-China is a recent memory. The sanctions making conscientious opposition highly problematical were far stronger in the 1670s than in the 1960s and 70s, but many of them continue to apply today. Among these sanctions, the most powerful was the belief that opposition was not only unpatriotic but even sinful, a rebellion against heaven. The divinity of order was a generally accepted truism in the seventeenth century, and the belief that 'the Duty of Obedience is the Original and Fundamental Law of Humane Societies'[41] is still widely held in our own day. Those who sought in the seventeenth century to justify dissent had to confront the argument, backed up by such biblical proof-texts as Romans 13, as well as countless sermons, that God had commanded us to obey our rulers: 'the powers that be are ordained of God. Whosoever therefore resisteth the power, re-sisteth the ordinance of God: and they that resist shall receive to themselves damnation.'[42] Open opposition required unusual tact or unusual courage: to oppose the government in speech or writing, especially in time of war, was to risk arrest for expressing treasonable sentiments against the head of that government. Some of the statements of loyalty to the King in such works as *The Growth of Popery* or even *The Rehearsal Transpros'd* may be considered blinds to avoid prosecution or get round the censorship. But those in power often ignored such discriminations and identified an attack on the King's advisers with an attack on the King. Moreover, the practical awareness that opposition would in all probability be futile, that the individual could do little or nothing to alter the course of events, would further argue, then as now, for acceptance of an unattractive war as a *fait accompli*. But to Marvell and his political allies, these considerations were subordinate to the claims of the individual conscience and the conviction that the war was unjust. As Peter Du Moulin says in his pamphlet addressed to Parliament that year, *England's Appeal from the Private Cabal at Whitehall, to the Great Council of the Nation, the Lords and Commons in Parliament assembled*:

And all men being equally concerned in the preservation of the Ship they sail in, though all do not sit at the Helm, it is every ones Duty, as well as their undoubted Right, to prevent as much as they are able, a fatal running upon Rocks, which may chance not to be discerned by others...All Christians should above all things enquire into the Justice of their Arms, before they either take them up, or refuse to lay them down.[43]

Marvell's intense opposition to the war led him to become involved with a clandestine political organization headed by Du Moulin, dedicated to breaking the alliance between England and France and bringing the war to an end. In his activities as a member of Du Moulin's organization, Marvell risked arrest for treason, since Du Moulin was a Dutch agent and England was at war with Holland. But for Marvell (as presumably for Du Moulin as well, a naturalized English citizen born a French Huguenot, who entered the service of William of Orange because of his implacable opposition to Louis XIV) the dangers of Popery, tyranny, and French power were great enough to call for extraordinary measures. Du Moulin's aim was to encourage anti-French sentiments among the Parliamentary opposition, and his views about the dangers of French influence came before long to be accepted by many members of Parliament. *England's Appeal*, as K. D. H. Haley has said, made a strong case in identifying the French alliance 'with the dangers of Popery at home, and consequently [led] public opinion and the Country Party in Parliament to turn against the war'. Later pamphlets distributed by Du Moulin's organization, including one which may have been written by Marvell, saw in the actions of the '*Popish* and *French Court* Party' during the parliamentary sessions of 1673 a design 'by the help of *French* Forces to introduce Popery into this Nation, and with it Arbitrary Government'.[44] The campaign against the Duke of York and his influence made use of verse satires such as 'Advice to a Painter to draw the Duke by' (1674), sometimes attributed (erroneously) to Marvell, and 'Upon his Majesties being made free of the Citty' (1674), as well as these prose pamphlets. In the two Parliamentary sessions of 1673 the Country Party were able to command a large majority on virtually every issue; the French ambassador, according to Haley, wrote to Louis XIV 'that there were not four people in the entire House' who did not favour peace with Holland and find English national interest to be 'in every way possible to oppose the plans' of the French monarch.[45] Faced with such unrelenting opposition in Parliament and no prospect of securing sufficient funds to continue the war, Charles signed a peace treaty with Holland in February 1674.

In the struggle for power between King and Parliament, reminiscent of 1641 to contemporary observers and to modern historians, Parliament now held a temporary ascendancy.[46] At this juncture, faced with the collapse of the Cabal ministry and the utter lack of 'men ... of credit and ability' able or willing to manage 'the Court's business in the House', Charles counter-attacked: he prorogued Parliament for over a year and used the time to build up an 'Episcopal Cavalier Party' in Parliament by means of appeals to patriotism and generous distribution of bribes.[47] Marvell's verse satires written at this time, like his letters and *The Growth of Popery*, pour scorn on the attempts by Charles and his ministers to regain control of the House of Commons by systematic bribery and by the 'Pageantry' of patriotic statues: 'To comfort the hearts of the poor *Cavalier*, / The late *King* on horseback is here to be shown' ('Statue at Charing Cross', lines 17–18).

They began therefore after fifteen Years to remember that there were such a sort of men in *England* as the Old Cavalier Party; and reckoned, that by how much the more generous, they were more credulous than others, and so more fit to be again abused. These were told, that all was at Stake, Church and State...That the Nation was running again into *Fourty One*, That this was the time to refresh their antient merit, and receive the Recompense double of all their Loyalty, and that hence-forward the Cavaliers should have the Lottery of all the Great and Small Offices in the Kingdom. (*Growth of Popery*, pp. 55–6)

The Earl of Danby, the architect of this policy, was the most capable of Charles's ministers, and his political astuteness made the need for concerted action and planning among the Country Party in the two Houses of Parliament even greater than before. In *The Growth of Popery*, the Earl of Shaftesbury and the Duke of Buckingham, leaders of the opposition in the House of Lords, are singled out for praise for their resolute resistance against the forces of absolutism. Both men had joined the opposition in 1673, after having held high court office for several years; to Marvell, the loss of place gave them their liberty:

But he was so far a Gainer, that with the loss of his Offices, and dependance, he was restored to the Freedom of his own Spirit, to give thenceforward those admirable Proofs of the Vigour, and Vivacity of his better Judgment, in Asserting, though to his own Imprisonment, the due Liberties of the *English* Nation. (pp. 51–2)[48]

Danby had taken the offensive in the 1675 session of Parliament by proposing an oath of loyalty to the Crown, which all members of Parliament and holders of office were required to sign, declaring it to be unlawful to take up arms against the King or 'against those that are Commissioned by him' and swearing never to 'Indeavour the Alteration of the Government either in Church or State'. Aided by the votes of the bishops, the court was able to command a majority in favour of the non-resistance oath in the House of Lords, and therefore it was necessary for Shaftesbury and his allies to fight a long holding action. Marvell praises their conduct in terms similar to those he had used to describe the gallant, outnumbered Country Party troops in 'Last Instructions':

They fought it out under all the disadvantages imaginable: They were overlaid by Numbers, the noise of the House, like the Wind, was against them, and if not the Sun, the Fire-side was always in their Faces; nor being so few, could they, as their Adversaries, withdraw to refresh themselves in a whole days Ingagement: Yet never was there a clearer Demonstration how dull a thing is humane Eloquence, and Greatness, how Little, when the bright Truth discovers all things in their proper Colours and Dimensions, and shining shoots its Beams thorow all their Fallacies. (*Growth of Popery*, pp. 57, 61)[49]

The two heroes especially commended for 'this brave Action' with 'a double proportion of Praise' are Shaftesbury and Buckingham, whose role as leaders of the opposition Dryden equally recognizes in attacking them in *Absalom and Achitophel*.

The Growth of Popery is part of a coherent Country Party propaganda campaign, organized under the overall direction of Shaftesbury, which culminated after Marvell's death in the attempt to exclude James II from the succession. One cannot of course predict how Marvell would have voted in the Exclusion Bill controversy, or what his reactions to the accusations of Titus Oates would have been; several of his close allies in 1675 followed the example of Halifax and voted against exclusion in 1679–81. But the charges of a conspiracy to impose popery and arbitrary government upon England, the main burden of *The Growth of Popery* and many other Country Party pamphlets in 1675–8, appeared to be borne out by the supposed revelations of Oates and the genuine revelations of Edward Coleman a few months after Marvell's death. Indeed, Marvell's pamphlet was reprinted post-humously at the height of the furor over the Popish Plot in support of the Whig cause. As Roger L'Estrange writes in a Tory reply to Marvell:

There was at that time no mention or thought of the PLOT...As the *designe* gets ground, so it gathers *confidence*; and that which in 77. would have been worth two or three hundred pound to the *Discoverer*, may be worth twice as much now in 79. to the *Publisher* and *Printer*. There may be [another] end in it, to *Canonize* Mr. *Marvell* (now in his grave) if not for a *Saint*, yet for a *Prophet*, in shewing how pat the *Popish Plot* falls out to his conjecture.[50]

As J. G. A. Pocock has remarked, Country Party pamphlets of 1675–7 are closely coordinated, come from 'the same stable', reflecting the views and serving the purpose of Shaftesbury and his closest supporters.[51] Such pamphlets as *A Letter from a Person of Quality* and *A Letter from a Parliament-Man to his Friend* are, like *The Growth of Popery*, appeals to the country, making public the proceedings of Parliament in order to stir up support for the Parliamentary opposition in the nation at large and strengthen the position of the Country Party in Parliament. Leading figures in the Parliamentary opposition met regularly to plan strategy before and during the Parliament sessions of 1675 and 1677, and though there is no documentary evidence linking Marvell to these meetings or to the Whig political association formed at this time, the Green Ribbon Club, it is likely that *The Growth of Popery* was written in direct consultation with Shaftesbury and other Country Party leaders. L'Estrange writes of *The Growth of Popery*:

You would have me guess at the Author...But I think I may call him *Legion*, for they are MANY; and there's a *Club* to his *Pen*, as well as to his *Pocket*. This I dare assure you, that the Author of *A Letter from a Parliament-man to his Friend in the Country, concerning the Proceedings of the House of Commons*, in 75. is very particularly acquainted with the Author of *An Accompt of the Growth of Popery, and Arbitrary Government*, &c. and the *Seasonable Argument*, &c. that followed it, in 77.[52]

As Caroline Robbins has suggested, *The Growth of Popery* may have been to some extent a collaborative enterprise. Marvell may

have relied on his own notes for a record of Parliamentary debates, and may have assembled the copious documentation of
proceedings in Parliament entirely unaided, but it is likely that
he had assistance.[53] The close relationship between *The Growth
of Popery* and another Country Party pamphlet of the same year,
*A Seasonable Argument to Persuade All the Grand Juries in
England to Petition for a New Parliament, or A List of the Principal Labourers in the Great Design of Popery and Arbitrary
Power*, suggests either common authorship or coordination between the two works as products of the same political organization.
L'Estrange calls *A Seasonable Argument* an abridged version of
The Growth of Popery, nineteen sheets reduced to three, 'as a
more Compendious Exposition' of the author's meaning. *The
Growth of Popery* provides evidence of a conspiracy, but omits
the names of the actual conspirators:

Some on the one side will expect, that the very Persons should have been
named; whereas he only gives evidence to the Fact, and leaves the male-
factors to those who have the power of inquiry ... That these to whom he
hath onely a publick enmity, no private animosity, might have the
priviledge of Statesmen, to repent at the last hour, and by one signal
Action, to expiate all their former misdemeanours.[54]

A Seasonable Argument, as the next logical step, supplies these
names, further substantiating the charges of a 'Great Design of
Popery and Arbitrary Power'. *A Seasonable Argument* lists over
two hundred members of the House of Commons in receipt of
bribes, pensions, or court places, with appropriate satiric comments for each:

Thomas King, esquire, a pensioner for 50 l. a session, &c., meat and drink,
and now and then a suit of clothes.

Sir John Shaw, once a vintner's boy, got of the Crown, out of the Customs
and by other ways, 60,000 l.[55]

This lengthy catalogue of petty venality and open theft, like the
similar catalogue of court troops in 'Last Instructions', builds up
in its cumulative effect a powerful indictment of a corrupt legislature, men who have bartered away their liberty and are willing,
if the price is right, to sell the English people into slavery. The
positive ideal implicit in the attack, as in 'Last Instructions' and
The Growth of Popery, is a Parliament composed of independent

97

agents who take their responsibilities seriously. Both *A Seasonable Argument* and *The Growth of Popery* are appeals to the electorate, urging petitions from all the counties of England that the sixteen-year-old Cavalier Parliament be dissolved and that new elections be held.

In urging the dissolution of Parliament, *The Growth of Popery* reflects the policy of Shaftesbury and his allies in the two houses of Parliament during the years 1675–7. Danby's success in assembling a party of court dependants in Parliament had led Shaftesbury to seek a dissolution, hoping for a commanding majority in new elections (a majority which the Whigs achieved when Parliament finally was dissolved in 1679). The necessity of dissolving a Parliament which had sat too long is a central theme in *The Growth of Popery*, as in such Shaftesburian pamphlets as *A Letter from a Parliament-Man to his Friend* and *The Debate or Arguments for Dissolving this present Parliament, and the calling frequent and new Parliaments* (1675). Indeed, in the Parliamentary session of February 1677, Buckingham and Shaftesbury argued that a long prorogation of fifteen months had dissolved Parliament *de facto*, a contention which Marvell supported in *The Growth of Popery*:

But if neither one Prorogation, against all the Laws in being, nor three Vitious Adjournments, against all Presidents, can Dissolve them, this Parliament then is Immortal. (p. 153)[56]

New elections were necessary, Marvell felt, because the institution of Parliament had become corrupted. In the view of Marvell and his Country Party allies, Parliament was failing to fulfil its constitutional responsibilities; confident that their actions would not be seriously questioned by a House of Commons most of whose members had sold their independent judgment for a sinecure or pension, the King's ministers could act with impunity. *The Growth of Popery* paints a portrait of a House of Commons whose average member, indifferent to 'the publick service', seeks election 'in design to make, and raise his fortune', is elected by chicanery, and once assured of a seat in Parliament behaves without conscience and without shame.

While men therefore care not thus, how they get into the House of Commons, neither can it be expected that they should make any conscience of what they do there...They list themselves streightways into some Court faction, and it is as well known among them, to what Lord each of them retaine, as when formerly they wore Coates, and Badges. (pp. 79–80)

Marvell's fullest analysis of the cavalier House of Commons occurs in *The Growth of Popery*, but a similar view of the dangers of corruption can be found throughout his satiric writings of the 1660s and 1670s, in 'Last Instructions', 'Clarindon's House-Warming', 'The Kings Vowes', the 'statue' poems, the parody speech from the throne. One category of M.P., the holder of governmental office, is according to Marvell unable by definition to act independently. When 'near a third part of the House have beneficial Offices under his Majesty, in the Privy Councill, the Army, the Navy, the Law, the Household, the Revenue . . . or in attendance on his Majesties person', the court can count on a solid bloc of votes. Such men, whether from feelings of obligation or a fear of losing the profitable offices they occupy, must vote with the court even when 'their hearts . . . are . . . with the Country', voting against their consciences on occasion. They are therefore 'to be looked upon as a distinct Body under another Discipline'. This strong attack on officeholders is in part a response to Danby's successful efforts to build up a court party by distributing spoils and applying party discipline on key votes. More significantly, it reflects the belief that 'the preservation of independence is the ultimate political good', and that the exercise of unbounded power and the pursuit of self-interest both necessarily corrupt (pp. 73–7).[57]

Only a tiny group of true patriots – the saving remnant we have seen praised in 'Last Instructions' and in other works by Marvell – direct their conduct by principles other than self-interest. It is for this reason, Marvell argues, that occasional patriots with no moral basis for their behaviour can never be relied upon: the Hobbesian calculus assumes that a man will behave well only when it appears to his advantage to do so. A sizeable number of M.P.s, Marvell says, are thwarted office-seekers, men 'hungry and out of Office' who pretend opposition to the court 'till some turn of State shall let them in the Adversaryes Place'. Though such men 'look Sullen, make big Motions, and contrive specious Bills for the Subject', their concern for the public interest is insincere; they 'onely wait the opportunity to be the

Instruments of the same Counsells, which they oppose in others'
(*Growth of Popery*, pp. 77–8). A third group of members, the
most corrupt of all, are men of no estates, who sell their votes
openly for enough money to live on.

Tables are kept for them at *White Hall*, and through *Westminster*, that
they may be ready at hand, within Call of a Question: all of them are
received into Pension, and know their Pay-day, which they never faile of:
Insomuch that a great Officer was pleased to say, *That they came about
him like so many Jack-daws for Cheese, at the end of every Session*. (p. 78)

Only the smallest of these groups, the 'hanfull of salt', the few
genuine committed patriots 'such as are above *hopes*, or *fears*, or
dissimulation, that can neither flatter, nor betray their King, or
Country', fulfil their trust as 'the Representers of the People of
England', protecting 'the Religion, Lives, Liberties and the Propriety of the Nation'. As for the rest of the members of the House
of Commons, Marvell says:

That poor desire of Perpetuating themselves those advantages which they
have swallowed, or do yet gape for, renders them so Abject, that they are
become a meer property to the Conspiratours, and must, in order to their
continuance, do and suffer such things, so much below and contrary to the
spirit of the Nation, that any honest man would swear that they were no
more an *English* House of Parliament. (pp. 74, 79, 150)

V

The basic political principles of *The Growth of Popery*, *The
Rehearsal Transpros'd*, 'Last Instructions to a Painter', and
Marvell's other post-Restoration writings are those of the classical
liberal tradition. Such scholars as Caroline Robbins, J. G. A.
Pocock, Z. S. Fink, and Bernard Bailyn have emphasized the
continuity of opposition political thought in the seventeenth and
eighteenth centuries. The tradition was conceived of as distinct
and coherent, and later writers often invoke the tradition by re-
citing a litany of names. Thus Wordsworth in 1802 praises 'the
later Sidney, Marvell, Harrington ... and others who called
Milton friend' as among the great practical moralists and ex-
ponents of liberty, while John Adams in 1776 claims that the true
principles of good government are stated in the writings of the
radical and republican theorists of the seventeenth century:

'Sidney, Harrington, Locke, Milton, Nedham, Neville'.[58] A work like *The Growth of Popery* needs to be seen in a broader context than that of the Shaftesburian opposition in the 1670s. Like Locke's *Two Treatises of Government*, similarly a product of the particular circumstances of opposition politics in the years 1679–1681, Marvell's tract should be seen in the overall context of libertarian political theory.

The chapter that follows is an attempt to place Marvell's political writings in the appropriate intellectual tradition. John Wallace has argued that Marvell was essentially a 'loyalist', whose primary concern was 'the necessity of regularizing' and rationally justifying assent to sovereign power. There are only two casual references to Locke in Wallace's book, none to Harrington, one to Algernon Sidney. As for Milton, according to Wallace, his political beliefs and Marvell's are 'most dissimilar': 'the course of their careers points to the basically different pattern followed by the loyalist and the revolutionary'.[59] My thesis, on the contrary, is that Marvell, Milton, and Locke, together with such figures as Harrington, Shaftesbury, Sidney, and Neville, are writers in a single tradition, just as Hobbes, Parker, and Filmer, along with such Tory satirists as Dryden, are writers in a second, rival tradition. The intellectual tradition in which Marvell's satiric and polemical writings can best be understood, and with which the next chapter will concern itself, may broadly be defined as Puritan libertarianism. The 'matrix of Marvell's political thought' may indeed, as Wallace says, be found during the Commonwealth period, but in an entirely different context and among an entirely different set of writers from those Wallace adduces.[60]

4 · CHRISTIAN LIBERTY

I

A single basic contrast dominates Marvell's later political writings. Though the circumstances of the works vary, each of them is essentially an attack on the theory and practice of absolutism and a defence of the liberty of the individual conscience. The grounds of these beliefs are religious: all men are equal in the eyes of God, and for one man to arrogate himself absolute power over another is to usurp God's prerogatives. Where such defenders of absolute monarchy as Parker saw non-resistance to authority as a binding obligation under any circumstances, so that even a blasphemous or criminal command of a sovereign must be obeyed, glorifying monarchical power as 'not meerely *humane*, but *Superhumane*, and indeed no lesse then a Power Divine' (*RT*, II, p. 253), Marvell like Milton considered such a total identification of secular power with God to be both blasphemous and absurd:

But therefore as it is unlawful to palliate with God and enervate his Laws into a humane only and Politick consideration; so it is on the other side unlawful and unnecessary, to give to Common and Civil constitutions a Divine Sanction, and it is so far from an owning of Gods Jurisdiction, that it is an Invasion upon it.[1]

To see God's will expressed in every command of the sovereign, Marvell argued in *The Rehearsal Transpros'd*, is to clothe a fallible human will with the trappings of divinity, to 'impose upon' God (*RT*, II, p. 249). The earthly and heavenly realms are discontinuous, and to invest mere human power with divine sanctions is the result of an 'Ignorance of Divine and Humane things' sufficient to lead one to 'jumble them so together that [one] cannot distinguish of their several Obligations' (*RT*, II, p. 247). Those men who worship earthly power, under colour of such doctrines as the divine right of kings, in fact serve Satan:

102

There has never been wanting among them such as would set the Magistrate upon the Pinnacle of the Temple, and shewing him all the Power, Wealth, and Glory of the Kingdoms of the Earth, have proferr'd the Prince all so that he would be tempted to fall down and worship them. (*RT*, II, p. 239)

To seek to 'erect an impregnable *Babel* of Power, that should reach to Heaven', Marvell argues, once again citing Scripture against his opponents, is the result of blind pride. Milton writes in a similar vein of wordly clergymen who 'bring the inward acts of the *Spirit* to the outward, and customary ey-Service of the body, as if they could make God earthly, and fleshy, because they could not make themselves *heavenly*, and *Spirituall*.'[2]

Marvell's political beliefs, like Milton's, are rooted in the concept of Christian liberty. The individual conscience is sacrosanct and should be exempt from all external compulsion; nothing is more important than a man's salvation, and in that earthly authority has no more role than earthly pleasures. Marvell shares the Puritan distrust of outward forms and ceremonies as a distraction from man's primary business on earth:

For Christianity has obliged men to very hard duty, and ransacks their very thoughts, not being contented with an unblameableness as to the Law, nor with an external Righteousness: it aims all at that which is sincere and solid and having laid that weight upon the Conscience, which will be found sufficient for any honest man to walk under, it hath not pressed and loaded men further with the burthen of Ritual and Ceremonial traditions and Impositions. (*RT*, II, p. 246)

Since 'the Mind is in the hand of God', it is unaffected by earthly power and earthly punishments. Indeed, in punishing a man for acts his conscience has compelled him to do, the state in Marvell's view is punishing a body which is an innocent, even unwilling agent. He uses the same witty metaphor as in 'A Dialogue between the Soul and Body' to suggest the uneasy marriage between body and soul, the difficulty of reconciling corporeal and spiritual values: 'The Body is in the power of the mind; so that corporal punishments do never reach the offender, but the innocent suffers for the guilty.' Consistently, Marvell holds that the attempt to regulate men's consciences or deny man his natural Christian liberty is an insult to man and God:

The Prince therefore, by how much God hath indued him with a clearer reason, and by consequence with a more enlightned judgment, ought the rather to take heed lest by punishing Conscience, he violate not only his own, but the Divine Majesty. (*RT*, I, pp. 111–12)

To Marvell, all earthly power is to be distrusted, since it is not of God. But in the fallen world, some authority, some laws are necessary. Though 'even Law is force, and the execution of that Law a greater Violence', yet 'God hath in general commanded and disposed men to be Governed' (*RT*, I, p. 111; II, p. 250). Marvell never deifies human authority in the manner of Hobbes, Parker, and Filmer, but at the same time he does not display the optimism about the nature of man characteristic of many later liberal theorists. The central event in human history is the fall:

And so also in the Government of the World, it were desirable that men might live in perpetual Peace, in a state of good Nature, without Law or Magistrate, because by the universal equity and rectitude of manners they would be superfluous. And had God intended it so, it would so have succeeded, and he would have sway'd and temper'd the Minds and Affections of Mankind so that their Innocence should have expressed that of the Angels, and the Tranquility of his Dominion here below should have resembled that in Heaven. But alas! that state of perfection was dissolv'd in the first Instance, and was shorter lived than Anarchy, scarce of one days continuance. (*RT*, II, p. 231)

Though Marvell does not present a full formal account of the institution of civil society, it is clear that he sees government as contractual in origin. In the passage quoted he identifies the state of nature characteristic of contract theory with the prelapsarian world. In this respect he agrees with Milton and disagrees with Locke, whose political theory is largely secularistic in its terminology. Milton writes in *The Tenure of Kings and Magistrates*:

No man who knows ought, can be so stupid to deny that all men naturally were born free, being the image and resemblance of God himself, and were by privilege above all the creatures, born to command and not to obey: and that they liv'd so. Till from the root of *Adams* transgression, falling among themselves to doe wrong and violence, and foreseeing that such courses must needs tend to the destruction of them all, they agreed by common league to bind each other from mutual injury, and joyntly to defend themselves against any that gave disturbance or opposition to such agreement.[3]

Government, the exercise of dominion by one man over others

who are his equals in the eyes of God, is the product of man's fallen nature. The fall is a fact that must be accepted, and power is an uncomfortable necessity which we must learn to live with; since 'we must nevertheless be content ... to inhabit such an Earth as it has pleased God to allot us' (*RT*, II, p. 231), our problem is how to make life tolerable – as Robert Frost puts it, 'what to make of a diminished thing'.[4] We cannot wish earthly power away, or pretend that kings are gods, or that the exercise of power somehow has a cleansing effect on man's nature. The central political question is not the theoretical basis of power but how to control it:

> But the modester Question (if men will needs be medling with matters above them) would be how far it is advisable for a Prince to exert and push the rigour of that Power which no man can deny them. (*RT*, II, p. 233)

Parker's position is to opt for tranquillity at all costs: '*Publick Peace and Tranquillity is a thing in it self so good and necessary, that there are very few actions that it will not render virtuous, whatever they are in themselves, wherever they happen to be useful and instrumental to its attainment.*'[5] In thus erecting expediency as a universal principle, Marvell argues, Parker not only jettisons all morality except as the civil power dictates, but debases man. Life with all its problems and complexities is preferable to a vegetable state, a lobotomized existence.

> Certainly if this course were once effectually taken, the whole year would consist of Halcyon Holy-dayes, and the whole world free from Storms and Tempests would be lull'd and dandled into a Brumall Quiet. (*RT*, II, p. 229)

To be 'row'd in state over the Ocean of Publick Tranquillity by the publick Slavery' (*RT*, II, p. 232), may be an appealing prospect to the Parkers of the world, but to deny man his natural, rational liberty is to reduce him to the level of a beast. Man's unique gift of reason is perhaps the source of his unhappiness, even as it raises him above all other animals. Only man is capable of anxiety, as the Body tells the Soul in Marvell's poem: 'But Physick yet could never reach / The Maladies Thou me dost teach' ('A Dialogue between the Soul and Body', lines 31–2). But man is denied the consolation of simpler, sinless animal existence, and bears the heavy weight of conscience; he is forced to choose, and is responsible eternally for the choices he makes. Conscience, defined as 'Humane Reason guided by the Scripture in order to Salvation', is 'that by which every man must be excused or accused' on the day of judgment (*RT*, II, p. 243). No other obligation can be more important. Rulers therefore should realize that they do not exercise a 'brutal magistracy' over 'cattle' but a less 'secure', more difficult, 'more honourable' rule over their fellow rational beings:

God has instated them in the Government of Mankind, with that incumbrance (if it may so be called) of Reason, and that incumbrance upon Reason of Conscience...Men therefore are to be dealt with reasonably: and conscientious men by Conscience. (*RT*, I, p. 111)

In *The Growth of Popery*, Marvell describes his ideal of government in similar terms, as appropriate to man's endowment of reason: a king 'keeping to these measures, may without arrogance be said to remain the onely Intelligent Ruler over a Rational People' (p. 4). In identifying the ideal of perfection in government with the British constitution, Marvell is not glorifying the status quo or addressing himself to patriotic conservative sentiment in the audience. Nor is he appealing, as D. I. B. Smith absurdly suggests of *The Rehearsal Transpros'd*, to 'complacency ... the art of the courtier at its most insinuating'.[6] Both *The Growth of Popery* and *The Rehearsal Transpros'd* recognize that those who exercise power almost always abuse it. Kings are fallible, and indeed are likely to be no less petty and vicious than ordinary men. The best constitution then will be one which blunts the ruler's capacity to do harm, while enabling him to act in ways that may be beneficial to the commonweal:

The Kings of *England* are in nothing inferiour to other Princes, save in being more abridged from injuring their own subjects: But have as large a field as any of external felicity, wherein to exercise their own Virtue and so reward and incourage it in others. In short, there is nothing that comes nearer in Government to the Divine Perfection, then where the Monarch, as with us, injoys a capacity of doing all the good imaginable to mankind, under a disability to all that is evil. (*Growth of Popery*, p. 5)

The system of government Marvell recommends is one in which 'nothing is left to the Kings will, but all is subjected to his Authority' (p. 4). The rule of law is opposed to the anarchic rule of individual will. In kings as in all other men since the fall, the will is 'infected' and, submitting to 'sensual Appetite' rather than 'sovran Reason', is likely to choose what is pleasurable over what is morally desirable.[7] Marvell's satiric poems of the 1670s regularly emphasize the need for external constraints on the boundless will of an irresponsible monarch who is certain, if left alone, to spend all the money 'intrusted' him on a round of 'delights... As if he should ne'er see an end on't.'[8] 'The Kings Vowes' describes Charles II as a monarch in whom will and appetite are one, uncontrolled by any internal or external restraints. Pleasure is his only law:

> I will have a *Privy Councill* to sit always still,
> I will have a fine *Junto* to do what I will,
> I will have two fine *Secretaryes* pisse through one quill
>
>   ...
>
> But whatever it cost I will have a fine whore
> As bold as *Alce Pierce* and as faire as *Jane Shore*,
> And when I am weary of her I'll have more.   (lines 31–9)

The tone of childish petulance is appropriate for an absolute monarch, whose morality as Marvell sees it is that of a child. The 'Mock Speech' of 1675, which like 'The Kings Vowes' adopts the persona of the monarch for satiric purposes, similarly treats Charles II as an overgrown baby, wilful and unthinking, mature only in his sexual desires:

I have a pretty good Estate I confess, but Godsfish I have a great Charge upon it. Here is my Lord Treasurer can tell you that all the Mony designed for the Summer Guards must of necessity be employ'd to the next Yeares Cradles and Swadling-Cloths. What then shall we do for ships? I only hint this to You, it is Your Business, not mine.[9]

A child was traditionally considered not fully a rational creature; though we are 'born Rational', we do not 'have actually the Exercise' of reason until the natural process of time allows us to come into our heritage of reason. An absolute monarch is a case of arrested development, outside the bounds of rationality as, in Locke's view, he is outside the bounds of civil society, as free as a wild beast from the civilizing restraints of normal communal life, 'still in the *state of Nature* ... in respect of those who are under his Dominion', with the natural liberty of that state 'increased with Power, and made licentious by Impunity'. 'Hence it is evident, that *Absolute Monarchy*, which by some Men is counted the only Government in the World, is indeed *inconsistent with Civil Society*, and so can be no Form of Civil Government at all.'[10]

The political writings of Marvell, like those of Locke, are directed at a specific opposition: the theory and practice of absolutism, as illustrated in the works of Filmer, Parker, Hobbes, and other proponents of absolute monarchy, and put into practice in contemporary England and France. France under Louis XIV was for Marvell as for many of his contemporaries synonymous with tyranny and 'arbitrary government'. In the limited monarchy of English tradition, on the other hand, law ruled and not the individual will:

For if first we consider the State, the Kings of *England* Rule not upon the same terms with those of our Neighbour Nations, who, having by force or by adresse usurped that due share which their People had in the Government, are now for some Ages in possession of an Arbitrary Power (which yet no Prescription can make Legall) and exercise it over their persons and estates in a most Tyrannical manner. But here the Subjects retain their proportion in the Legislature: the very meanest Commoner of *England* is represented in *Parliament*, and is a party to those Laws by which the Prince is sworn to Govern himself and his people. (*The Growth of Popery*, p. 3)[11]

Under an absolute ruler, argued the proponents of limited monarchy, no man can call anything his own; the King has title to all things and, by a kind of *droit du seigneur*, can enjoy them at his pleasure or leave them in his subjects' hands. Hobbes denied any right of private property; all individual possessions and all political liberties are granted by the sovereign and are therefore alienable.[12] The liberties of the subject, Hobbes said, depend on 'the silence of the law', and extend only so far as the sovereign desires. 'In cases where the sovereign has prescribed no rule, there the subject hath the liberty to do, or forbear, according to his own discretion. Such liberty is . . . in some times more, in other times less, according as they that have the sovereignty shall think most convenient.' Under such a doctrine, sovereignty is unlimited and indivisible; in Parker's words, 'The Supream Government of every Commonwealth wherever it is lodged, must of necessity

be universal, absolute, and uncontroulable, in all affairs whatsoever, that concern the Interests of mankind, and the ends of
Government.'[13]

Where the theorists of absolutism felt that the sovereign 'must
of necessity be above the Laws', the proponents of limited monarchy believed in the supremacy of law. Tyranny, wrote Locke,
or '*the exercise of Power beyond Right*, which no Body can have
a Right to', occurs 'when the Governour ... makes not the
Law, but his Will, the Rule'.[14] The belief in the government
of laws, rather than of men, is based on the assumption that even
the best men are susceptible to the temptations of power. Even
if an absolute monarch is a virtuous man and exercises restraint,
'the People are not safe', writes Marchamont Nedham, '*because
... it is in his power to be wicked if he please*'. In the fallen
state, no man can be trusted with absolute power. Power is a
strong intoxicant, and man's passionate, concupiscent nature often
leads him to throw off the reins of reason. 'The Interest of Freedom', says Nedham, 'is a Virgin that everyone seeks to de-
flower ... So great is the Lust of mankinde after dominion, there
follows a rape upon the first opportunity.'[15] The absolute monarch, knowing no law but his own will, is likely to be ruled by
the impulse of the moment; thinking himself absolutely free and
all other men and women his bondservants, he is in fact the slave
of his passions. To James Harrington and other theorists of the
mixed state, law is codified reason, protecting man from the
tyranny of boundless desire. 'If the liberty of a man consist in the
Empire of his *reason*, the absence whereof would betray him unto
the *bondage* of his *passions*: Then the *liberty* of a *Commonwealth*
consisteth in the *Empire* of her *Lawes*, the absence whereof would
betray her unto the *lusts* of *Tyrants*.'[16] In the English system of
mixed government as Marvell describes it in the *Growth of
Popery*, the King rules not by fiat but by consent of the governed,
expressed through their representatives in Parliament. The will of
the prince is hedged in by 'Laws either fram'd, or consented to
by all, that should confine and limit' his authority.[17] A number of
these restrictions are listed in the introductory paragraphs of the
Growth of Popery:

No Mony is to be levied but by the common consent. No man is for Life,
Limb, Goods, or Liberty at the Soveraigns discretion: but we have the same

Right (modestly understood) in our Propriety that the Prince hath in his Regality; and in all Cases where the King is concerned, we have our just remedy as against any private person of the neighbourhood, in the Courts of *Westminster* Hall or in the High Court of *Parliament*. His very Prerogative is no more than what the Law has determined. His Broad Seal, which is the Legitimate stamp of his pleasure, yet is no longer currant, than upon the Trial it is found to be Legal. He cannot commit any person by his particular warrant. He cannot himself be witnesse in any cause: the Ballance of Publick Justice being so delicate, that not the hand only but even the breath of the Prince would turn the scale. (p. 4)

Hobbes, Parker, and other proponents of absolutism feared individual liberty as tending to anarchy. 'The specious name of liberty,' Hobbes wrote, had given men the 'habit . . . of favouring tumults, and of licentious controlling the actions of their sovereigns,' with the resultant 'effusion of . . . much blood' in endless, futile wars (*Leviathan*, xxi, pp. 140–1). Parker saw the claim of natural freedom as a slogan by which men justified their own selfish desires:

For if their wild and capricious humors are not severely bridled by the strictest Laws and Penalties, they soon grow headstrong and unruly, become alwaies troublesome, and often fatal to Princes. The minds of the Multitude are of a fierce and eager temper, apt to be driven without bounds and measures, whithersoever their Perswasions hurry them: and when they have overheated their unsetled heads with religious rage and fury, they grow wild talkative and ungovernable; and in their mad and raving fits of zeal break all the restraints of Government, and forget all the laws of order and sobriety. (*Discourse*, p. 13)

In emphasizing the role of 'religious rage and fury' in governing men's political behaviour, Parker is drawing like Hobbes on memories of the Civil War. 'Religion then,' Parker writes with Hobbesian coolness, 'is either useful or dangerous in a Commonwealth, as the temper of mind it breeds is Peaceful or Turbulent.'[18] If religious belief is capable on the one hand of being 'the strongest Bond of Laws, and only support of Government', it is on the other hand capable of sanctioning rebellion, stirring up men's passions under the pretence of godly zeal, encouraging wild and restless men to imagine that they are 'led on by the spirit of God' to commit the most heinous of crimes, 'to disturb the Publick peace, kill Kings, and overthrow Kingdoms'. Both men define true religious belief as that which is supportive of authority: morality consists of obedience, and in obeying the secular authority, God's representative, man can be confident that he is obeying God. It is erroneous to think of Jesus as in any way subversive of the wordly rulers of his day; indeed, according to Parker, the Christian dispensation serves to confirm these rulers and all others in their authority, handing them a blank cheque which they may fill in as they please:

Our Blessed Saviour...came not to unsettle the Foundations of Government, or to diminish the natural Rights of Princes, & settle the conduct of humane affairs upon new Principles, but left the Government of the world in the same condition he found it.[19]

False or dangerous religious belief, according to Parker and Hobbes, is individualistic rather than corporate in nature. 'Private Will and Judgment' are anarchical, unreliable, a threat to the stability of society. The governments of the world, Parker says, have 'never been ... disturb'd so much by any thing as Conscience'.

This has ever rival'd Princes in their Supremacy, and pretends to as uncontroulable an Authority over all the Actions and affairs of humane life, as the most absolute and unlimited Power durst ever challenge.

To claim that the conscience is 'subject and accountable to God alone', that a subject can disobey the command of a sovereign if in his conscience he feels that obeying this command would be morally wrong, is, Parker and Hobbes argue, to exalt private whim and reduce the state to anarchy. If men were to act on such beliefs, no civil government could function.

Most mens minds or Consciences are weak, silly, and ignorant things, acted by fond and absurd principles, and imposed upon by their vices and their passions; so that were they entirely left to their own conduct, in what mischiefs and confusions must they involve all Societies? Let Authority command what it please, they would doe what they list.[20]

The remedy for the inconveniences of freedom proposed by the seventeenth-century theorists of absolutism is that of Dostoevsky's Grand Inquisitor: if free choice leads to chaos and misery, allows men's destructive impulses to reign unchecked, mere self-preservation will compel men to surrender any power of individual judgment they might otherwise claim to a higher authority, who will choose for men and direct their actions. There must be 'one

Supreme and Publick Judgment, to whose Determinations the private Judgment of every single Person should be obliged to submit it self' (*Discourse*, pp. 28–9). Men are deluded if they consider themselves independent agents, and their private likes and dislikes are nugatory in comparison with the overriding necessity of civil order. Parker's position is clearcut: thought is free, but nothing else is. Men may hold whatever beliefs they wish, as long as they do not express them; their actions, writings, and religious practices must be regulated by the state, and only those conducive to public order should be allowed. In political, ethical, and religious questions, men should follow the directions of authority rather than the dictates of conscience:

In cases and disputes of a publick concern, private men are not properly *sui Juris*, they have no power over their own actions, they are not to be directed by their own judgments, or determined by their own wills; but by the commands and determinations of the Publick Conscience. And if there be any sin in the command, he that imposed it, shall answer for it; and not I, whose whole duty is to obey: the commands of Authority will warrant my obedience, my obedience will hallow, or at least excuse my action, and so secure me from sin, if not from error . . . And in all doubtful and disputable cases it is better to erre with *Authority*, than be in the right against it. (*Discourse*, p. 308)

Though there are differences among the theorists of order, Hobbes, Parker, and Filmer, their disagreements are family quarrels and their basic position is identical:[21] their distrust and fear of 'private Judgment' is accompanied by a pessimism about human nature unaccompanied by any faith in grace or redemption, a conviction that civil peace and tranquillity comprise the *summum bonum* and civil war the worst of evils, and, central to their thought, the belief that the powerful forces of chaos within man can only be controlled and a reasonable degree of happiness secured if men submit to an absolute, indivisible sovereign power totally beyond their control.

The state of man can never be without some incommodity or other; and . . . the greatest, that in any form of government can possibly happen to the people in general, is scarce sensible in respect of the miseries, and horrible calamities, that accompany a civil war, or that dissolute condition of masterless men, without subjection to laws, and a coercive power to tie their hands from rapine and revenge. (*Leviathan*, XVIII, p. 120)

Or as Parker writes, with his unfortunate tendency to provide an unintended parody of the position he is arguing:

The miseries of Tyranny are less, than those of Anarchy; and therefore 'tis better to submit to the unreasonable Impositions of *Nero*, or *Caligula*, than to hazard the dissolution of the State, and consequently all the Calamities if War and Confusion, by denying our Subjection to Tyrants. (*Discourse*, p. 215)

Marvell's position against Parker, like Locke's against Filmer and Milton's in his prose writings, is that there are other evils worse than disorder and that absolute obedience is due only to God: kings are men like any others, and to worship them is to worship Baal. Caligula, Parker's ineptly chosen example of a ruler to whom all subjects, whatever their private reservations, must submit, had deified himself in precisely this manner:

He built a Temple to himself, and appointed Priests to his own Divinity . . . But more than this he commanded that his Image should be set up in the Temple at *Jerusalem*, and that the Temple should be devoted only to him and he there to be worship'd under the name of the *New Jupiter*. (*RT*, ii, pp. 217–18)

Where Parker and other clerical proponents of absolutism seek to invest the holders of earthly power with a cloak of divinity, the writers in the liberal tradition seek to strip away the mystery. Necessity and order, the honorific words so often cited in urging non-resistance, are subjective terms, as Marvell points out in his comments on Parker's frequent recourse to 'Necessity upon Necessity' as an argument.[22] Throughout history, politicians in power have invoked necessity when they wished to get round possible opposition. Public order as Marvell and Locke see it is a good, but not an absolute good, to which all else must be sacrificed.

Polyphemus's Den gives us a perfect Pattern of such a Peace, and such a Government, where in *Ulysses* and his Companions had nothing to do, but quietly to suffer themselves to be devour'd. And no doubt *Ulysses*, who was a prudent Man, preach'd up *Passive Obedience*, and exhorted them to a quiet Submission, by representing to them of what concernment Peace was to Mankind; and by shewing the inconveniences might happen, if they should offer to resist *Polyphemus*, who had now the power over them. (Locke, *Two Treatises*, ii, ch. xix, par. 228)

The doctrine of the 'Publick Conscience', in Marvell's view, is an absurdity. To act against the dictates of one's conscience, to do something one feels to be morally wrong in deference to authority, 'must render' one 'an Hypocrite to God, and a Knave amongst Men' (*RT*, I, p. 53). Parker may 'revile and debase Conscience', treating it as 'a thing ... inconsiderable' (*RT*, II, p. 243), but Marvell in the Puritan tradition sees conscience as man's most precious possession, his guide through life, that by which the 'warfaring Christian', confronted with the 'baits and seeming pleasures' of the world, may 'yet abstain, and yet distinguish, and yet prefer that which is truly better': 'My gentler Rest is on a Thought, / Conscious of doing what I ought.'[23] The ultimate stakes for which each man must play are salvation or damnation; no man can escape responsibility for his actions. Marvell states his position on the inalienability of conscience most explicitly in *A Short Historical Essay*:

A good Christian will not, cannot atturn and indenture his conscience over; to be represented by others...The Soul is too precious to be let out at interest upon any humane security, that does or may fail, but it is only safe when under God's custody, in its own cabinet. (p. 21)

The differing attitudes of Marvell and the authoritarian theorists toward the rival claims of order and liberty stem ultimately from their opposed views of man and the universe. In keeping with his materialism, Hobbes defined liberty in essentially mechanistic terms, as 'the absence of ... external impediments of motion' (*Leviathan*, XXI, p. 136). In his view, any arguments predicated on the sovereignty of conscience, of spiritual values, of individual morality, were literally nonsensical, since they assumed the reality of something that did not exist. 'The *universe* ... is corporeal, that is to say body ... and that which is not body, is no part of the universe: and because the universe is all, that which is no part of it, is *nothing*; and consequently *nowhere*' (*Ibid.*, XLVI, p. 440). Parker is less systematically a materialist than Hobbes, but agreed with him in scoffing at the idea of grace as 'a Phantasm, and an Imaginary thing' and in effectively denying the existence of a spiritual realm separate in any way from the temporal; Marvell characterizes his adversary, with considerable accuracy, as one 'who having never seen the receptacle of Grace or Conscience at an Anatomical Dissection, may conclude therefore that there is no such matter'. To Marvell, the realm of spirit was not only real, but the primary reality. The assumption that only the visible and tangible world exists was according to him the product of human arrogance and blindness: 'If things of Sight such Heavens be, / What Heavens are those we cannot see?'[24]

The authoritarian theorists were similarly dogmatic in their conception of the obligation of obedience. Whatever their individual differences in mode of argument or in the theoretical underpinnings of their positions, they agreed in holding categorically that no man born of parents into civil society could be free, just as no descendant of Adam could be free of Adam's sin.[25] Law to them was identified with civil peace, restraint, the assertion of the ruler's will and the forced submission of his subjects. For Marvell and Locke, on the other hand, law was not the negation of liberty but its necessary complement; rather than restraining liberty, laws assure liberty. As Locke writes:

For *Law*, in its true Notion, is not so much the limitation as *the direction of a free and intelligent Agent* to his proper Interest, and prescribes no farther than is for the general Good of those under the Law. Could they be happier without it, the *Law*, as a useless thing would of it self vanish; and that ill deserves the Name of Confinement which hedges us in only from Bogs and Precipices. So that, however it may be mistaken, *the end of Law* is not to abolish or restrain, but to *preserve and enlarge Freedom*: For in all the states of created beings capable of Laws, *where there is no Law, there is no Freedom*. For *Liberty* is to be free from restraint and violence from others which cannot be, where there is no Law. (*Two Treatises*, II, ch. vi, par. 57)

No man created by God can be absolutely free: here the liberal theorists and their opponents are in agreement. Milton's Satan shows how the demand for absolute liberty is the mirror image of the demand for absolute power, and how the pursuit of this dangerous and chimerical ideal is inevitably self-defeating. Marvell too compares 'that sober Liberty which men may have' with the vain hope of living utterly without restraint. The attack on the radical sectaries in *The First Anniversary* contrasts drunkenness with sobriety, a passionate self-seeking with a prudent concern for others, nakedness with the clothing necessary in civilized society. Cromwell is praised for his rational self-restraint; though after 'the Wars Flood' recedes, 'the large Vale' of England lies open and defenceless before him, 'subject to [his] Will', he refuses to act with the liberty of a tyrant, but serves as a 'Husbandman', tilling the field for the common good: 'And only didst for others plant the Vine / Of Liberty, not drunken with its Wine' (lines 284–9). The form of government under the Protectorate differs from that under the restored monarchy, but Marvell's basic ideal remains in both instances 'an intelligent Ruler over a Rational People', liberty under law. The radical sectaries who oppose Cromwell, as Marvell characterizes them in *The First Anniversary*, seek an absolute liberty which is incompatible with civil society. Liberty to them is the power to destroy, to 'deface' both 'the Scriptures and the Laws . . . / With the same liberty as Points and Lace'. They would reduce man to a state of Adamite nakedness, but though they pretend kinship with Adam, their true allegiance is to Satan:

> Oh Race most hypocritically strict!
> Bent to reduce us to the ancient Pict;
> Well may you act the *Adam* and the *Eve*;
> Ay, and the Serpent too that did deceive.
> *(First Anniversary*, lines 315–20)

Norman Cohn's interesting account of similar doctrines of the 'free spirit' in the Middle Ages and the seventeenth century shows clearly how the belief that 'one can be so united with God that whatever one may do one cannot sin' could lead to a deification of impulse, the identification of liberty with the power to gratify one's desires, often at the expense of others. Indeed, in some of the passages Cohn quotes, the potential for tyranny implicit in the cry for absolute liberty is painfully apparent. One hears the voice of the Hobbesian monarch (or the King of 'The Kings Vowes'):

I belong to the Liberty of Nature, and all that my nature desires I satisfy...When a man has truly reached the great and high knowledge, he is no longer bound to observe any law or command, for he has become one with God. God created all things to serve such a person, and all that God ever created is the property of such a man...It would be better that the whole world should be destroyed and perish than that a 'free man' should refrain from one act to which his nature moves him.[26]

Liberal theorists like Locke and Milton agreed with Hobbes

that the inconveniences of the state of nature cause man to abandon this '*State of Perfect Freedom*' for civil society.

> Thus Mankind, notwithstanding all the Privileges of the state of Nature, being but in an ill condition, while they remain in it, are quickly driven into Society. Hence it comes to pass, that we seldom find any number of Men live any time together in this State. The inconveniences, that they are therein exposed to, by the irregular and uncertain exercise of the Power every Man has of punishing the transgressions of others, make them take Sanctuary under the establish'd Laws of Government. (*Two Treatises*, II, ch. ii, par. 4; ch. ix, par. 127)

But the liberal theorists did not see liberty and order as incompatible: rather than surrendering his original freedom of action absolutely and irrevocably in return for the protection of a sovereign, man in liberal contract theory retains his freedom, delegating power to a government as a revocable trust. However great one's theoretical freedom may be in the state of nature, in practical terms one can only enjoy freedom under the aegis of law.

> For Freedom is not, as we are told, *A Liberty for every Man to do what he lists*: (For who could be free, when every other Man's Humour might domineer over him?) But a *Liberty* to dispose, and order, as he lists, his Person, Actions, Possessions, and his whole Property, within the Allowance of those Laws under which he is; and therein not to be subject to the arbitrary Will of another, but freely follow his own. (*Two Treatises*, II, ch. vi, par. 57)

Locke and Marvell see civil society as defined by the control of power rather than by the surrender of rights. Since men must live in the society of their fellows ('But 'twas beyond a Mortal's share / To wander solitary there', 'The Garden', lines 61–2), they exchange a hypothetical absolute freedom suitable only on an unpopulated earth for that limited, rational freedom 'which man may have' (*First Anniversary*, line 289). Man does not abandon his natural liberty by entering into society any more than by recognizing the authority of God. As Marvell writes in *The Rehearsal Transpros'd*: 'No man hath devested himself of any Natural Liberty as he is a Man, by professing himself a Christian, but one liberty operates within the other more effectually, to strengthen themselves better by that double Title' (*RT*, II, p. 245).

According to liberal contract theory, laws are instituted to protect the liberties of the individual from invasion by the arbitrary strength of others. Hobbes and Parker, in contrast, identify law as the will of the sovereign; to them morality begins at the barrel of a gun. Though both occasionally speak of laws of nature, and of moral obligation which exists *in foro interno*, if not *in foro externo*, in practice they believe the law to be mere 'words and paper, without the hands and swords of men'. What the sovereign declares to be the truth becomes the truth, both in politics and religion, and men are compelled to obey, even if they inwardly dissent: 'The makers of civil laws, are not only declarers, but also makers of the justice and injustice of actions: there being nothing in men's manners that makes them righteous or unrighteous, but their conformity with the law of the sovereign' (*Leviathan*, XLII, p. 368; XLVI, p. 448). Both Parker and Hobbes are thoroughgoing Erastians: the sovereign not only has the power to regulate religious worship, but can ordain and establish any religion he pleases. To hold that 'Princes have Power to bind their subjects to that Religion that they apprehend most advantageous to publique Peace and Tranquillity' (Parker, *Discourse*, p. 12), Marvell argues, is to erect idols to a mortal god.

'Tis true, the Author for fashion-sake speaks in that Book of Religion and of a Deity, but his Principles do necessarily, if not in terms, make the Princes Power *Paramount* to both those, and if he may by his uncontroulable and unlimited universal Authority introduce what Religion, he may of consequence what Deity also he pleases. Or, if there were no Deity, yet there must be some Religion, that being an Engine most advantageous for Public Peace and Tranquillity. (*RT*, I, p. 65)

Indeed, Parker goes so far as to say that the magistrate has 'Power to make that a Particular of the Divine Law, that God has not made so' (*Discourse*, p. 80).[27] The liberal theorists do not worship power in this way, but see it as at best a necessary evil. The ruler does not exist as solitary lord and master, inhabiting a different world from other men, but is bound by a network of subtle obligations both to his creator and his fellow creatures. Law serves the common good, rather than the interest of the ruler:

I do suppose therefore that the true stress and force of Laws lyes in their aptitude and convenience for the general good of the People; and no Magistrate is so wanton as to make Laws meerly out of the pleasure of

Legislation, but out of the prospect of some utility to the Publick...
God...could not institute Government to the prejudice of mankind, or
exact obedience to Laws that are destructive to the Society. (*RT*, II, p. 251)

Law is not absolute and unchanging, but subject to modification,
interpretation, even tacit abandonment according to circumstances. If laws prove 'inconvenient in the practice', they fall into
disuse:

And therefore it is very usual to make at first Probationary Laws, and for
some term of years only; that both the Law-giver and the Subject may see
at leisure how proper they are and suitable to the effect for which they
were intended. And indeed all Laws however are but Probationers of time;
and, though meant for perpetuity, yet, when unprofitable, do as they were
made by common consent, so expire by universal neglect, and without
Repeal grow Obsolete. (*RT*, II, p. 251)

Where to Hobbes and Parker, government is based on fear of
punishment ('What man ... does not find himself governed by
them he fears, and believes can kill or hurt him when he obeyeth
not?'), (*Leviathan*, XLVI, p. 448) to Locke and Marvell, government is grounded on rational consent. To deprive man of his
natural liberty is to derogate from the glory of God, who created
man with the capacity of reason, enabling him to exercise the
heavy responsibility of free choice.

When God gave him reason, he gave him freedom to choose, for reason is
but choosing; he had bin else a meer artificiall *Adam*, such an *Adam* as he
is in the motions. We our selves esteem not of that obedience, or love, or
gift, which is of force. (Milton, *Areopagitica*, *CPW*, II, 527)

Since men are 'rational creatures', no government which does not
treat them as such is worthy of the name; 'it had been a melancholy Empire,' Marvell writes, 'to have been only Supreme
Grasiers and Soveraign Shepherds' (*RT*, I, p. 111). Or, as Locke
says, in a clear statement of the libertarian position he shares with
Milton and Marvell:

The *Freedom* then of Man and Liberty of acting according to his own
Will, is *grounded on* his having *Reason*, which is able to instruct him in
that Law he is to govern himself by, and make him know how far he is left
to the freedom of his own will. (Locke, *Two Treatises*, II, ch. vi, par. 63)

II

Each of Marvell's prose works dealing with the issue of liberty of conscience is an occasional piece, embedded in an immediate context which is likely to seem remote from the modern reader. *The Rehearsal Transpros'd*, *Mr. Smirke*, and *Remarks upon a late Disingenuous Discourse* are all written in defence of other writers who had come under attack, and each makes up part of a pamphlet war. Their very titles and sub-titles – 'Remarks', 'Animadversions', 'Annotations' – point to their occasional, even ephemeral nature. The two parts of *The Rehearsal Transpros'd*, for example, written in part to defend the dissenting minister John Owen against abusive attack on him by Parker, are the sixth and thirteenth items in a lengthy series, including four works by Parker and two by Owen. In writings so attuned to transient political realities and concerned with point-by-point refutation of an opponent, indebted even in their structure to the work being 'anatomiz'd' or animadverted upon, it is often difficult to distinguish the essential from the accidental. Marvell's verse satires similarly respond in detail to immediate circumstances and usually seek to disable or refute particular adversaries. Given the instability of Restoration politics, the shifts in allegiance made necessary by political circumstances (so that, for example, the King, seen as a potential ally in *The Rehearsal Transpros'd* and 'Last Instructions', becomes the chief object of attack in some of the satiric poems of the 1670s), the problems imposed by censorship and the danger of prosecution for sedition, the need to 'observe *decorum*' in works intended for different audiences and serving different ends, it is to be expected that the particular positions argued in the various works will show some inconsistencies.[28] Nevertheless, one can extrapolate a consistent overall view of liberty of conscience from Marvell's various writings, which accords with the basic political and religious principles set forth in these works.

Though Marvell's religious affiliations are not entirely clear, his position in matters of Christian doctrine and discipline is stated explicitly in such works as *The Rehearsal Transpros'd* and *A Short Historical Essay*. He consistently maintains the Puritan view that religious belief is entirely an individual matter, to which external, established forms are irrelevant.

Every man is bound to *work out his own Salvation with fear and trembling*, and therefore to use all helps possible to his best satisfaction; hearing, conferring, reading, praying for the assistance of God's Spirit; but when he hath done this, he is his own Expositor, his own both Minister and People, Bishop and Diocess, his own Council; and his Conscience excusing or condemning him, accordingly he escapes or incurs his own internal Anathema. (*Short Historical Essay*, p. 20)

His hostility toward the 'innumerable rabble of Rites and Ceremonies' (*RT*, II, p. 238), as well as his depiction of life as a spiritual battlefield in which the resolved soul is bombarded by 'the Batteries of alluring Sense' ('Resolved Soul', line 47), ally him with the Puritan left of the Commonwealth period. He denies the high-church Anglican position that the clergy comprise an order distinct from laymen and that a church is defined by civil establishment, formal ordination, and discipline: a church to him, as to Milton and the left-wing Independants and sectaries of the 1640s and 1650s, was a voluntary organization of Christian believers, members of the body of Christ. Men like Parker arrogate to themselves the title of the Church of England, but the true Church of England are the 'Faithful' (*Short Historical Essay*, p. 23), some of whom for reasons of conscience are unable to conform to the established religion. If the visible unity of Christendom is broken, Marvell argues, the fault lies entirely with those 'Ingrossers' (*RT*, II, p. 212) who, departing from 'the good and ancient wayes of Christianity' (cf. *RT*, II, p. 238) and ignoring their proper pastoral duties, allow abuses to creep into the church.[29] A periodic, continuous Reformation is necessary both in church and state: 'For all Governments and Societies of men, and so the Ecclesiastical, do in process of long time gather an irregularity, and wear away much of their primitive institution' (*RT*, II, p. 239).

But though *The Rehearsal Transpros'd*, *Mr. Smirke*, and *A Short Historical Essay* are sympathetic to the dissenters, none is written explicitly from a dissenter's point of view. There is no reason not to take Marvell literally when he writes in *The Rehearsal Transpros'd*: 'Not on the other part to impute any errors or weakness of mine to the Nonconformists, nor mistake me for one of them, (not that I fly it as a reproach, but rather honour the most scrupulous:) for I write only what I think befits all men in Humanity, Christianity and Prudence toward Dissenters' (*RT*, II, p. 186). Disclaimers of this kind, as Legouis points out, are in part diplomatic. Marvell has chosen to write *The Rehearsal Transpros'd* from the point of view that is most rhetorically effective. The pose of a neutral, fair-minded observer, a wit rather than a zealot, a Christian unconcerned with doctrinal distinctions, protects the author against the claim of undue 'Bias and Partiality' (*RT*, II, p. 242), and is more likely to gain him the support of readers who consider themselves moderate, uncommitted to either party in the dispute; as Dryden writes in the preface to *Absalom and Achitophel*: 'If I happen to please the more Moderate sort, I shall be sure of an honest Party; and, in all probability, of the best Judges; for, the least Concern'd, are commonly the least Corrupt ... But, they are not the Violent, whom I desire to please.'[30] In its wit and suavity, set off to maximum advantage by the blustering of Parker, *The Rehearsal Transpros'd* was adroitly aimed at catching the ear of Charles II, which an appeal by an avowed dissenter might well not have succeeded in doing. In the words of Burnet, 'one may judge how pleasant these books [the two parts of *The Rehearsal Transpros'd*] were; for the last king, that was not a great reader of books, read them over and over again'.[31]

Nevertheless, the persona Marvell assumes in *The Rehearsal Transpros'd* would appear essentially to reflect his own position, that of a man who, though he himself conformed to the Church of England, respected the conscientious scruples of his fellow Christians who did not so conform. The answers to *The Rehearsal Transpros'd* by Parker and his allies resort to *ad hominem* attacks on Marvell of the most scurrilous kind (accusing him among other things of a homosexual relationship with Milton), but they do not generally call him a dissenter. He is 'the most sufficient States-man' of 'the GOOD OLD CAUSE', active in the cabals of republicans and zealots, a base hireling 'who had formerly been a whiffling Clerk to a *Usurper*, and afterwards turn'd Broker for all *Phanatick Ware*', a coffee-house wit intent only on gaining the applause of the rabble, surrounded by an admiring '*Auditory*' of '*White Aprons*' and apprentices, whose books 'are made free of all the Trades', given away in the shops with 'every Pound of Candles'. But though his adversaries do their best to tar him with the brush of dissent, associating him with the greasy caps and unstable judgments of the mob, they represent him as an intriguing politician and ambitious wit, rather than as himself a dissenter, more an Achitophel than a Hudibras.[32] There is no evidence that Marvell was actually a member of a dissenting congregation after the Restoration, no record of his attendance at conventicles. A recent study of dissenters in the period 1661–89 lists thirty-seven Members of Parliament who were certainly or probably nonconformists, and Marvell's name is not among them, though he is listed along with others active in the Country Party as friends to nonconformity. His description of the religious affiliations of his father, a clergyman of Puritan inclinations who died before the outbreak of the Civil War, would in all probability fit himself as well: 'he was moreover a Conformist to the established Rites of the Church of England, though I confess none of the most over-running or eager in them' (*RT*, II, pp. 203–4).[33]

In some ways Marvell's attitude toward liberty of conscience is akin to that of the latitudinarian Anglicans of the 1630s and 1640s. In search of precedents which his opponents could not accuse of Puritanism, he frequently cites Anglican moderates of this period in support of his position – most notably his old acquaintance John Hales, whom he praises as a model Christian divine, 'one of the clearest heads and best prepared breasts in Christendom', exemplifying 'a peaceful and unprejudicate Soul and the native simplicity of a Christian-spirit', and whose *Tract concerning Schism* (1642) he quotes at length in *The Rehearsal Transpros'd*, but also William Chillingworth, Jeremy Taylor, Archbishop James Ussher, Bishop John Davenant, and Bishop Joseph Hall.[34] The moderate Anglicanism of these men and their successors, though a minority view among the leaders of the church both in the years immediately before the Civil War and after the Restoration, represented a substantial body of Anglican opinion even in the heyday of Laudian authoritarianism. In the next generation, such figures as Herbert Croft and John Wilkins, who unsuccessfully tried to bring about some easing of the legal restrictions on dissent during the 1660s and 1670s, held views on liberty of conscience and on Christian doctrine substantially similar to those of Hales and Chillingworth. By 1688, after the rise to power and influence of such politically astute latitudinarian clergymen as Burnet and Tillotson and the accession of William III, the views of the low-church Anglicans had come even in the higher councils of the church to eclipse the high Tory attitudes associated with Parker and Laud. But in 1675, when Marvell wrote *Mr. Smirke* in defence of the Anglican moderate position as represented by Bishop Herbert Croft in *The Naked Truth*, the attitude of Croft and Hales toward the unity of Christendom and the folly of persecution was still that of an embattled minority largely excluded from positions of political and ecclesiastical power and attacked by the dominant Laudians as 'betrayers of the church'.[35]

Where in *The Rehearsal Transpros'd* the author takes pains to dissociate himself from those whose cause he is defending, in *Mr. Smirke* he embraces that cause as his own (p. 11). Throughout the work, as well as in a letter addressed to Croft shortly after its publication, Marvell speaks of 'our Church'. But the common perspective which Marvell finds in himself, Hales, and Croft is not so much Anglicanism, however defined, as Protestant Christianity. A central belief of the latitudinarian moderates was that Christianity was essentially one; all Protestant Christians are 'Brethren' and 'Fellow-Servants', children of the same father, and their doctrinal disagreements, 'in their nature indifferent', are insignificant as compared to their overall agreement.[36] The latitudinarians characteristically distinguished between the fundamentals of faith, 'necessary to be known and beleeved to the salvation of Christians', and subsidiary questions of doctrine and discipline about which devout Christians may hold varying opinions. To multiply articles of belief, insisting upon doctrinal uniformity, they argued, can only rend the fabric of Christian unity. 'For why should man be more rigid then God? Why should any error exclude any man from the Churches Communion, which will not deprive him of eternal Salvation?'[37]

In *Mr. Smirke* and the *Short Historical Essay* appended to it, Marvell, like the latitudinarians, argues that the articles of Christian faith are simple and universal:

And as in a Seed, the very Plain and Upright of the Plant is indiscernably express'd, though it be not branch'd out to the Eye, as when it germinates, spreds, blossoms, and bears fruit; so was the Christian Faith seminally straitned in that virtual sincerity, Vital Point, and Central vigour of

Believing with all the heart that *Jesus Christ* was come in the Flesh, and was the Son of the Living God. And, would men even now Believe that one thing thorowly, they would be better Christians, then under all their Creeds, they generally are both in Doctrine and Practice. (*Mr. Smirke*, pp. 26–7)

Like Croft and like the earlier Anglican moderates, Marvell identifies these fundamentals of faith with the Apostles' Creed; additional creeds, confessions, or statements of faith to which men are forced to subscribe, he argues, are not only unnecessary but injurious. The multiplication of doctrinal tests and anathemas is in Marvell's view an attempt to give divine sanction to human pride and contentiousness: to make salvation dependent on an exclusive formula, 'an exact Forme of Words, not Expressed in Scripture', requiring men to 'Declare too that no Man else can be saved' without subscribing to particular specified details of doctrine, is 'Dangerous', 'Unwarrantable', and contrary to Christian charity and common sense (*Mr. Smirke*, p. 22). Ambitious men, ignoring the word of God, are apt to substitute 'a Gibbrish of their Imposing'; such framing of creeds is likely to be 'a pitiful humane business, attended with all the ill circumstances of other worldly affairs'. Marvell's ironic treatment of the epic battles of Arians and Athanasians, partisans of *homoousios* and *homoiousios*, at the Council of Nice anticipates Gibbon in its cool satiric approach toward factional dispute, yet central to his account of these controversies is a strong commitment to an ecumenical ideal of Christianity:

In digging thus for a new deduction, they undermined the fabrick of Christianity; to frame a particular Doctrine, they departed from the general Rule of their Religion; and...violated our Saviour's first Institution of a Church, not subject to any Addition in matters of Faith, nor liable to Compulsion, either in Belief or in Practice. (*Short Historical Essay*, pp. 19–20)

A second resemblance between the views of Marvell and those of the Anglican latitudinarians was his attitude toward separation and schism. Like Hales, Croft, and the author of *The Conformist's Plea for the Nonconformist* (1683), he held that, though it would be preferable for dissenters to unite themselves with the main body of the church, conscientious Christians were not to be condemned if 'their Judgements and Consciences cannot comply with what is injoyned' and they feel themselves unable to conform: 'A man would suffer something rather than commit that little error against his Conscience, which must render him an Hypocrite to God, and a Knave amongst Men' (*RT*, I, pp. 52–3). Marvell cites Hales's *Tract concerning Schism* in support of his position: men are too quick to accuse others of heresy, investing their own opinions with the cloak of divinity, using the pejorative terms 'heresy' and 'schism' as a substitute for the patient marshalling of rational arguments.

Heresy and schism, as they are in common use, are two theological... scarecrows, which they, who uphold a party in religion, use to fright away such, as making inquiry into it, are ready to relinquish and oppose it, if it appear either erroneous or suspicious. For as Plutarch reports of a painter, who having unskilfully painted a cock, chased away all cocks and hens, that so the imperfection of his art might not appear by comparison with nature; so men willing for ends to admit of no fancy but their own, endeavour to hinder an inquiry into it by way of a comparison of somewhat with it, peradventure truer, that so the deformity of their own might not appear.[38]

When a separation or schism exists, when Christian unity is fragmented, the blame according to the latitudinarians lies with those who precipitate the separation by attempting to force their will on others, not with those who break away: 'Not he that separates, but he that occasions the separation is the schismatic.'[39] Here as elsewhere the views of Marvell and the latitudinarians find a parallel in liberal contract theory. In both civil and ecclesiastical constitutions, Marvell argues in *The Rehearsal Transpros'd*, order is a desirable end, but not an absolute, sovereign necessity overriding all other considerations. Rebellion and disobedience are not desirable, may even be 'unlawful', but under certain conditions they 'prove unavoidable' because of 'the guilt of those men who have always design'd to secure their own misdemeanors by publick oppression' (*RT*, II, pp. 239–40). As Locke puts it, rulers who 'set up force ... in opposition to the Laws' are properly to be considered rebels, and not those who atempt to resist them.[40]

Some statements by Marvell are more reminiscent of Puritan defenders of liberty of conscience during the Commonwealth period than of the Anglican latitudinarians, while others are commonly held positions, not identified with any particular group. The emphasis on Christian charity and forbearance, on 'that great and fundamental Law of Mercy' (*RT*, II, p. 249), throughout *The Rehearsal Transpros'd*, is perhaps more characteristically Anglican than Puritan, though we find similar statements by such radical Puritans as William Walwyn. Pragmatic arguments against persecution and tyranny abound in *The Rehearsal Transpros'd*, and similar citations of evidence from 'the History of all Ages' to show that 'nothing has alwayes succeeded better with princes than this Clemency of Government', where 'the sanguinary course' has always failed (*RT*, II, p. 234), may be found in such writers as the Puritan John Owen and the Anglican Jeremy Taylor. The philosophical basis of Marvell's defence of liberty of conscience is his conviction that, since the spiritual and corporeal realms are entirely distinct, faith by its very nature cannot be forced. Though Puritan and Anglican writers often draw different conclusions from this initial premise, we find similar arguments that by definition 'no Man can be forc'd to believe', frequently using homely concrete analogies to drive the point home, in many treatises written during the thirty years previous to *The Rehearsal Transpros'd*.[41]

The prose writings of Milton, of William Walwyn, of Hales, of Jeremy Taylor, like Marvell's works, express what one might call a Christian scepticism, a belief that, though truth in itself is 'a perfect shape most glorious to look on', the ways of God cannot be known readily in the fallen world, where the 'lovely form' of the virgin Truth has been 'hewd ... into a thousand peeces, and scatter'd ... to the four winds'. However confident we may be that we are in the right, the possibility always remains that we have been deceived; there is no such thing as certainty except in heaven. Truth is not the exclusive property of a single group, and the only way to find it is to search for it.

From that time ever since, the sad friends of Truth, such as durst appear, imitating the carefull search that *Isis* made for the mangl'd body of *Osiris*, went up and down gathering up limb by limb still as they could find them. We have not yet found them all...nor ever shall doe, till her Masters second comming. (*Areopagitica, CPW*, II, 549)

The common doctrinal position of all these writers is that man has been given the capacity of reason in order to enable him to search out the truth: to neglect this gift, to allow oneself to be led in matters of religion by 'man's authority thrust upon us under divers shapes', is, these authors maintain, no better than to 'lie still, and sleep, and require the use of other men's eyes or legs'.[42]

It is no good reason for a mans Religion, that he was born and brought up in it...For my part, I am certain that God hath given us our Reason, to discern between Truth and Falsehood, and he that makes not this use of it, but believes things he knows not why; I say, it is but chance that he believes the truth, and not by choice: and that I cannot but fear, that God will not accept of this *Sacrifice of fools*.[43]

Yet within this common framework of agreement among the defenders of liberty of conscience, certain distinctions can be made. In several respects Marvell's view of Christian liberty differs from that of the Anglican moderates and much more closely resembles that of libertarian Puritans like Milton and Roger Williams. Hales and Chillingworth, like the latitudinarians of the post-war generation, were prominent figures in the development of rational theology in the seventeenth century, the conscious effort 'to free religion from Enthusiasm and Fanaticism, and to establish it upon its true rational grounds and foundations'.[44] As Joseph Glanvill writes in 'Anti-fanatical Religion and free Philosophy' (1675), the latitudinarian moralists, 'in order to the cure of the madness of their Age, were zealous to make men sensible'.[45] To Chillingworth and his friend and patron Viscount Falkland, as later to Tillotson and Locke, God did not speak to man by blinding individual revelations, but through his rational faculties, in ways open to public inspection. 'Visible Arguments' to them were always preferable to 'invisible' ones: to follow 'the never failing rules of Logick', 'drawing conclusions out of premises' by means of 'right Reason ... written by God in the hearts of all men', Chillingworth wrote in *The Religion of Protestants the Safe Way to Salvation*, was to follow God.[46] The latitudinarians thus set themselves resolutely against what they considered the excesses of 'wild Extatical Enthusiasts' and fanatics, attacked as spurious and contrary to 'the sober *use* of *Reason*' and decorum any claims of '*Illuminations*', '*Raptures*', or 'false pretences to the *Spirit*' associated with the radical Puritan sects, while at the same time urging, within limits, the right of Protestant Christians to persist in religious attitudes and practices which may be erroneous. Marvell agreed with them that the state had no right to judge in matters of doctrine, but in no sense shared in the neoclassical dislike of Puritan enthusiasm and of the doctrine of the inner light.[47] Indeed, Marvell's adversary Parker, who was as thorough and unsubtle a Baconian as he was a Hobbesian, was in this respect far more attuned than Marvell to the temper of the new age. To Parker, the programme of the Royal Society and the doctrine of 'the sober Christians of the Church of *England*' were virtually interchangeable: both were bastions against irrationalism, the 'frenzies of a bold and ungovern'd Imagination' allowed to run unchecked in the 'fulsome and lushious Metaphors' of vain philosophy, dissenting sermons, and attempts at metaphysical wit.[48]

Marvell's own theological beliefs, in contrast with those of the latitudinarians, and with those of Parker and his allies, were essentially Puritan. His vocabulary is that of the 1640s rather than the rationalist 1670s: 'that serious business of Regeneration, Justification, Sanctification, Election, Vocation, Adoption, which the Apostle *Paul* hath, besides others, with so much labour illustrated and distinguish'd' (*RT*, II, p. 287). Theologically, the latitudinarians were anti-Calvinists, abhorring the Calvinist doctrines of predestination and irresistible grace, emphasizing the necessity of good works to salvation.[49] Marvell, though like Milton and other Puritan libertarians he departs from Calvinist orthodoxy in several respects, writes within the overall framework of Puritan belief. He is careful to cite precedents among reformed theologians for his relatively heterodox position on predestination, while at the same time arguing that the citation of authority has little bearing in matters of conscience. He attacks Parker for his 'too high conceit of mens good Works; as if, contrary to the stream of the Scripture, we could be thereby justified' (*RT*, II, pp. 267–8), emphasizes the spiritual dimension in religion beyond mere 'Mortal Virtue' (*RT*, I, p. 46), and lays particular stress on the need to overcome the effects of original sin by individual repentance and spiritual regeneration, 'those allowed and obvious Truths of Faith, Repentance, and the New Creature'.[50] 'To render men capable of Salvation,' he writes in *The Rehearsal Transpros'd*, 'there is a more extraordinary influence of Gods Spirit required and promised' (*RT*, II, 267): in poems and prose works, he consistently puts forth the view that men must humbly submit themselves to divine judgment and petition for divine grace, rather than presume on their own imputed merits.

Marvell's attitude toward 'Ritual and Ceremonial traditions' (*RT*, II, p. 246) can also clearly be distinguished from that of the latitudinarians. The latitudinarians cautioned against the rigid insistence on ceremonies, matters indifferent in themselves, as unnecessarily provocative; for the church to insist, for example, on the wearing of surplices 'when the People are so passionate against them', Croft wrote, 'savours more of passion likewise in Governours than Religion'. But the moderate, prudential attitude characteristically expressed in their writings, sympathetic toward ritual and ceremony in themselves but unwilling to force them on others, equally critical of those who were 'so eager either for or against' ceremonies, is quite different from militant Puritan iconoclasm.[51] Marvell's view of Laudian attempts to '*Magnificate* the Church with triumphal Pomp and Ceremony' (*RT*, I, p. 131) is uncompromisingly Puritan – as, indeed, one would expect from the author of the nunnery episode of 'Upon Appleton House' and 'A Dialogue, between the Resolved Soul, and Created Pleasure'. 'Ceremonies and Decorations' to him were not only 'new Inventions' and impositions, but were in their nature contrary to 'the Primitive Christianity' (*Mr. Smirke*, p. 11) and the 'plainness of fashion' appropriate to Protestantism: the scorn is apparent in his catalogue of '*Candles, Crucifixes, Paintings, Images, Copes, bowing to the East, bowing to the Altar*, and so many several Cringes & Genuflexions, that a man unpractised stood in need to entertain both a Dancing Master and a Remembrancer' (*RT*, I, pp. 131–2).[52]

The distrust of authority, civil or intellectual, expressed throughout Marvell's writings, suggests another difference between Marvell and the Anglican moderates who, feeling a primary loyalty to the Church of England, tended to favour comprehension of dissenters within the national church rather than legal toleration of dissent. The distinction is not merely a semantic one. The relationship of the moderates with the dominant Laudian wing of the Anglican Church was ambivalent: in their anti-Calvinist theology they were at one with the Laudians, and they regularly stated their loyalty to mother church even while urging that 'as Children, are to obey their Parents, so Parents ought not to provoke their Children to disobedience'. Hales and Chillingworth believed that Christians of all persuasions should join in a single communion and that for the sake of civil peace men should conform to the national church of whatever place they happened to be, simply not participating in any parts of the service they disliked.[53] The Anglican moderates of this generation were temperamentally conservative, allied by instinct and background to the old regime, and when war broke out all chose the royalist side. During the late 1660s and 1670s latitudinarians such as Wilkins and Tillotson were active in pressing schemes for comprehension of dissenters within the church. But again their position was essentially one of moderate conservatism. Though Tillotson and his associates were willing to modify the liturgy of the Church of England to accommodate Presbyterian objections against church ritual, they opposed widespread toleration, considering it a 'Trojan Horse', a method of legalizing and perpetuating sectarianism.

Is it not to every considerate Man as clear as the Sun at Noon-day . . . that nothing can be a Bulwark of sufficient force to resist all the Arts and Attempts of popery, but an *establish'd National Religion*, firmly united and compacted in all the parts of it? Is it not plain to every Eye, that little *Sects* and *separate Congregations* can never do it?[54]

Dissenting leaders such as John Owen consistently opposed these schemes of comprehension, seeing them as attempts by those in authority to weaken dissent by splitting moderate Presbyterians who could find shelter under the aegis of the national church from more radical Independents, Baptists, Quakers, and others who felt they could not in conscience conform even to a modified establishment. In general, the Anglican moderates deplored separatism, though they expressed a great deal of sympathy for the separatists. Even Croft, probably more favourably inclined toward dissenters than any other member of the Anglican hierarchy, ultimately comes down in favour of incorporation of dissenters into the Church of England, rather than their right to follow religious practices of their own choosing.

The rhetorical strategies of *The Rehearsal Transpros'd* and *Mr. Smirke*, addressed primarily to an audience of royalists and Anglicans of 'the more Moderate sort' whom the author seeks to enlist as allies against the forces of absolutism, preclude any open expression of radical separatist views. Nevertheless, the conception of liberty of conscience which emerges from these works is quite distinct from that of the latitudinarian moderates and far closer to that expressed during the Civil War by such figures among the Puritan left as Roger Williams and Milton and later by Locke: that there should be no established church and that, subject to certain minimal restrictions, men should be free to practise whatever religion they choose. Such a position is stated in ringing, unequivocal terms by Marvell's nephew and close associate William Popple, in the preface to his English translation of Locke's *Letter Concerning Toleration* (1689):

Our Government has not only been partial in Matters of Religion; but those also who have suffered under that Partiality, and have therefore endeavoured by their Writings to vindicate their own Rights and Liberties, have for the most part done it upon narrow Principles, suited only to the Interests of their Sects...Absolute Liberty, Just and True Liberty, Equal and Impartial Liberty, is the thing that we stand in need of.[55]

'Absolute Liberty . . . Equal and Impartial Liberty' is an attractive formula, but one that virtually no one during the period was able to hold consistently; nearly all proponents of liberty of conscience between 1640 and 1688 felt it necessary to impose certain restrictions, either on doctrinal or on prudential grounds. Even Roger Williams, who in 1644 boldly urged toleration with no doctrinal limitations whatsoever, 'a permission of the most *Paganish, Jewish, Turkish,* or *Antichristian consciences and worships*', was unwilling to extend such toleration to those who refused '*civill obedience*' to the state or violated the civil law. Most Protestant theorists during the seventeenth century automatically excluded Popery from toleration, on political rather than religious grounds; as Locke wrote near the end of the century, 'that Church can have no right to be tolerated by the Magistrate, which is constituted upon such a bottom, that all those who enter into it, do thereby, *ipso facto*, deliver themselves up into the Protection and Service of another Prince'. Milton shared this position and so, it is clear from *The Growth of Popery* as well as *The Rehearsal Transpros'd*, did Marvell.[56] Other Protestant theorists sought to impose more severe restrictions. The history of seventeenth-century Puritanism is of course filled with men who wished only, in Popple's words, 'to vindicate their own Rights and Liberties ... upon narrow Principles', and who, once they gained power, were metamorphosed into strict guardians of doctrinal purity and public order. But though no theorist, including Marvell, Milton, and Locke, argued a case for unrestricted and absolute liberty of conscience, it is wrong to assume that all the partisans of liberty during the period were simply hypocrites awaiting their share of the spoils. A consistent libertarian position, always a minority view, may be found within the Puritan tradition in the writings of such men as Walwyn, Williams, and Milton and in the speeches of the Leveller leaders during the Army Debates of 1647-9. It is this libertarian Puritanism, with its characteristic attitudes toward civil power, toward the demands of conscience, toward liberty and necessity, and toward the relationship of the spiritual and corporeal realms, to which Marvell is most closely allied.

The rise to power during successive stages of the English revolution of the 'Presbyterian' and the 'Independent' group meant that the libertarians normally directed their arguments against other, less tolerant Puritans who believed that 'when the Back doth smart under the Rod, the ear is open to discipline and instruction'.[57] The belief was widespread among Puritans that, on both moral and prudential grounds, 'that which is good must be commended ... That which is evil must be forbidden ... No evil that is in the Power of the Magistrate to suppresse, ought to be tolerated.' Men, according to this view, are weak and need to be led: it is better to force men to be good than to abandon them to sin. When faced with a choice between morality and freedom, both in themselves desirable but not always reconcilable, many Presbyterian and Independent theorists, as A. S. P. Woodhouse has pointed out, opted to redefine Christian liberty in highly restrictive terms, subordinating the ideal of liberty to that of reformation.

A wandering sheep forced at first by Discipline, may at last blesse God for that violence; but being left to it self, and its own fancies and desires, may for ever curse the Authors of such a *Liberty*...The understanding is naturally as prone to errour, as the will is to evil...A childe may easily be enticed from his own parents by an Apple.[58]

Against this position, the Puritan libertarians argued that God had created the soul free and that, after man's sins had deprived him of his initial freedom, Christ's sacrifice had set the soul free once more. Men thus were wrong in trying to entangle the conscience 'that Christ set free' in bonds of their own making.[59] In *The Rehearsal Transpros'd*, Marvell rejects all attempts to restrict the scope of Christian liberty in theory or practice, defining it as 'the Restauration of the Mind of Man to its Natural Liberty from the *Mosaical* Law' (*RT*, II, p. 244).

> As our Saviour has exacted those duties which are necessary with more declarative strictness from Christians, then was under any other Religion, and thereby bound the Conscience to a severer scrutiny within it self over all our performances; so hath he gratified them on the other part with larger exemptions and Priviledges from things Indifferent and Unnecessary...But whatsoever general Rules, Laws and Precepts are given in Scripture, and more particularly in the New Testament...do make up the great Charter of Christian Liberty. (II, p. 246)

According to this view, all authority which seeks to limit the conscience in its pursuit of truth is illegitimate. The libertarian position on the sovereignty of conscience is clearly stated in Milton's *Treatise of Civil Power*:

> If then we count it so ignorant and irreligious in the papist to think himself discharged in Gods account, beleeving only as the church beleevs, how much greater condemnation will it be to the protestant his condemner, to think himself justified, beleeving only as the state beleevs...Every true Christian able to give a reason for his faith, hath the word of God before him, the promised Holy Spirit, and the minde of Christ within him... a much better and safer guide of conscience, which as far as concerns himself he may far more certainly know than any outward rule impos'd upon him by others. (*CPW*, VII, 246–7)

To the arguments of conservatives that unchecked liberty would lead to 'license and confusion', that the unstable multitude would be 'seduced by false doctrines', the libertarians replied that truth need not be afraid of falsehood: to fear the consequences of freedom is to doubt God's providence, 'showing a great diffidence in the spirit of God, and in Christ, as if he would not provide for the maintaining his own truth in the world'.[60] Truth, according to Milton's *Areopagitica* and such contemporary radical libertarian pamphlets as William Walwyn's *The Compassionate Samaritane* and Henry Robinson's *Liberty of Conscience*, as well as the speeches of the army radicals in the Whitehall debates of 1648–9, can not flourish under 'a perpetuall childhood of prescription', but only in an atmosphere of freedom: 'give her but room, & do not bind her when she sleeps'.

It is true that if liberty were given for men to teach what they will, there will appear more false Teachers then ever, yet it were better that many false doctrines were published...then that one sound truth should be forcibly smothered or wilfully concealed...Doe we suspect that errour should vanquish truth?...We may plot, contrive and endeavour whatsoever our owne depraved natures will suggest to us against it, but great is the power of truth, and it will prevaile at last.[61]

Perhaps the central distinguishing doctrine of the radical Puritan libertarians is their belief in the absolute separation of the corporeal and spiritual realms. This is a belief which Marvell entirely shares. In *The Rehearsal Transpros'd* , *Mr. Smirke,* and *A Short Historical Essay* he argues at length that the civil power has no jurisdiction over men's consciences and that 'the Government of Religion' (*RT*, I, p. 64) is entirely outside the magistrate's concern.

Christianity, if rightly exercised upon its own Principles, would render all Magistracy useless. But although he, *who was Lord of all, and to whom all Power was given both in Heaven and in Earth*, was nevertheless contented to come in the form of a Servant, and to let the Emperours and Princes of the World alone with the use of their Dominions; he thought it good reason to retain his Religion under his own cognizance and exempt its Authority from their jurisdiction. In this alone he was imperious, and did not only practise it himself against the Laws and Customs then received, and in the face of the Magistrate; but continually seasoned and hardened his Disciples in the same confidence and obstinacy...

It plainly appears that according to natural right, and the apprehension of all sober Heathen Governours, Christianity as a Religion, was wholly exempt from the Magistrates jurisdiction or Lawes, farther than any particular person among them immorally transgressed, as others, the common rules of human society. (*Short Historical Essay*, pp. 3, 34)

The position argued here is a radical one and differs from that held in turn by Anglican, Presbyterian, and Independent spokesmen during the Civil War period while each group was in ascendancy: the belief that the Christian magistrate should act as 'a *Nursing Father*' to religion, with responsibilities which included

propagating the true religion, restraining men from impious practices, and punishing transgressions of the moral law. In his
'Discourse about Toleration' (1649), Owen, later Marvell's ally
against Parker but far more conservative than Marvell in his view
of the relationship between civil power and religion, states a view
which was widely held at the time: 'Hath the *Magistrate* nothing
to doe, in, or about Religion? Is he to depose the *care* thereof?
Shall men... be suffered to devoure one another as they please?'[62]
Marvell's position is that the Christian magistrate is in no sense
different from the pagan magistrate ('For what power had the
Emperours by growing Christians, more than those had before
them? None. What obligation were Christian Subjects under to
the Magistrate more than before? None', *Short Historical Essay*,
p. 34) and that God's law and the civil law are entirely separate.
Parker's extreme Erastianism makes him an easy target for
reductio ad absurdum parody, but in ridiculing the view that
'whatsoever is enacted on Earth is at the same time enacted in
Heaven', that 'every man who transgresses in Cartwheels, and
the number of Horses in his Team, or that buries not in Flannel'
(*RT*, II, p. 248) is delivered over to Satan, Marvell is attacking
not only Parker's total subordination of the spiritual to the secular,
but any attempt to combine or confuse the two. His own view
is clear-cut: 'He that will do the Clergyes drudgery, must look for
his reward in another World' (*RT*, I, p. 134). 'An humane Law,'
Marvell states flatly, 'can create only an humane obligation' (*RT*,
II, p. 250); since men are '*free*' and '*the servants of God*', their
behaviour must be ruled by the principle that where the civil
power and the command of God can be 'contradistinguished, not
man but God is to be obey'd' (*RT*, II, p. 248).

Marvell's position depends upon the radical segregation of the
orders of nature and grace, which A. S. P. Woodhouse has shown
to be central to the thought of Milton and of such writers on the
Puritan left as Roger Williams. Such a conception of two separate
orders or spheres, both created and ruled by God but 'by different
dispensations' and with 'different goods which pertain to them',
is central to Marvell's poetry – to 'A Dialogue between the Soul
and Body' as well as 'A Dialogue, between the Resolved Soul,
and Created Pleasure', to 'The Mower's Song' and 'To his Coy
Mistress' as well as 'On a Drop of Dew'.[63] The weapons of faith,

Marvell like the libertarians of the Civil War period remarks again and again, are spiritual and not carnal: in the words of Roger Williams, '*God* needeth not the helpe of a materiall *sword* of *steele* to assist the *sword* of the *Spirit* in the affaires of *conscience*.'[64] Disdaining 'that Spiritual Armour, which the Apostle found sufficient against the assaults of whatsoever enemy, even of Satan', Marvell writes in *Mr. Smirke*, those who would force the conscience choose 'Weapons of another Warfare'. 'They would establish the Christian Religion by a *Mahometan* way... Why may they not, as well as force men to Church, cram the Holy Supper too, down their throats... and drive them into the Rivers by thousands to be baptized or drowned?' (p. 8, Sig. g2ᵛ, g3ʳ). For the civil magistrate to seek to punish heresy, imposing the magistrate's version of the true faith on all under his jurisdiction, is 'to take *Christ Jesus*, and make him a temporall *King* by force',[65] and thus to succumb to the temptation of earthly power which Jesus rejected when Satan offered it in the wilderness. The kingdoms of the earth, according to the radical libertarians, were indeed Satan's domain; all 'the powers and kingdoms of this world', Milton wrote in *A Treatise of Civil Power*, 'are upheld by outward force only':

Christ hath a government of his own, sufficient of it self to all his ends and purposes in governing his church; but much different from that of the civil magistrate; and the difference in this verie thing principally consists, that it governs not by outward force...because it deals only with the inward man and his actions, which are all spiritual and to outward force not lyable.[66]

Marvell's views on civil power and religious liberty are developed in a series of pamphlets written in the 1670s, while the writers who presented similar views a generation earlier – Walwyn, Robinson, and Williams in the 1640s, Milton in 1659 – wrote under quite different circumstances. Marvell's political writings between 1654 and 1659 are defences of the Cromwellian regime, which he like Milton served as Latin secretary and propagandist. The writers of the Commonwealth period whose views on authority and conscience most closely resembled those of Marvell, with the exception of Milton, generally refused to support the Protectorate. Marvell's political allies during 1654–9, as we have seen, tended to be more conservative in their attitude toward civil power: one cynical political maxim is that suspicion of power usually varies inversely with proximity to it. We thus have the curious phenomenon of Marvell in *The First Anniversary* attacking Levellers and sectaries who in many ways were his natural allies, or at least shared some of his central religious and political beliefs. By the 1670s a dozen years of persecution and exile from the seats of power had obliterated many of the doctrinal distinctions and rivalries characteristic of Puritanism during the Commonwealth. One needs to be cautious in extrapolating Marvell's religious beliefs of the 1670s into the 1650s, when he wrote the bulk of his non-satiric poems, and one must resist the temptation to assume that in political writings ideas somehow exist independently of their historical context. Nevertheless, a consistent attitude toward the claims of conscience and the power of the state can be found in all Marvell's writings, early and late, and this position strikingly resembles that argued by the Puritan libertarians of the 1640s and 1650s.

One can distinguish two major strands in the attacks by Marvell and the earlier generation of Puritan libertarians on the 'unnatural Copulation of Ecclesiastical and Temporal' (*RT*, II, p. 238) – first, the belief that religious faith is entirely an internal matter, and secondly, the belief that earthly power is in itself corrupting. The radical Puritans defined church membership as wholly voluntary: 'God accepts only of willing service, such as we perform of our owne free election, not by compulsion.' In such a view, an established national church, to which men are constrained to give their allegiance, is at best irrelevant to man's salvation and, insofar as it encourages hypocrisy and mere formal adherence to outward rites and ceremonies, can hinder God's work of salvation, serve to 'make the blood of Christ ineffectuall'. Why, asks Henry Robinson, do we seek the 'false lustre of a Nationall Church? Do we think that Gods salvation is also Nationall? ... This is the worke of man and not of God.'[67] Marvell does not in his writings attack the concept of an established church as such, but he consistently defines a true church as a 'Congregation of the Faithful' (*Short Historical Essay*, p. 23), independent of any system of clerical organization as of any element of compulsion; individual conscientious Christians, 'instructed and animated' by Scripture 'in their duty to God, in despight of Suffering' (p. 3) and regenerated by faith, testify to their membership in the invisible church militant. No considerations of expediency or public order can relieve man of the responsibility of choice in the spiritual matters that concern him most:

> Is it not reason...to allow that men should address themselves to such Minister as they think best for their souls health?...What sick man, but, if a Physician were inforced upon him, might in good prudence suspect that it were to kill him, or that, if the next heir and the Doctor could agree, he would certainly do it?
>
> . . .
>
> But I know not why the Mouth of the Church should pretend to be the Brain of the Church, and understand and will for the whole Laity... We are all at the same Ordinary, and pay our souls equally for the Reckoning. (*Mr. Smirke*, Sig. g³; G1)⁶⁸

In an extended discussion in *The Rehearsal Transpros'd*, Marvell upholds a position which Woodhouse has identified as characteristic of Williams, Milton, and the army radicals in the theological and political controversies of the 1640s and 1650s: the claim that the coming of Jesus had 'abrogated...the *Mosaical Law*...in perpetuity' (*RT*, II, p. 245). More conservative Puritans, such as Ireton and his allies in the Whitehall debates, rejected the potential antinomianism of this position, arguing that magistrates retained the power assigned them in the Old Testament as keepers of the Tables of God's commandments: 'sin is to be restrained as it was then, and that which was sin then is sin now.'⁶⁹ Marvell's view and that of the radicals was that 'the great Charter of Christian Liberty' (*RT*, II, p. 246), given to men in the New Testament, had rendered invalid the rigid, restrictive morality of the Old Law, as it freed men from the practice of those ceremonies for the worship of God prescribed in the Old Testament. As Milton writes:

> Then was the state of rigor, childhood, bondage and works, to all which force was not unbefitting; now is the state of grace, manhood, freedom and faith; to all which belongs willingness and reason, not force.

In the theocracy of the Old Testament, the magistrate, 'appointed, instituted, and directed by God himself', could legitimately compel obedience to the true faith.⁷⁰ But, Marvell argued, no monarch since the coming of Jesus bore any such 'express Revelation...

Inspiration of a Prophet, nor Unction' from heaven (*RT*, II, p. 250) confirming him in his rule and allowing him to arrogate to himself the right to act as God's representative.

A further characteristic uniting the writers of the libertarian left is a thoroughgoing distrust of power, ambition, and wealth. To these men, as to Marvell, a crown or a badge of office did not raise a man into a sphere above ordinary fallible mortals, and 'prosperity' was by no means 'a mark of the true Church'.[71] The possession of worldly goods, in their view, was not a sign of inward grace; as Marvell writes in *The Rehearsal Transpros'd*, 'those that can go upright under the load of wealth, make up the lesser part of mankind, and for the most part they that seek it more earnestly do the worst deserve it' (*RT*, II, p. 237). Christ's apostles were men of 'low condition and meane estate', 'poore and unlearned Fishermen and Tent-makers'. The true Christian realizes how meaningless 'externall State, pomp, riches' are in the eyes of God, and thus scorns the corrupt values of the world.[72] In *The Rehearsal Transpros'd*, Marvell contrasts Parker, the well-fed pluralist, intent on worldly advancement and indifferent to the welfare of his parishioners, with the good shepherds who maintain the principles of primitive Christianity, 'Godly... Ministers, who take care of the peoples Souls committed to their charge and reside among them.'

> You in the mean time, as if you were an Exempt of the Clergy, and as Parson can transmit over the Cure of Souls to your Curate, saunter about City and Countrey whither your gilt Coach and extravagance will carry you, starving your People and pampering your Horses, so that a poor man cannot approach *their heels* without dying for it. (*RT*, II, p. 212)

In *A Short Historical Essay*, Marvell, like Milton and Williams, locates the initial falling-away from 'the good and ancient ways of Christianity' (*RT*, II, p. 238) in the establishment of Christianity as state religion under the Emperor Constantine. At the time of Constantine, Marvell writes, a 'New Disease', a 'Pestilence' had 'diffused it self most remarkably thorow the whole body of the Clergy' (*Short Historical Essay*, p. 9): the disease of worldliness, the lust for wealth and power. From that time forward, the clergy, corrupted by the taste of worldly power, far too often 'follow'd the Courts of Princes, and intangled themselves in secular affairs, beyond what is lawful or convenient to the Sanctity of their Vocation' (*RT*, II, p. 238). In similar terms, Williams argues that under Constantine Christianity, drugged by comfort or swollen with ambition, 'fell asleepe on the beds of carnal ease'.[73] What is properly spiritual had in this view been contaminated by temporality, the 'wreaths of Fame and Interest' ('The Coronet', line 16), Satan winds through all earthly things. The only remedy, as Marvell and the radical libertarians saw it, was the total separation of church and state. They viewed the values of Christianity and the values of the world as incompatible, and therefore felt it necessary that the clergy avoid all secular employment, as a corollary to their belief that secular princes should have no power over the religious practices of their subjects. 'Truly I think the reason that God does not bless them [the clergy] in Affairs of State', Marvell remarks in *The Rehearsal Transpros'd*, 'is, because he never intended them for that imployment' (I, p. 134). In keeping with his concern for practical morality rather than theological niceties, he ends *A Short Historical Essay* with a series of recommendations to would-be clergymen:

That, betaking themselves to the Spiritual Warfare, they ought to disintangle from the World. That they do not ride for a Benefice, as if it were for a Fortune, or a Mistress...That they take the Ministry up not as a Trade. (pp. 37–8)[74]

III

Though the context in each case is secular, the terms in Marvell's evocations of the ideal government are openly or implicitly theological. In describing the British limited monarch as 'the onely Intelligent Ruler over a Rational People' (*Growth of Popery*, p. 4) and claiming of the British constitution that 'there is nothing that comes nearer in Government to the Divine Perfection' (p. 5), Marvell is suggesting that, though man's state is fallen, it may be possible to 'repair the ruins of our first parents'.[75] In the perspective of Marvell's Christian irony, man remains a rational being even in his fallen state, for all the proofs he constantly gives of his irrationality. Like Milton, Marvell reminds us of the 'Divine Perfection' man threw away at his first fall to warn us of the folly of throwing it away once again. The sad likelihood that man will make a desert out of a peaceful and flourishing landscape, where 'the whole Land at whatsoever season of the year does yield him a plentiful Harvest' (*Growth of Popery*, p. 4), that like Eve and Satan he will succumb to the temptation of greater power and dissatisfaction with what he has, does not negate a poet's responsibility to provide a 'warning voice' (*Paradise Lost*, IV, line 1). In his satires and political writings, Marvell is a realist in recognizing the brutal cynicism with which men in power feed their insatiable wills and an idealist in urging alternative standards of conduct, in insisting that it is not yet too late.

Marvell's characteristic ironic tone reflects an awareness that, however much we may regret it, the world is fallen and that we must therefore chasten our expectations. The morality implicit in much of Marvell is that of the education of Adam and Eve in the last books of *Paradise Lost*: though we may be tempted to 'give ear to proud and curious Spirits' (*RT*, II, p. 231), to fall prey either to 'a vast opinion of [our] own sufficiency' (I, p. 15) or to despair, ultimately we must learn 'to be content with such bodies, and to inhabit such an Earth as it has pleased God to allot us' (II, p. 231). Underlying both the outward-looking, militant irony of Marvell's satires and the impersonal, detached, freely proliferating ironic wit which is Marvell's signature in his lyrics is a further form of irony turned inward, Christian wit. Man's lot, with the body and soul uneasily coexisting as irreconcilable and inseparable enemies, is itself ironic. His 'vain Head, and double Heart' ('A Dialogue between the Soul and Body', line 10) assure both that his unresolved paradoxes will cause him pain and that he will be incapable of finding any solution or relief. Man, as Marvell sees him, is doomed to feel the anguish of parallel lines, wracked by a yearning to 'joyn', yet helplessly extending side by side into infinity ('The Definition of Love', line 23).

Yet, as a final twist of irony, in man's weakness and frustration lies his strength. It is his consciousness, his capacity for feeling guilt, pain, and loss, his unique though sometimes unwelcome gift of retrospective awareness, the weight of conscience which he cannot, even if he wished to do so, 'atturn and indenture' over to others (*Short Historical Essay*, p. 21), that enables man to find a path to freedom. It is by the 'Opposition of the Stars' ('The

Definition of Love', line 32) that love is defined: 'Magnanimous Despair' (line 5) enables the lovers of 'The Definition of Love' to attain a perfection denied ordinary lovers, whose 'Tinsel' (line 8) joys soon fade. The couple of 'The Definition of Love' have been initiated into experience, unlike the happy innocents 'with whom the Infant Love yet playes', described in stanza 1 of 'The Un-fortunate Lover', who imagine themselves secure in a vegetative pastoral contentment, unaware of their inability 'to make im-pression upon Time' (line 8). Gifted with consciousness, the post-lapsarian lovers of 'The Definition of Love' are able to defy the 'Tyrannick pow'r' (line 16) of fate, which in separating them can only intensify their love. In 'The Unfortunate Lover', the pains and frustrations of love in the fallen realm are emphasized, rather than any possible transcendence, yet here too the lover gains a form of apotheosis in resisting the forces of envious fate, 'cuffing the Thunder' (line 50) and dying in music. Here perhaps it is the confrontation of pain which gives man his identity.

Neither earthly tyrant nor outer necessity, Marvell argues, has the absolute power their partisans claim. A belief in an essential human freedom which no outward force can touch is central to Marvell's thought, as to Milton's. In his verse and prose satires, as in such poems as 'An Horatian Ode', 'The Definition of Love', 'To his Coy Mistress', and 'Upon Appleton House', Marvell consistently emphasizes the role of free choice in a providentially ordered universe. The conception of an iron necessity which rendered all human action futile and made all talk of moral choice superfluous, a necessity 'that was pre-eternal to all things, and exercised dominion not only over all humane things, but over *Jupiter* himself and the rest of the Deities and drove the great Iron nail thorough the Axel-tree of Nature', was antipathetic to him. The doctrine of a 'Universal Dictatorship of Necessity over God and Man', so attractive to predestinarians and apologists for earthly rulers ('I have some suspicion', he writes of Parker in *The Rehearsal Transpros'd*, 'that you would have men under-stand it of your self, and that you are that Necessity'), in Marvell's view robs the universe of any meaning and simply deifies power (II, p. 230). Marvell rejected Hobbist reason of state as he rejected Calvinist predestination: to him, man is a reasonable creature and therefore free. No form of outward necessity can negate man's responsibility to choose between right and wrong, to determine, with the aid of his conscience, 'Humane Reason guided by the Scripture' (II, p. 243), how to behave in his daily life. The soul is given an 'immortal Shield', and must 'learn' to bear its weight ('Resolved Soul', lines 1–2). Neither truth nor morality, as Milton says in *Areopagitica*, can flourish in a climate of prescription, 'unexercis'd and unbreath'd' (*CPW*, II, 515); through exercise, through exposure to experience, the resolved soul learns to discriminate.

Like Milton, Marvell consistently sought to reconcile a belief in a divine providence (in Milton's definition, 'that by which God the father views and preserves all created things and governs them with supreme wisdom and holiness, according to the conditions of his decree') with a belief that man was a free agent responsible for his own acts.[76] In their emphasis on man's freedom, Marvell, Milton, and the Puritan libertarians directly or by implication challenged the orthodox Calvinist belief in predestination. Because their view of morality stressed the role of free choice and man's endowment of rationality in this way, rejecting any form of determinism as they rejected earthly authority, the libertarians frequently came under attack by guardians of Calvinist doctrinal purity. The last of Marvell's prose works, *Remarks upon a late Disingenuous Discourse* (1678), is a defence of the dissenting clergyman John Howe against attacks by more orthodox Calvinists for upholding the doctrine of free will against rigid predestination. Though the circumstances of the 1670s, when the Puritans had long been out of power and Calvinist theology was no longer dominant in England, differed greatly from the prevailing climate of opinion in the Commonwealth and Protectorate years, nevertheless Marvell's position in *Remarks* is closely akin to that of such libertarian radicals of the 1640s as John Goodwin and to Milton in *De Doctrina Christiana*, as well as in *Paradise Lost*. Like Milton, Marvell is careful to distinguish between God's prescience or omniscience and any form of necessitarianism, arguing that God's foreknowledge of events in no way implies a predestination that limits man's ability to choose freely among alternatives. In *Remarks*, Marvell repeatedly draws the distinction between 'a thing so plainly reveal'd in the Word of God as his Prescience is, and so agreeable to all rational apprehension, and a Notion so altogether unrevealed as this universal Predetermination yet appears, and so contrary if not to the whole scope and design of Divine Revelation, yet to all common understanding and genuine sense of right Reason' (pp. 76–7).[77] To the Calvinist doctrine of predestination, Marvell and the libertarians opposed the Lutheran doctrine of justification by faith: though they by no means make man's redemption depend on man alone, unaided by God's grace, they reject the view of man as the purely passive object of God's decrees.[78] Sinners, in Milton's and Marvell's view, are responsible for their own sins: 'as to Evil', Marvell writes, citing biblical proof-texts, 'that also of St. James, is sufficient conviction, cap. I. v. 13, 14. *Let no man say, when he is tempted, I was tempted by God; God cannot be tempted with Evil, neither tempteth he any man:* But every man is tempted, when he is drawn aside by his own lusts and enticed.' To deny man the freedom to use his God-given reason to choose an appropriate course of action, Marvell argues, is to make God the author of sin:

But how much doth *It* reflect upon God and that Religious sense which we ought to cherish of him...when it makes God to have determined Innocent *Adam*'s Will to the choice of eating the fruit that was forbidden him?...To *Illustrate* (as it pretends) so black a thing, it parallels God's moving him to that Act rather than to another, *with a Writing-Master's directing his Scholars hand.* If the Cause be not to be defended upon better terms than so, what Christian but would rather wish he had never known Writing-Master, than to subscribe such an Opinion; and that God should make an innocent Creature in this manner to do a forbidden Act, for which so dreadful a vengeance was to insue upon him and his posterity? (*Remarks*, pp. 4–5, 125–6)

Such works as *The Rehearsal Transpros'd, The Growth of Popery*, and 'Last Instructions', like *Remarks*, are grounded in a conception of freedom and experience which can be described as libertarian or non-Calvinist Puritan. A similar view is implicit in many of Marvell's lyrics, which tend either to be aids to the embattled soul (Marvell at his most Miltonic, as in 'A Dialogue, between The Resolved Soul, and Created Pleasure') or, more often, reflections on, or definitions of, the human condition. Education into experience is his recurrent theme, and experience, as with Vaughan and the romantic poets, is normally defined in terms of loss. The central irony of human existence is man's fallen,

alienated state in which he longs after a recovered wholeness
'beyond a Mortal's share' ('The Garden', line 61). The realm of
freedom and unchanging truth in Marvell's poems is often explicitly Christian: the unenlightened and puzzled mower and the
weeping nymph, introduced to a reality of unrelieved pain so out
of consonance with anything they had previously known, the
imperious infant T. C. as yet protected from any such knowledge,
the coy mistress who wishes to deny its existence, are distinguished
from the converted shepherd in 'Clorinda and Damon' or the
resolved soul, both of whom recognize that 'Where the Creator's
skill is priz'd, / The rest is all but Earth disguis'd' ('Resolved
Soul' lines 35–6). Yet if Marvell's moral universe is Miltonic,
there is a fundamental difference in attitude between the two
poets. The acute pain of the nymph, her sense that the rules have
changed, that a universe hitherto comprehensible has suddenly
been deprived of harmony and meaning ('It cannot dye so.
Heavens King / Keeps register of every thing', 'The Nymph
complaining for the death of her Faun', lines 13–14) has its
Miltonic parallels, but no answer is even implied to the nymph's
agonized questions. It is striking how often Marvell's poems are
left unresolved: 'The Nymph complaining for the death of her
Faun' is like a version of *Paradise Lost* ending with Book IX.
Marvell's attitude toward the naifs and infants who populate his
poems is ambivalent: the hard freedom of truth is consistently
shown to be morally preferable to enslavement to pleasing fictions,
and yet in common with Vaughan, Blake, and Wordsworth
Marvell sees the capacity of imaginative or mythopoeic sympathy,
so much a prey to circumstances, so fragile when exposed to the
harsh air of experience, as representing one of the few ways by
which man can free himself from his surroundings. What children
lose, the poet retains: the poetic imagination unites the gifts of
innocence and experience. In somewhat similar terms, John
Creaser has identified Marvell's wit with gaiety transfiguring
dread, 'the mind's declaration of independence from the Fall' and
its attendant train of fears and sorrows.[79] And yet for Marvell the
realist, the mind's sovereignty over contingencies can never be
complete. He keeps returning in his poems to the one inescapable
fact which defines the human condition, the question which can
never be answered:

146

What luckless Apple did we tast,
To make us Mortal, and Thee Wast?
    ('Upon Appleton House', lines 327–8)

The extended dialogue in Marvell between hope and despair, between the fervent belief that '*Paradice's only Map*' ('Upon Appleton House', line 768) lies open before us and the forlorn conviction that the world is 'not, what once it was', but a 'rude heap' (lines 761–2), in which we are irreparably and irremediably cut off from the good for which we long, is the dialogue at the heart of seventeenth-century Puritanism. Both Marvell and Milton see the situation of the blind and shorn Samson as representative, not least in his ultimate solitude. Without any certainty outside the inner court of conscience, man can never know with any certainty whether he has been saved. Marvell consistently emphasizes the exposed isolation of the man who seeks to follow the imperious demands of conscience, with its 'prickling leaf' which 'shrinks at ev'ry touch' (lines 357–8): a temporary respite from the pains of existence is possible, but essentially for Marvell the man of conscience, restless and questioning, rejecting the voice of worldly authority in all its forms, rejecting even the consolation of a sense of solidarity with fellow believers, is left alone with his own unanswerable questions.[80]

The firm conviction that God directs all things does not in itself make for serenity, since the ways of God are not only unfathomable but often incompatible with human ideas of justice, to say nothing of our preferences. Even those who dedicate themselves to the service of God, 'such as thou hast solemnly elected, / With gifts and graces eminently adorn'd / To some great work', Milton writes in *Samson Agonistes* (lines 678–80), are often thrown down 'lower then thou didst exalt them high' (line 689): 'Just and unjust, alike seem miserable, / For oft alike, both come to evil end' (lines 703–4). In moments not of promised glory but 'on evil days though fall'n, and evil tongues; / In darkness, and with dangers compast round, / And solitude' (*Paradise Lost*, VII, lines 26–8), the conviction that God provides for his servants is difficult indeed to sustain.[81] It is tempting at such a time to succumb to despair, to see, as Marvell did in his later years, not a 'wish'd Conjuncture' of the destined moment and the chosen people, but the actual 'Conjuncture' of a tyrannous, 'absolutely powerful' king, a supine parliament ('we are all venal Cowards, except some few'), and a disease seemingly spreading from the court to infect the entire nation. 'In such a Conjuncture, dear *Will*,' he writes to his nephew William Popple in 1670, 'what Probability is there of my doing any Thing to the Purpose?'[82]

When in 'Last Instructions' Marvell compares England in its state of decline to the bound Samson, there is no suggestion of a possible regeneration, no sense that the dark ways of providence will suddenly be illumined, that suffering will turn by unforeseen ways into triumph. Instead, the lines suggest only ignominy, in evoking the former greatness and potential for good which have been laid waste by man's folly and venality. The possibility is broached that the 'wondrous gifts' of God will indeed be 'frustrate' (*Samson Agonistes*, line 589), that God has averted his eyes from the English. In punishment for their iniquities, the English, reduced to spectators, are forced to watch the Dutch navy sail undisturbed into British waters and destroy or capture those British ships which once, 'Oaken Gyants of the ancient race, / ... rul'd all Seas' ('Last Instructions', lines 577–8).

> The Seamen search her all, within, without:
> Viewing her strength, they yet their Conquest doubt.
> Then with rude shouts, secure, the Air they vex;
> With Gamesome Joy insulting on her Decks.
> Such the fear'd *Hebrew*, captive, blinded, shorn
> Was led about in sport, the publick scorn.   (lines 731–6)

The 'Black Day' (line 737) of England's humiliation, so different from the 'blest Day' (*First Anniversary*, line 155) for which Marvell had seen presages under the reign of Cromwell, is made more painful by the memory of past glories and blighted promise. The imagery of rampant disorder explicitly provides standards by which the state of England in 1667 may properly be judged, but the lines do not suggest any immediate solution, except insofar as shame may lead to a resolve to bring about change:

> Thee, the Year's monster, let thy Dam devour.
> And constant Time, to keep his course yet right,
> Fill up thy space with a redoubled Night.
> When aged *Thames* was bound with Fetters base,
> And *Medway* chast ravish'd before his Face...

Now with vain grief their vainer hopes they rue,
Themselves dishonour'd, and the *Gods* untrue.
('Last Instructions', lines 740–52)

Pain and ignominy are often the human lot, and at times no response is possible other than sterile and fruitless mourning or the recognition that all joys, all hopes are transitory. Implicit in the laments for fallen England in 'Upon Appleton House' and 'Last Instructions', as in those passages in *Paradise Lost*, x, where Adam mourns his own separation from the glory, happiness, and beauty he has known, is the conviction that the decrees of God are unalterable. To Marvell as to Milton, wisdom begins with the acceptance of man's fallen state. ''Tis pride that makes a Rebel': to inveigh against divine providence, Marvell says in a letter to Sir John Trott on the death of a son, is 'the over-weening of our selves and our own things'.[83] One major lesson the Christian learns from experience is 'Humility': 'A Soul that knows not to presume / Is Heaven's and its own perfume' ('Resolved Soul', lines 29–30). Only if we recognize our fallen condition and accept the limitations imposed by it, Marvell says, can we hope to transcend it.

Freedom then is possible, according to Marvell, only after we have come to learn that 'the world will not go the faster for our driving' (*RT*, I, p. 135). The recognition that we can never know 'where Heavens choice may light' (*First Anniversary*, line 147), that men at all times labour in darkness, that even when we seek to serve God's cause our efforts are likely to end in utter defeat in a world in which injustice rules, need not lead to despair, but to a kind of exhilaration. Free from the distraction of false hopes, we can confront the truth openly, without recourse to comforting evasions:

The Grave's a fine and private place,
But none I think do there embrace.
('To his Coy Mistress', lines 31–2)

'The poet's time' occurs when the cause of virtue appears most desperate, when outward fortune appears implacably hostile, when his weaker allies have fled in dismay. It is at that time, when the temptation is greatest to succumb to despair or to abase oneself at the altar of success, that the poet finds courage to endure in his recognition that virtue alone is free:

> Then is the Poets time, 'tis then he drawes,
> And single fights forsaken Vertues cause.
> He, when the wheel of Empire, whirleth back,
> And though the World's disjointed Axel crack,
> Sings still of ancient Rights and better Times,
> Seeks wretched good, arraigns successful Crimes.
>
> ('Tom May's Death', lines 65–70)

5 · MARVELL'S SATIRES: THE SEARCH FOR FORM

I

Marvell's historical position as a satirist is in no way comparable to his place in the history of the Renaissance lyric; rather than being an assured master building on the example of his predecessors, Marvell the satirist has an uncertain touch, and his satires represent an uneasy marriage between the metaphysical and the Augustan. Their most striking quality allies them to earlier Renaissance poetry, especially the metaphysical line in the seventeenth century: a proliferating wit, throwing off unexpected comparisons which, at times grotesquely, take on an independent life:

> He gathring fury still made sign to draw;
> But himself there clos'd in a Scabbard saw
> As narrow as his Sword's; and I, that was
> Delightful, said there can no Body pass
> Except by penetration hither, where
> Two make a crowd, nor can three Persons here
> Consist but in one substance.
> ('Fleckno, an English Priest in Rome', lines 95–101)

> *Excise*, a Monster worse than e're before
> Frighted the Midwife, and the Mother tore,
> A thousand Hands she has and thousand Eyes,
> Breaks into Shops, and into Cellars prys.
> With hundred rows of Teeth the Shark exceeds,
> And on all Trade like *Casawar* she feeds:
> Chops off the piece where e're she close the Jaw,
> Else swallows all down her indented maw.
> She stalks all day in Streets conceal'd from sight,
> And flies like Batts with leathern Wings by Night.
> ('Last Instructions', lines 131–40)

His shape exact, which the bright flames infold,
Like the Sun's Statue stands of burnish'd Gold.
Round the transparent Fire about him glows,
As the clear Amber on the Bee does close:
And, as on Angels Heads their Glories shine,
His burning Locks adorn his Face Divine.
But, when in his immortal Mind he felt
His alt'ring Form, and soder'd Limbs to melt;
Down on the Deck he laid himself, and dy'd,
With his dear Sword reposing by his Side.
And, on the flaming Plank, so rests his Head,
As one that's warm'd himself and gone to Bed.   (lines 679–90)

What ethic river is this wondrous Tweed,
Whose one bank vertue, other vice does breed?
Or what new perpendicular does rise
Up from her stream, continued to the skies,
That between us the common air should bar
And split the influence of every star?
                    ('The Loyal Scot', lines 85–90)[1]

But a market, they say, does suit the king well,
Who the Parliament buys and revenues does sell,
And others to make the similitude hold
Say his Majesty himself is bought too and sold.
                    ('The Statue in Stocks-Market', lines 21–4)

These passages differ greatly in style and tone (and of course in context), but they share certain characteristics. They are all strings of conceits, examples of the quickness and fertility of invention which Dryden emphasizes in his definition of wit:

Wit in the poet, or wit writing...is no other than the faculty of imagination in the writer which, like a nimble spaniel, beats over and ranges through the field of memory, till it springs the quarry it hunted after; or, without metaphor, which searches over all the memory for the species or ideas of those things which it designs to represent. (Dryden, *Essays*, I, 8)

It is doubtful that Dryden or any other neoclassical critic would cite these passages by Marvell to illustrate the complementary quality of judgment, 'accuracy', or aptness, by which, according to neoclassical canons of taste, the fancy needs to be bounded and circumscribed; by these standards, they are typical of the 'wild and lawless' nature of wit which threatens to 'outrun the judgment' (*Ibid.*, I, 98).

In all of them, heterogeneous materials are yoked by violence together: with the exception of the last passage, which uses a popular style and homely comparisons, all employ metaphors which are learned, self-conscious, and *outré*, and the comparisons in the last example are no less incongruous and shocking, both in their violation of social decorum and in the revaluation forced on the reader. Yet on reflection, each of them turns out to be surprisingly 'accurate' and appropriate to its circumstances. Each seeks 'to make the similitude hold', to illuminate reality by the unexpected comparisons, showing that royalty and the market-place have more in common than one would think, that the divisions of custom and prejudice have neither celestial nor terrestrial basis, and that a quarrel on a staircase can illustrate both the laws of physics and the doctrine of the Trinity. By metaphorical analogy, the universe is made coherent. Metaphysical wit can be defined as lies in the service of truth: rhetorical distortions, logical sleight-of-hand, argument by 'Metaphors and Allegories' (which, as Parker says, literally considered 'is nothing else but to sport and trifle with empty words, because these Schems do not express the Natures of Things, but only their Similitudes and Resemblances'), which light up the contours of reality like a lightning-flash, reveal the truth hidden under the veil of custom.[2]

Each of the passages follows a different poetic model; Marvell has not a single style, but a whole armoury of styles varying according to the individual context and the different genres in which he works. The passages quoted show the variety of approaches possible within the single broad genre of satire. The first is in the manner of Donne's satires, imitating their abrupt movement, involved syntax, avoidance of end-stopped lines, and recondite imagery. In the second, the models are different and so, in consequence, are the versification, syntax, and type of imagery: here Marvell is writing mock-epic verse in closed heroic couplets, and draws on the tradition of epic and romance, with particular echoes of Spenser and Milton. The allegorical imagery is pictorial and expansive in the Spenserian manner. As with *The Faerie Queene*, the reader is simultaneously aware of the literal narrative and of the moral and historical allegory. The wit lies in the full and precise detail with which the allegory is carried out: each phrase of epic description not only calls up the image of a properly fearsome monster, but dramatizes the effects of the tax bill Marvell is attacking and, in terms of the general moral allegory, demonstrates the dangers of arbitrary power, the greed with which governments, unless they are checked, can swallow up the property of defenceless citizens. The third passage is again heroic, and again draws on Renaissance models – in this case, the Renaissance epyllion, the Ovidian mythological narrative. Here the strained imagery seeks to depict the exact moment of metamorphosis, the interpretation of the earthly and the spiritual; this is Marvell at his most baroque and fantastic, and one can cite equivalents in baroque painting and sculpture, such as Bernini. The fourth passage begins with relatively straightforward statement, in a couplet phrased with typical Augustan balance, but then proceeds to two further couplets whose imagery is more complex and learned, in the metaphysical style. There is a strong element of the grotesque in the lines, and an implicit appeal to common sense; though there is a less specific model here than in the other passages, the example of Cleveland underlies the poem, as Marvell wittily seeks to refute Cleveland's 'The Rebel Scot' in more or less Clevelandesque terms. The last passage finds its models in popular poetry and its practical, down-to-earth analogies are suitable to its intended audience. It is the only one of the passages outside the tradition of learned wit and the only one which does not declare its allegiance to 'European, that is to say Latin, culture', illustrating that aspect of Marvell which Eliot and, after him, such critics as Leishman, Colie, and Kermode have emphasized; the figures of Horace, Virgil, and Ovid are present behind the first three passages.[3] In all five of the passages, abstractions are visualized, and the unexpected literalness with which the ideas are rendered into images creates a sense of shock: the soldered limbs, the split stellar influence, the stalking monster with her indented maw, the two bodies striving to occupy a single space, are of a piece with the vegetable love, the brain vaulted as a model, the soul deaf with the drumming of an ear, and the unfortunate lover braving the tempest.

The metaphysical conceit can be a unifying device when linked with a firm structure of argument. But in a succession of couplets or quatrains united only by a common origin, an assigned topic on which they can display a series of dazzling variations, the effect of freely proliferating wit is more likely to be centrifugal than centripetal. There are various strategies by which Marvell seeks to give overall form to his satires: the close following of a model, the direct refutation of an adversary by using the adversary's own words, particular attention to the decorum of occasion and genre. But none of these is sufficient in itself to hold a long poem together; they may suggest a general direction for the poem, but do not provide a principle governing the articulation and disposition of parts. The problem is compounded when, as with the court and university wits of Marvell's day, a poem is conceived as 'a Tissue of Epigrams', loosely stitched together.[4] Leishman has shown how common it was for a poet-courtier in the seventeenth century to use an occasion as an excuse for a display of virtuosity. Such titles as 'A forsaken Lady to her false Servant', 'A Black patch on Lucasta's Face', 'My mistris commanding me to returne her letters', 'A flye that flew into my Mistris her eye', 'Upon Master W. Mountague his returne from travell', suggest the tendency in occasional poems written within an enclosed society to become merely counters in a game, instruments of social intercourse.[5] When a poem not only follows the general pattern of an epistle or an epigram, but in fact serves the function of a letter or a ready commentary on any situation that might arise in a courtier's life, then its form is likely to be rudimentary, unless it can draw on the aid of stanzaic pattern or structure of argument, or unless it can find a rhetorical and thematic scheme of organization suitable to a long discursive poem.

It is precisely the combination of freely flowing wit and loose, occasional structure which makes Marvell's satires often seem invertebrate. The structural difficulties here are not limited to satire as a genre, but are characteristic of all poetry with a strong topical element. The principles of organization in such poems as 'Upon Appleton House' and *The First Anniversary* are no easier to discern than those in 'Last Instructions' and 'The Loyal Scot'. Legouis has characterized 'Last Instructions' and *The First Anniversary* as essentially 'rimed chronicle', a series of observations tied to a chronological progression of concrete historical details.[6] The method of 'Upon Appleton House', as I have argued in chapter two, is that of 'occasional meditation', in which the imagination expatiates freely upon natural particulars. The difference between 'Last Instructions' and 'Upon Appleton House' is less in method than in the object of the poet's meditations: one deals primarily with the political and one with the natural world, though both show these two realms as intertwined. Yet if occasional meditation provides a general method of procedure in the two poems, a series of miscellaneous reflections chosen at random from 'the infinite multitude of objects' will not in itself give a poem a coherent form.[7] 'Upon Appleton House' is more than a ramble round Fairfax's estate, with appropriate meditations on what the poet observes, and 'Last Instructions' is more than a ramble through recent history. 'Upon Appleton House' suggests one way of organizing a long discursive poem: its structure is essentially thematic. The poem is a meditation in time of civil war, in which the infinite variety of 'Scene' gives rise repeatedly to the same questions: can one regain '*Paradice's only Map*', find a secure refuge from the destructiveness of war and the painful consciousness of loss? In his satires, Marvell seeks similarly to give thematic unity to his disparate topical materials. He also tries other devices which might impose form on the flux of events: rhetorical patterning, control of point of view, dramatization of ideas, attention to decorum of speaker, language, and situation, the creation of fictional personae and plots. If Marvell is less successful in finding an appropriate form for his satires than his near-contemporaries Rochester and Dryden or the major satirists of the next century, the fault in part lies in his reliance on the occasional method and the conceit, characteristic devices of an earlier age. Though his experiments as a satirist are not always successful and his command of overall form is inconsistent and uncertain, the brilliance of his individual effects and the alert poetic intelligence displayed throughout makes even his failures attractive.

II

Perhaps the central problem any satirist must face is that of validation. The reader must be persuaded that the satirist is a man to be trusted, must be brought round to share the satirist's judgments and accept as valid his standards of desirable and undesirable conduct. Some contemporary theorists have sought to distinguish between 'persuasive' and 'punitive' satire, claiming that in the latter the satirist's negative judgment of the object of attack is 'accepted a priori by the audience': 'No new judgment is invited; no course of action is urged; no novel information is produced,' but instead the audience takes pleasure in 'the abuse of an accepted figure of fun'.[8] Such a distinction can be misleading: Shadwell was not generally accepted as a dunce by Dryden's original audience, but had a considerable contemporary reputation as a dramatist, and *Absalom and Achitophel* is expressly directed at 'the more Moderate sort', 'the least Concern'd' and therefore 'the best Judges' (best because least likely to be 'Corrupt' in their allegiance to factional interest), not at those who already felt Shaftesbury and his allies to be a danger to the state. 'He who draws his Pen for one Party, must expect to make Enemies of the other. For, *Wit* and *Fool*, are Consequents of *Whig* and *Tory*: And every man is a Knave or an Ass to the contrary side' (Preface, *Poems*, I, 215). The poet's task is to bring about a revaluation, convincing the reader that the impressive front which Shadwell or Shaftesbury or May or Parker or Clarendon presents to the world is a hollow sham:

> Besides, his goodly Fabrick fills the eye,
> And seems design'd for thoughtless Majesty;
> Thoughtless as Monarch Oakes, that shade the plain,
> And, spread in solemn state, supinely reign.
>
> (*MacFlecknoe*, lines 25–8)

All satire is an expression of hostility and much of it contains an element of snobbery, asserting the common membership of author and audience in a group defined as superior, from which the satiric victim is excluded. Satire enables the reader vicariously to satisfy the impulses to hurt others, which normal canons of politeness keep men from expressing directly; to watch an enemy being 'stript and whipt' pleases both the aggressive instinct and the herd instinct in man.[9] But satire of any lasting merit can never appeal simply to unthinking group loyalties or prejudices: it must prove its case. The premises upon which *MacFlecknoe* is based are stated in the poem and Dryden assumes that the audience will agree to them as self-evident: 'Tautology' (line 30), 'stupidity' (line 18), 'dullness' (line 16) are intellectual and literary vices, where wit and sense are virtues. What Dryden seeks to prove in his poem is that Shadwell, for all his abilities at self-advertisement, his armour of 'new Impudence, new Ignorance' (line 146), is properly to be ranked among the fools rather than the wits. *The Medall* differs from *Absalom and Achitophel* in being addressed to Dryden's fellow Tories rather than to the uncommitted, yet it too relies on arguments rather than party loyalty, seeking to demonstrate that the Whigs' acclaimed hero and the doctrines of popular sovereignty he espouses are vicious and dangerous. In opposition to the flattering images which 'Ideots run in crowds to see, / ... more the Favourite of the Town / Than either Fayrs or Theatres have shown' (lines 2, 4–5), Dryden paints a rival portrait of Shaftesbury, his beliefs, and his past and present actions. The literary and social satires so popular during the Restoration period – Buckingham's *The Rehearsal*, Rochester's 'An Allusion to Horace', Rochester's 'A Letter from Artemisia in the Town to Chloe in the Country', the comedies of Etherege, with their Sir Fopling Flutters and Lady Cockwoods – tend to be Horatian raillery at folly rather than Juvenalian attacks on vice. But they too operate by defining two categories, showing that the object under scrutiny belongs to one category rather than the other, and by implication urging the audience to follow one pattern of behaviour in preference to another.

The defences of satire by Marvell, Dryden, Pope, and Swift all present satire as a serious literary art, 'of the nature of moral philosophy, as being instructive'.[10] In several passages, Marvell is explicit about the theoretical basis of his satire: it is directed at those 'formerly of another mind' (*RT*, I, p. 145), and seeks to makes converts. In the apologiae included in 'Last Instructions', 'The Loyal Scot', and *The Rehearsal Transpros'd*, Marvell argues that satire encourages 'the Good' in the hope of increasing their number, while it exposes 'the Bad' ('Loyal Scot', line 240) to the 'Spectacle' of public 'Shame' ('Last Instructions', lines 389–91). Like Swift and Pope he thus claims to be performing the function of 'publick instruction' (*RT*, II, p. 185), identifying himself with truth and virtuous conduct rather than with faction or prejudice, 'To VIRTUE ONLY and HER FRIENDS, A FRIEND.'[11] Far more than the Augustans, Marvell presents the satiric impulse in religious terms; the poet speaks out because he must (*difficile est saturam non scribere*),[12] acting as any public-spirited citizen ought to act, but the authority he cites is that of conscience, God's voice within man.

> I must confess that when all these things centred together upon my imagination, and I saw that none of his Superiors offer'd to interpose against an evil so great in it self, and as to me appear'd so publick in the consequence and mischief, I could hold no longer, and I, though the most unfit of many, assumed upon him the Priviledge (if any such Priviledge there be) of an English *Zelote*. (*RT*, II, p. 169)

In his repeated attacks upon Parker's 'presumption and arrogance' (II, p. 170), Marvell invokes not only the classical standards of 'Reason or Laughter' (II, p. 187), common sense and moderation, but specifically Christian ideals of humility and reverence before God.[13]

A satirist's apologia is a literary device like any other; the relationship between a satirist's claimed motivation for writing and his actual historical motivation, however interesting a question in its own right, is irrelevant to the issue of validation in satire. Nevertheless, it is legitimate to ask why we should accept the satirist's claim to be the friend of virtue, a member of the intellectual or moral elect. Why should we accept Marvell's judgment of Fleckno, May, and Parker, Dryden's judgment of Shadwell, Rochester's judgment of Dryden, Pope's judgment of Cibber? The problem is shown acutely in paired poems like 'An Allusion to Horace' and *MacFlecknoe* or 'Last Instructions' and *Annus Mirabilis*, which take mutually exclusive views of the same topic, presenting directly competing claims for the reader's belief. Validation in literature is based on an implicit compact: the author provides the material which makes validation possible, but the leap into faith is one which the reader must make. One should not underestimate the strength of readers' resistance. When Marvell claims that *The Rehearsal Transpros'd* 'wrought a sensible alteration in all that took it' (II, p. 156), he is being too optimistic in assuming that the satirist's skill in compounding his medicine will automatically work its cure. Swift, the most profound of the eighteenth-century theorists of satire, emphasizes the difficulties any satirist must face in gaining the reader's assent.

Though satire may be aimed at moral reform, few people are willing to be reformed and apply the satirist's lessons to themselves:

Satyr is a sort of Glass, wherein Beholders do generally discover every body's Face but their Own.

'Tis but a *Ball* bandied to and fro, and every Man carries a *Racket* about Him to strike it from himself among the rest of the Company.[14]

III

Of Marvell's early satires, the one whose approach to the problem of validation and form is simplest is 'The Character of Holland'. An author writing a satire in time of war against an enemy nation need not worry much about means of gaining his audience's assent: he can appeal directly to patriotic feelings and national prejudices. There are no autobiographical passages in 'The Character of Holland' aimed at establishing the satirist's ethos as an honourable and trustworthy man, but something of the same function is served, more crudely, by the inclusion of a large number of honorific terms associated with the English ('our *Infant Hercules*' line 138, 'our better *Rome*' line 142, 'the obsequious Air and Waters' line 129) and denigratory terms associated with the Dutch. The poem contains a great many easy jokes at the '*Burgomaster of the Sea*' (line 114), 'pickled *Heeren*' (line 34), '*Half-anders*' (line 53), Dutch drunkenness and corpulence, which rely on class snobbery and jingoism. Much of the poem consists of direct insults: 'How fit a Title clothes their *Governours*, / Themselves the *Hogs* as all their Subjects *Bores*' (lines 79–80). Though the bilingual puns here (boer/boor/boar, hog and the official title Hoog-mogenden) leaven the insults with a certain amount of wit, the effect of the lines is to invoke complacent feelings of English superiority, reinforced by scorn at the Dutch for speaking such a peculiar language. Passages of this sort may gain immediate assent, but are not likely to survive their immediate circumstances. Though 'The Character of Holland' is intended as persuasive, in stirring up feeling against the Dutch, its intent cannot be called moral, in the sense that Marvell, Dryden, Pope, and Swift argue in their apologiae that satire should be.

Marvell's poem is directly indebted to two seventeenth-century

models: the satiric poems of John Cleveland and the prose
'Character' fashionable throughout the century. Cleveland was
the most popular of mid-century satirists, with twelve editions of
his poems between 1647 and 1653. His 'Character of a London-
Diurnall' (1644) and 'Character of a Diurnall-Maker' (1654)
were among the first prose characters turned to the service of
partisan politics, and show the same qualities of extravagant wit
as his verse satires. In verse and prose, Cleveland seeks to adapt
the metaphysical conceit to satiric purposes. In invective satire like
'The Character of Holland' or Cleveland's writings, the satirist's
invention is turned toward finding as many clever, defamatory
things to say about his subject as possible. Though neatness of
wording may make the sting of the barbs sharper, the basic
stylistic ideal in invective is copiousness, and the invective satirist
need only stop when he has run out of breath:

A library of Diurnalls is a wardrobe of frippery, 'tis a just Idea of the
Limbo of Infants. I saw one once that could write with his toes, by the
same token I could have wished he had worne his copyes for socks, 'tis he
without doubt from whom the Diurnalls derive their pedigree, and they
have a birth-right accordingly, being shuffled out at the beds feet of
History...To supply this smallnes they are fain to join forces, so they are
not singly, but as the custome is, in a croaking Committee, They tug at the
Pen, like slaves at the Oare, a whole bank together, they write in the
posture that the *Swedes* give fire in, over one anothers heads.

> See, see, how close the Curs hunt under a sheet,
> As if they spent in Quire, and scan'd their feet;
> One Cure and five Incumbents leap a Truss,
> The title sure must be litigious.
> The *Sadduces* would raise a question,
> Who must be *Smec* at th' Resurrection.
> Who cook'd them up together were to blame,
> Had they but wyre-drawne and spun out their name,
> 'Twould make another Prentices Petition
> Against the Bishops and their Superstition.[15]

Both passages use an occasion as a topic for witty elaboration:
the first takes as its theme the 'smallnes' of diurnals and their
anonymous authors, as compared to the grander scope of history,
and the second attacks as absurd the joint composition of a
pamphlet by five 'Club-Divines' under the acronymic pseudonym

Smectymnuus. The imaginative energy in each is attractive and serves to validate the satiric attack: the reader gives his emotional assent because he is carried away on the flow of the author's fancy and seals a tacit alliance with the author in understanding and laughing at his jokes. Yet the diffuseness in each passage ultimately detracts from its effectiveness as satire.

The model of the prose character, on the other hand, may have given Marvell some hints on how to give a satiric poem a firmer structure. The prose character also consists of variations on a theme, but the emphasis on definitive conciseness, 'in little comprehending much', catching the essence of a character in a few brushstrokes, implies an artistic ideal of unity and control, rather than copiousness. The definition of the form, 'What a Character Is', in Sir Thomas Overbury's *Characters or Witty Descriptions of the Properties of Sundry Persons* (1614), suggests by its analogies from painting and music that the essence of the character is unity in multiplicity.

To square out a character by our English level, it is a picture (real or personal) quaintly drawn, in various colours, all of them heightened by one shadowing.

It is a quick and soft touch of many strings, all shutting up in one musical close; it is wit's descant on any plain song.[16]

Though 'The Character of Holland' at first glance appears to be relatively formless Clevelandesque satire, a stream of witty insults directed at the Dutch, it in fact has a definite (if simple) overall structure. The first hundred lines make up a 'character', on the general pattern of the prose 'witty descriptions of the properties of sundry persons', applied in this case to a nation rather than an individual. The 'character' is arranged under four separate topics: the physical characteristics of Holland (lines 1–36), the government of the Dutch (lines 37–54), 'next in order', their religion (lines 55–76), and finally their lack of 'Civility' (lines 77–100). Descriptive detail, prominent in the prose characters, plays a role in each of the sections, but is most pronounced in the fourth, with its vivid comic pictures of the quarrelling Dutch sea-captains, reeling with drink, and the housewives sitting over a smoking stove at church.

Within this overall structure, the poem can be seen to have a loose thematic unity. Such phrases as 'indigested vomit of the Sea' and 'Off-scouring of the *Brittish Sand*' not only function as wittily outrageous denigration of the satiric adversary, but fit into a coherent metaphorical pattern based on physical fact: the topography of the Netherlands, below sea-level and forced to fight a constant battle with the sea in order to reclaim its land.

> *Holland*, that scarce deserves the name of *Land*,
> As but th' Off-scouring of the *Brittish Sand*;
> And so much Earth as was contributed
> By *English Pilots* when they heav'd the Lead;
> Or what by th' Oceans slow alluvion fell,
> Of shipwrackt Cockle and the Muscle-shell;
> This indigested vomit of the Sea
> Fell to the Dutch by just Propriety.   (lines 1–8)

Geography is presented as emblematic of character. 'Just Propriety' – not the decorum of politeness but the satirist's decorum of the true image – reveals Holland as the sea's unwanted residue and the Dutch as 'anxious', materialistic, and wholly preoccupied with the accumulation of what after all is no more than dirt. The daily battle with the sea is presented not as heroic (as it is in popular myth – the boy with his finger in the dike), but as both 'sordid' and 'mad', a violation of natural order.

> Glad then, as Miners that have found the Oar,
> They with mad labour fish'd the *Land* to *Shoar*;
> And div'd as desperately for each piece
> Of Earth, as if 't had been of *Ambergreece*;
> Collecting anxiously small Loads of Clay,
> Less then what building Swallows bear away;
> Or then those Pills which sordid Beetles roul,
> Transfusing into them their Dunghil Soul.   (lines 9–16)

The imagery of land and sea which runs throughout the poem suggests a form of validation more subtle and ultimately more convincing than the appeal to national prejudices: the association of the Dutch with terrestrial, cosmological, and moral disorder. In comparing the Dutch dikes to a '*watry Babel*', built with the presumptuous aim of containing the sea, Marvell uses a comparison he employs to similar effect in 'Upon Appleton House' and *The Rehearsal Transpros'd*.[17] References to the 'daily deluge' (line 27), in which 'the Injur'd Ocean' (line 23) seeks to regain the land stolen from it, serve much the same function. Marvell's touch here is light: the *adunata* are comic, with a deliberate note of the grotesque. Lines such as these, like the equivalent passages in the meadow section of 'Upon Appleton House', pay tribute to the ability of wit to invert normal perspectives and make unexpected juxtapositions as well as to the power of nature:

> A daily deluge over them does boyl;
> The Earth and Water play at *Level-coyl*;
> The Fish oft-times the Burger dispossest,
> And sat not as a Meat but as a Guest.   (lines 27–30)

The imagery in the sections of the poem devoted to the government and religion of the Dutch can similarly be seen as 'wit's descant' on the 'plain song' of Holland's physical situation between land and sea: thus 'he that *drains*' becomes the king of the '*drowned*' (line 42), as the one-eyed man is king among the blind, and the man who best can wield a pump or shovel comes to act as magistrate, 'grows as 'twere a *King of Spades*' (line 50). Shrewd observation, fanciful metaphorical elaboration, outrageous puns all serve to convict the Dutch of disorder.

The 'character' proper ends with line 100; the remaining fifty-two lines (omitted in the unauthorized printings of 1665 and 1672) extend the imagery of order and disorder, land and sea, with particular reference to the circumstances of 1653. The Anglo-Dutch War is presented in the last section of the poem as wholly due to Dutch treachery and ambition. The English are treated as entirely blameless, ruled by honour, 'court'sie' (line 103), 'ancient Rights and Leagues' (line 107), where the Dutch are as lacking in 'Civility' abroad as at home (lines 101–2), dishonourably attacking their nominal ally without warning. A series of sea-battles is presented in the manner recommended for epideictic rhetoric by Aristotle and later theorists: praise of one's own side and dispraise of one's opponents, celebrating English victories and explaining away or papering over English reverses.[18] If the Dutch lose a battle, then 'the torn Navy stagger'd with him home, / While the Sea laught itself into a foam' (lines 121–2). But if a battle ends to the disadvantage of the English, then ''Tis true since that (as fortune kindly sports,) / A wholesome Danger drove us to our Ports' (lines 123–4), where the

English can be safe from the greater danger of storms. Here as earlier in the poem the Dutch are characterized as rebels against the natural order, whose 'vain Attempt' (line 119) is deservedly met by scornful laughter.

Marvell's other political poems contemporaneous with 'The Character of Holland' are panegyrics, and the final section of 'The Character of Holland' combines panegyric and satire. As such, it resembles 'The Loyal Scot' and 'Last Instructions' – or, for that matter, *The First Anniversary*, which, though primarily a panegyric, includes a satiric attack on the '*Chammish* issue' of Cromwell's enemies (lines 293–320). The patriotic element is particularly marked in this part of 'The Character of Holland', with its appeal to the loyalties of a nation at war and to the ideal of imperial dominion, with Holland playing '*Carthage* overcome' by England's Rome (lines 141–2). Yet the cautionary note in the closing lines recalls the political realism of 'An Horatian Ode' in that the glimpse vouchsafed of a glorious imperial future is hedged round with conditions: 'Provided that they be what they have been, / Watchful abroad, and honest still within' (lines 147–8). A similar quality of realism is present in the lines describing the British navy's winter in port. The witty conceit reflects some awkward facts: an embarrassing retreat and a Parliamentary inquiry into whether the English losses were caused by corruption and incompetence. But, as the poet's wit gracefully suggests, temporary reverses may prove beneficial:

> The *Common wealth* doth by its losses grow;
> And, like its own Seas, only Ebbs to flow.
> Besides that very Agitation laves,
> And purges out the corruptible waves.   (lines 131–4)

The imagery here suggests that apparent disorder may turn out to be order after all; nature, represented by the sea against which the Dutch constantly and foolishly struggle, can teach a moral lesson to those alert enough to recognize it.

A different approach to the problems of validation and form is represented by 'Fleckno, an English Priest in Rome'. Where 'The Character of Holland' pays little attention to establishing the ethos of the author or narrator, 'Fleckno', in keeping with Aristotle's dictum that the 'ethical argument' is more effective

than any other in convincing an audience, takes care to build up
the character of a sympathetic and credible narrator.[19] 'The
Character of Holland', in appealing to patriotic sentiments, makes
frequent use of the first person plural but never employs the first
person singular pronoun. In 'Fleckno', two of the three characters
are insistent bores who intrude on the third character's privacy,
and the intrusiveness of the pronouns echoes the poem's action: as
the narrator is unable to escape Fleckno's endless recitations of
bad verse, holds his 'burning Ear' toward the drone of verse 'and
when that could not hear' turns his head to present the other
(lines 31–3), the reader is confronted with the obtrusive 'he' and
the uncomfortable 'I' in virtually every line. The theme of
'Captivity' (line 168) is given further physical manifestations in
the setting, a series of confined spaces rendered with comic
realism:

> I found at last a Chamber, as 'twas said,
> But seem'd a Coffin set on the Stairs head.
> Not higher then Seav'n, nor larger then three feet.
> Only there was nor Seeling, nor a Sheet,
> Save that th'ingenious Door did as you come
> Turn in, and shew to Wainscot half the Room.   (lines 9–14)

'Fleckno' and 'The Character of Holland' have the same
shrewd eye for the telling detail, the ingenious, grotesque comparison. But politics has no role in 'Fleckno', which is concerned
with the war between the wits and the fools, not with that between
the English and Dutch. 'Fleckno' is a poem about poetry, and its
sphere of action is private, not public. In its comic, anecdotal way
it touches on several of Marvell's major themes: the need to
choose and the difficulty of choosing, the rival claims of the active
and contemplative life, the soul's encounter with experience.
For all its knockabout comedy, the poem is explicitly ethical in its
concerns, like the satires of Horace, Juvenal, and Persius, and
deals with problems of judgment and behaviour.

As a literary satire, 'Fleckno', in common with poems on
similar themes by Dryden, Rochester, and Pope, raises the
question of how one distinguishes wit from folly. Here the author
needs to convince us that Fleckno and the quarrelsome fop who
comes to visit are in fact fools, worthy of our contempt, in contrast

with the narrator whose values we accept. Marvell's method is to show us the characters in action, selecting for his portrait those physical details and metaphorical comparisons which will foreclose sympathy, preventing us from seeing the character in other than an unfavourable light. It is hard for us to take seriously the poetic pretensions of a figure 'swaddled' in his own poems, which he peels off to read.

> Of all his Poems there he stands ungirt
> Save only two foul copies for his shirt:
> Yet these he promises as soon as clean.
> But how I loath'd to see my Neighbour glean
> Those papers, which he pilled from within
> Like white fleaks rising from a Leaper's skin!
> More odious then those raggs which the *French* youth
> At ordinaries after dinner show'th,
> When they compare their *Chancres* and *Poulains*. (lines 129–37)

The element of insult, relatively crude and simple, in the use of heavily loaded negative words like 'loath'd' and 'odious' carries less satiric weight than the visual evocation of the scene, the imaginative creation of a disordered universe where poems are worn as clothing and diseases displayed as badges of honour. There is more than a touch of cruelty in the jokes at Fleckno's poverty and much of the humour, as in 'The Character of Holland', is crudely aggressive: satire is not above appealing to the satisfaction the comfortably-off feel in not being poor, the healthy feel in not being sick, or the English feel in not being Dutch. But Pope's defence of *The Dunciad* against objections that poverty ought not to be the subject of ridicule applies equally well to 'Fleckno'. The would-be poet and the roaring boy are ridiculous not out of involuntary deficiencies but out of 'self-conceit'.

If Obscurity or Poverty were to exempt a man from satyr, much more should Folly and Dulness, which are still more involuntary, nay as much so as personal deformity. But even this will not help them: Deformity becomes the object of ridicule when a man sets up for being handsome: and so must Dulness when he sets up for a Wit. They are not ridicul'd because Ridicule in itself is or ought to be a pleasure; but because it is just, to undeceive the honest and unpretending part of mankind from imposition, because particular interest ought to yield to general, and a great number who are not naturally Fools ought never to be made so in complaisance to a few who are.[20]

The distinction between wit and folly is thus presented as a matter of judgment. Spenser, according to Milton, is 'a better teacher than *Scotus* or *Aquinas*' because he presents practical examples of the need to 'distinguish, and . . . prefer that which is truly better'; the satirist similarly seeks to 'expose the bad' in order to school the judgments of his readers.[21] A second ethical consideration important in 'Fleckno' is more problematical: even if one is able to make ethical and aesthetic discriminations, one still needs to live in the world. The opening lines of the poem ('Oblig'd by frequent visits of this man . . . I sought his lodging') suggest that sociability, politeness, and the invisible network of obligation are issues in the poem, and themselves pose moral problems. As Duncan-Jones points out, the narrator, however uncomfortable he may feel at being trapped in the presence of two strident bores, never behaves other than politely, never allows an expression of annoyance to escape his lips, acts consistently as 'Mediator' (line 155) between his two vain and touchy companions.[22]

> The place doth us invite
> By its own narrowness, Sir, to unite.
> He ask'd me pardon; and to make me way
> Went down, as I him follow'd to obey.   (lines 103–6)

The narrator's good manners, as contrasted with his quarrelsome companions, always 'furious', 'with anger full', 'struck dead' at each trivial mischance, help make him a sympathetic figure, and so does his status as victim, undergoing 'Martyrdom' at their hands. Sociability and courtesy here, however, are not presented simply as praiseworthy, but as the source of conflict. It is understandable that a young man visiting a foreign country would be drawn to his compatriots and that an aspiring poet would seek out his fellow poet (the narrator's youth is brought out in line 25 and his concern for 'divine...*Poetry*' in lines 6–7, while the Italian setting, mentioned in the title, provides much of the incidental imagery). But poetry is essentially an anti-social vocation, allowing no compromise; behind the comic exaggeration, there is a concern with the role of 'Tryal' in everyday life.

> But I, who now imagin'd my self brought
> To my last Tryal, in a serious thought

Calm'd the disorders of my youthful Breast,
And to my Martyrdom prepared Rest.
Only this frail Ambition did remain,
The last distemper of the sober Brain,
That there had been some present to assure
The future Ages how I did indure.   (lines 23–30)

Any serious implications here (brought out, for example, by the echo of 'Lycidas' in line 28) are held in check by the humour of the situation. Yet the narrator's difficulties, transposed to a different plane, are those of the resolved or restless soul in Marvell's religious poetry, hoping to 'bath...and be clean, / Or slake its Drought' ('Clorinda and Damon', lines 15–16), or baffled to discover the serpent's 'winding Snare' ('The Coronet', line 21) inextricably tangled around his votive offering.

If we compare 'Fleckno' with Donne's 'Satyre IV', on which it is partly based, we find that Donne's narrator is not bothered by any such constraints of politeness. Donne's poem is anti-court satire, in which the narrator, on a chance visit to the court, encounters 'a thing more strange, then on Niles slime, the Sunne / E'r bred' (lines 18–19), a walking compendium of all the vices of the court, who confirms him in his resolution never again to leave his 'wholesome solitarinesse' (line 155) for the specious splendours of the courtier's life. Donne uses religious imagery similar to that in 'Fleckno' to draw a clear-cut distinction between the two worlds represented by the narrator and the courtier he meets:

Well; I may now receive, and die; My sinne
Indeed is great, but I have beene in
A purgatorie, such as fear'd hell is
A recreation to' and scant map of this.
My minde, neither with prides itch, nor yet hath been
Poyson'd with love to see, or to bee seene,
I had no suit there, nor new suite to shew,
Yet went to Court.[23]

The narrator's own values are presented more explicitly in Donne's 'Satyre IV' than in 'Fleckno', and as a result moral issues are posed in terms of a clear and unequivocal contrast of irreconcilable opposites: truth against falsity, freedom against imprisonment, things that last against ephemeral 'newes' (line 93), fashion, gossip, 'household trash' (line 98). As in the con-

temporaneous 'Satyre III' and the later Holy Sonnets, Donne
portrays worldly values as the province of the world, the flesh,
and devill'.

> Shall I, nones slave, of high borne, or rais'd men
> Feare frownes? And, my Mistresse Truth, betray thee
> To th'huffing braggart, puft Nobility? (lines 162–4)

The narrator's attitude toward his intrusive companion is not
nearly as polite and complaisant as in 'Fleckno': he is curt,
insulting, 'sullen' (line 91), openly shows his displeasure and his
eagerness to shake the courtier off. His aversion takes physical
manifestations, with little regard to normal canons of politeness:

> I belch, spue, spit,
> Looke pale, and sickly, like a Patient; Yet
> He thrusts on more...
> So I sigh, and sweat
> To heare this Makeron talke in vaine. (lines 108–10, 116–17)

In Horace's *Satire* I, ix, which serves as model for both Donne
and Marvell, the narrator's discomfort at the bore's intrusion is
equally apparent, but the emphasis there is on the intruder's
leech-like persistence, his inability or refusal to recognize that he
is not welcome. Unlike the equivalent characters in the two
English poems, Horace's interloper has a practical end in mind,
wanting an introduction to the wealthy Maecenas; the poem thus
contrasts true and false conceptions of friendship and of patron-
age. Donne's narrator resembles the 'plain-dealer' figure frequently found in seventeenth-century literature. Like Wycherley's
Manly or Molière's Alceste, or like the malcontent of Jacobean
drama, he refuses to flatter, rejects court manners and court
values, and openly expresses his dissatisfaction with the mores of
his society. But in Donne and Horace, the choice between virtue
and vice is straightforward, where in 'Fleckno', *The Plain-Dealer*,
and *Le Misanthrope* (to say nothing of *Hamlet* or *The Revenger's
Tragedy*), the pursuit of uncompromising truth is seen as problematical. The moral questions posed by Molière and Wycherley in
the juxtaposition of the protagonist with a more complaisant com-
rade, who is respectful of the social amenities and willing to
compromise with worldly standards, are in Marvell's poem
embodied in the single figure of the narrator, trapped by his

politeness in an awkward situation. Where Donne explicitly urges the need to follow truth in one's daily affairs, Marvell reminds us, with wry humour, how difficult it is to live up to such an ideal.

> Who should commend his Mistress now? Or who
> Praise him? both difficult indeed to do
> With truth. (lines 163–5)

'Fleckno' illustrates the ideal of creative imitation widely held in the seventeeth and eighteenth centuries. If its aims of realism and its casual, sometimes digressive first-person narration give monologue satire the air of being an impromptu, in which the events of everyday life and the observations of the satirist pass by in unedited flow, formal verse satire in fact operates within strictly defined parameters. Indeed, the frequency with which a small number of Roman models were imitated by English and European satirists perpetuated the structural design of the earlier poems in the later.[24] Formal satire is essentially plotless, or at least has no plot in the Aristotelian sense, the imitation of an action with clearly defined beginning, middle, and end, each event moving toward a conclusion. Instead, it presents a panorama of the passing scene, in which folly or vice is revealed as such to the audience but not brought to any conclusion; in deliberately leaving the poem's basic situation unresolved, the satirist is in a sense appealing to the members of the audience to provide their own resolution by applying the lessons of the poem to their own lives.[25] The structural design of monologue satire is dependent upon its ethical purpose (as philosophy brought to the tea-table). Some form of encounter or confrontation is characteristic of the genre: a figure or a series of figures is detached from the crowd, brought into the foreground, and contrasted with the narrator, either as an object of attack or as an interlocutor, friendly or unfriendly. Though the view of Dryden that a formal satire necessarily attacks a specific vice and recommends a specific virtue is too schematic, failing to take account of the variety within the genre, formal satire can be seen as having a unity of theme, equivalent to the Aristotelian unity of action:

A perfect satire...ought only to treat of one subject; to be confined to one particular theme; or at least, to one principally. If other vices occur in the management of the chief, they should only be transiently lashed, and not be insisted on, so as to make the design double. As in a play of the English fashion, which we call a tragi-comedy, there is to be but one main design; and tho' there be an underplot, or second walk of comical characters and adventures, yet they are subservient to the chief fable, carried along under it, and helping to it: so that the drama may not seem a monster with two heads.[26]

In all significant respects, 'Fleckno' follows the pattern of Roman formal satire. It is a monologue, quasi-dramatic, full of incidental action and dialogue, but unified by theme rather than plot; its main action, the narrator's encounter with first one, then another bore, is episodic, concluding only in that the narrator (like the narrators in Horace and Donne) manages by good luck to escape from his temporary captivity. The poem has two major figures who are shown in an adversary relationship; the third character, who has no direct equivalent in Horace or Donne, can be seen as 'underplot'. Though Marvell follows the details in Horace and Donne less closely than was the practice in the 'imitations' of Rochester, Oldham, Pope, and Johnson, like these satirists he uses individual parallels to suggest repetitive patterns of vice and folly.

What Marvell chooses to imitate in 'Fleckno' is not simply Roman formal satire, but Donne's imitations of Roman formal satire. Thus the stylistic characteristics of 'Fleckno' – rapidity, abruptness, enjambement, witty striking conceits – resemble those of Donne, as the stylistic characteristics of 'The Character of Holland' resemble those of Donne's follower Cleveland. Both 'Fleckno' and 'The Character of Holland' are attempts at meta-physical satire; the superiority of 'Fleckno' comes in part from the superiority of Donne as a model (Cleveland's poems are a faint and distorted reflection of Donne's), and in part from its more promising approach to the problem of overall form. The conceits in 'Fleckno', like those in 'The Character of Holland', are derived from the occasion. But in 'Fleckno' the structure of the poem keeps the connection from seeming tenuous; the overall pattern of formal satire, with its thematic unity, provides a discipline which prevents the poem from fragmenting.

Fleckno is satirized in each of his functions, 'Priest, Poet, and Musician' (line 2). His poetry is 'ill made' (line 144) and 'hideous' (line 20), his religion is empty idolatry, and his music, rather than being an echo of the heavenly harmony, intended for the service of God, simply reflects his empty belly:

> Now as two Instruments, to the same key
> Being tun'd by Art, if the one touched be
> The other opposite as soon replies,
> Mov'd by the Air and hidden Sympathies;
> So while he with his gouty Fingers craules
> Over the Lute, his murm'ring Belly calls,
> Whose hungry Guts to the same streightness twin'd
> In Echo to the trembling Strings repin'd.
>   I, that perceiv'd now what his Musick ment,
> Ask'd civilly if he had eat this Lent.   (lines 37–46)

Much of the effect here comes from the contrast between the more exalted normal poetic uses of such musical imagery (found in such poems as 'Musicks Empire' and *The First Anniversary*) and the undignified reality of hunger and rumbling guts. Fleckno's behaviour throughout the poem, with its multiple violations of decorum, illustrates the distinction between folly and self-knowledge with which the poem is centrally concerned. Rapt in self-admiration, Fleckno is unaware that his dinner companions are not eager to hear him recite, unaware of the grotesqueness of his appearance and dress, unaware that his poetry is inspired only by hunger and vanity.

In poetry and in religion, Fleckno is presented as serving a false ideal. The many jokes at Roman Catholicism in the poem not only appeal to popular anti-Papist sentiments, but serve to characterize Fleckno and to anatomize his folly. As with Donne's poems, the images reflect an emblematic view of the universe:

> Nothing now Dinner stay'd
> But till he had himself a Body made.
> I mean till he were drest: for else so thin
> He stands, as if he only fed had been
> With consecrated Wafers: and the *Host*
> Hath sure more flesh and blood then he can boast.
> This *Basso Relievo* of a Man,
> Who as a Camel tall, yet easly can
> The Needles Eye thread without any stich,
> (His only impossible is to be rich)

Lest his too suttle Body, growing rare,
Should leave his Soul to wander in the Air,
He therefore circumscribes himself in rimes;
And swaddl'd in's own papers seaven times,
Wears a close Jacket of poetick Buff.   (lines 57–71)

This series of dazzling conceits presents Roman Catholic dogma
as contrary to reason, a system of beliefs appropriate to a fool like
Fleckno. Fleckno's extreme thinness is made the emblem of a false
spirituality which seeks to deny the imperatives of 'flesh and
blood'. Such an attitude, as Marvell presents it, is the mirror
image of the excessive worldliness of which Marvell accuses the
bishops in *The Rehearsal Transpros'd* – in both cases, an inability
to distinguish between 'Divine and Human things' (II, p. 247).
A religious faith which so easily embraces the 'impossible', ignoring the restraints of common sense, seeking out of vanity to alter
'the shape of Mans body, and...the frame of the world' (II,
p. 231) into something more convenient, is in Marvell's view
necessarily 'fraudulent' ('Upon Appleton House', line 214). The
grotesque comic conceit of the body rarefied out of existence and
the soul wandering in air (a comic parallel to the manacled soul of
'A Dialogue between the Soul and Body') suggest the extent to
which Fleckno deludes himself. False religion, bad poetry, and
false ideas of courtesy are shown as having the same root, self-love.

Like 'Fleckno', 'Tom May's Death' is a lampoon, an attack on
a named, historically identifiable opponent. The problem the
author of such a poem faces is how to keep the poem from seeming a petty squabble, motivated by personal animosity, factionalism, or spite. The method Marvell chooses in 'Tom May's
Death' is akin to that followed by Dryden and Pope in their
satires. More explicitly than in 'Fleckno', the poet seeks to
demonstrate the seriousness of his aims, enlisting the reader's
support by convincing him that the poem is written in a 'gen'rous
Cause' and that writing it is 'an action of virtue' – philosophy
rather than thuggery. As examples of what Brower calls 'the
poetry of allusion', seeking to bring 'the larger light of European
literature and a European past into verse of local public debate',
both 'Tom May's Death' and 'Fleckno' illustrate Marvell's links
with the emerging aesthetic of neoclassicism. If the method of
'Fleckno' is imitation, the method of 'Tom May's Death', like

that in *MacFlecknoe* and *Absalom and Achitophel,* is allusive comparison: the poem creates a framework of allusion through which the past can throw a long shadow over the present.[27]

'Tom May's Death' is based on 'Romane...similitude', comparisons between the state of England and the state of Rome. In his use of Roman analogy, Marvell follows the example of Ben Jonson, who appears in the poem as Marvell's satiric spokesman. In his satiric comedy *Poetaster,* Jonson brings on stage the figures of Horace and Virgil, standard-bearers for immortal poetry, to satirize the hack poet Crispinus (John Marston), just as Marvell uses the figure of Jonson the censor to satirize May. Jonson writes in the epilogue to *Poetaster* that he

> ... therefore chose AUGUSTUS CAESARS times,
> When wit, and artes, were at their height in *Rome,*
> To shew that VIRGIL, HORACE, and the rest
> Of those great master-spirits, did not want
> Detractors, then, or practisers against them:
> And by this line (although no *paralel*)
> I hoped at last they would sit downe, and blush.[28]

The difference between Marvell and May lay not in their attitudes toward the past – both shared the widespread Renaissance belief that history served as a storehouse of examples applicable to the present – but to the particular lessons they sought to draw from history. To see May as a 'Foul Architect' who failed to 'see / How ill the measures of these States agree' (lines 51–2) would not preclude the possibility of a better architect able both to see better and to build better.

In seeking to convince the reader of his definition of virtue and vice, the admirable and contemptible, Marvell uses a number of devices, all intended to support the basic contrast between the 'Mercenary Pen' (line 40) of May and the 'severe' (line 31) conception of the responsibilities of the artist represented in the poem by Jonson. To some extent, Marvell relies on the argument from authority, both in using the stern, judicious figure of Jonson as guardian of and spokesman for the values espoused in the poem and in associating these values with classical Rome. Marvell's judgment on May is further impersonalized and given external sanctions by being expressed in a seemingly objective action. A method Marvell uses extensively both in 'Tom May's Death' and in *The Rehearsal Transpros'd* is parody, in which he fashions a weapon from his opponent's words, sinking May's sword 'in his own Bowels' (line 24). Directly or indirectly, he seeks to refute the position argued in May's *History of the Parliament* and other writings, offering a rival set of historical parallels to contrast with what he sees as May's doctrinaire republicanism. But the primary means of validation in this poem is the 'ethical argument', by which the poet shows that his opponent, unlike himself, is not worthy of trust or respect. The ethical argument is omnipresent in 'Tom May's Death', both in the many unsavoury details which seek to discredit the character and motives of May, portraying him as a 'Malignant' (line 42) rather than unbiased and reliable historian, and in the moving portrait of the true poet, which explicitly states the poem's ethical norms.[29]

The standards by which May is judged in the poem are fundamentally aesthetic and moral; as in *MacFlecknoe*, the political element is secondary. Marvell portrays May as a man whose god is his belly, where the true poet is ruled by a disinterested love of virtue and justice. The poem is thus openly didactic, fitting Dryden's general description of satire in providing examples of correct and incorrect behaviour. Its charge against May is that he has 'prostituted ... our spotless knowledge and the studies chast' (lines 71-2) for entirely venal reasons. May masquerades as a serious historian, classical scholar, and poet, professing 'to follow that one Rule, Truth, to which all the rest (like the rest of Morall Vertues to that of Justice) may be reduced'.[30] But in reality, Marvell argues, his opponent is nothing but a 'Gazet-writer' (line 60), a 'Tankard-bearing Muse' (line 61). May's motivations, as presented in 'Tom May's Death', are petty and 'base' (line 71) – jealousy, ambition, 'malice' (line 56), the pursuit of (largely alcoholic) pleasure, the unprincipled pursuit of success.

The alleged inconsistencies between 'Tom May's Death' and 'An Horatian Ode', written three months earlier, have puzzled critics, to the extent that attempts have been made to exclude it from the Marvell canon.[31] The critical problem raised by 'Tom May's Death' is essentially twofold: whether the politics of 'Tom May's Death' are compatible with Marvell's other writings, and whether in the attack on May's republicanism Marvell descends from 'principle' to 'propaganda'. Some critics find 'Royalist fervour' in the poem, but there is no need to posit an early royalist phase for Marvell, bracketing 'Tom May's Death' with the suppositious 'Elegy upon the Death of my Lord Francis Villiers' as works written before his political conversion.[32] 'Tom May's Death' is of a piece with his many other attacks on timeservers, apostates, and apologists for those in power, entirely consistent with the aesthetic and ethical principles he expressed both before and after the Restoration. The attitude toward 'ancient Rights and better Times' in 'Tom May's Death' is identical with that in the commendatory poem to Lovelace written one or two years earlier and close to that in 'Upon Appleton House', written a year or two later. The treatment of poetic ambition and 'wit corrupted' is similar in the poem to Lovelace, 'Fleckno', and 'Tom May's Death', all of which contrast the disinterested pursuit of truth with the potentially corrupting influence of pride, poverty, self-interest, and the desire for acceptance or worldly success.

'An Horatian Ode' and 'Tom May's Death', far from being incompatible, are in many ways companion pieces, reflecting a similar time of disorder and uncertainty. The opening lines of 'Tom May's Death' not only describe May's sudden, undignified death in vivid comic terms, but suggest that all men are likely to be 'hurry'd hence', unable to control events in a world which rarely conforms to men's desires. Though May's death is seen as an emblem of all human fate, May himself is presented as characteristic of a particular type of man – the merely worldly (in the Christian terminology of *The First Anniversary*, the unregenerate, 'unconcern'd, or unprepar'd'), unable to recognize any perspective beyond the physical demands of food and drink, unable even to imagine a landscape other than that which surrounds him every day:

> As one put drunk into the Packet-boat,
> *Tom May* was hurry'd hence and did not know't.
> But was amaz'd on the Elysian side,
> And with an Eye uncertain, gazing wide,
> Could not determine in what place he was. (lines 1–5)

'Tom May's Death' attempts to provide a means of making sense of the seemingly meaningless flux of events, a guide for conduct at a time when 'the wheel of Empire, whirleth back' (line 67) and the customary foundations of the world are shaken. Rather than being an anomaly among his works, then, 'Tom May's Death' expresses a view of providence, freedom, and the historical imperatives of 'the times' at one with that in the vaguely royalist commendatory poem to Lovelace and elegy on Lord Hastings (1648–9), the balanced sympathies of 'An Horatian Ode' (1650), and the openly Cromwellian *The First Anniversary* (1655).[33]

The most problematical element in 'Tom May's Death', the almost Hobbesian treatment of rebellion so at variance with Marvell's later account of the causes of the Civil War, need not be taken as reflecting the poet's political convictions, but as instrumental in his strategy of persuasion.[34] As a satirist, Marvell seeks to disable his adversary and to refute his basic assumptions, a Dryden later did with Shadwell. His implicit argument is that May's version of '*Romes* example' (line 53), as presented in *The History of the Parliament* (1647), his verse translation of Lucan's *Pharsalia* (1627), and elsewhere, is both partial and 'Malignant' (line 42), and that alternatives are possible. May's true affinities, he maintains, are not with the classical poets who sing of 'ancient Heroes' (line 15), but with the enemies of civilization, '*Vandale, Goth*' (line 41). The references to Spartacus, Brutus, and Cassius, like the description of the Virgilian and Dantesque underworld at the end of the poem, are meant as demonstrations to the reader of the legitimate and illegitimate use of historical parallels.

Twentieth-century critics who debate whether '*Spartacus*' (line 74) refers to Essex, Fairfax, or Cromwell rather miss the point: Spartacus encapsulates the spirit of rebellion, and to 'turn the chronicler to *Spartacus*' is seen as the ultimate apostasy, to seek to justify rebellion even when the rebel is an illiterate slave (the argument *a fortiori* – he who would praise Spartacus would praise anybody). The scornful reference to '*Brutus* and *Cassius* the Peoples cheats' (line 18) again seeks to discredit May's republican assumptions: the lines suggest that all republicans and regicides, however much they try to delude themselves and others by insisting on the nobility of their motives, renege on their promises and 'cheat' those who would find in them images of disinterested virtue. Marvell is here opposing one traditional interpretation of classical history to another. May follows such classical authors as

Tacitus, Juvenal, and Plutarch in seeing Brutus and Cassius, Cato and Cicero, as heroes of liberty; the terms of his eulogy of Brutus and Cassius in Book III of *The History of the Parliament* are meant to reflect directly upon the English Civil War, portraying the two opposing sides as the forces of liberty and tyranny, motivated on the one hand by principle and on the other by the desire for personal gain ('Whether the parallel will in some measure fit this occasion or not, I leave to the Reader').[35] In refutation, Marvell follows the example of Dante in presenting Brutus and Cassius as archetypal traitors. Marvell once more turns May's penchant for classical parallels against him in the descriptions of the underworld near the end of the poem ('Sulphrey *Phlegeton*', the jaws of Cerberus, 'the perpetual Vulture' gnawing at the sinner's vitals, Ixion lashed to his wheel), which echo Virgil and Dante in showing the punishments inflicted on traitors, deceivers, and over-reachers as justified by their crimes: "'Tis just what Torments Poets ere did feign, / Thou first Historically shouldst sustain' (lines 90–6). The wit and packed allusiveness in thus finding a punishment suitable for the poet-historian May is characteristic of Marvell.

'Tom May's Death' thus takes its origin as a debate between two positions, and as such the opponent necessarily provides much of the material. In *The Rehearsal Transpros'd* and *Mr. Smirke*, as in many polemical works of the seventeenth century, such a 'Living Dissection' (*RT*, I, p. 185) is undertaken by means of quoting the opponent's words in detail and seeking to refute his arguments *seriatim*. In 'Tom May's Death', as in *Absalom and Achitophel* and *MacFlecknoe*, on the other hand, individual debating points are subordinated to a unifying myth or allegory, which is embodied in a plot. Unlike the episodic 'The Character of Holland' and 'Fleckno', the poem has a clearly defined beginning, middle, and end. It begins with May's sudden arrival in the Elysian Fields, 'With an Eye uncertain, gazing wide' (line 4), confused at his unfamiliar surroundings. The action then continues with the appearance 'in the dusky Laurel shade' (line 13) of Ben Jonson, May's attempt to force an entry 'among the Learned throng' (line 28), and (lines 39–96, over half of the poem) Jonson's speech refuting May's claims to a place by the side of the great poets of the past. The conclusion is as sudden and dramatic as the beginning and resembles the conclusions of *MacFlecknoe* and *The Vision of Judgment* – May's disappearance 'in a Cloud of pitch' (line 99), after Jonson 'by irrevocable Sentence' (line 97) had condemned him to eternal torment in Hades. Marvell's verdict on May is thus embodied in the central action, which first pronounces and then presents May's physical expulsion from the pantheon of the poets:

> If that can be thy home where *Spencer* lyes
> And reverend *Chaucer*, but their dust doth rise
> Against thee, and expels thee from their side...
> Nor here thy shade must dwell; Return, Return,
> Where Sulphrey *Phlegeton* does ever burn...
> And streight he vanisht in a Cloud of pitch,
> Such as unto the Sabboth bears the Witch. (lines 85–90, 99–100)

The plot of 'Tom May's Death', like the rather similar plot of *MacFlecknoe*, not only suggests to the reader that May's claims to poetic stature are bogus, it demonstrates this judgment in action.

Marvell's use of parody in 'Tom May's Death' helps to define the ideal of poetry with which Marvell is centrally concerned in the work. Parodic refutation of May's own words is one of the means by which he seeks to demolish May's claims to be a 'son' of Ben Jonson and a fit candidate for the laureate in Jonson's place. The first words Jonson speaks in the poem, which indicate to the translator May that he himself has been doubly 'translated' (line 26), parody the opening lines of May's version of the *Pharsalia*:

> Cups more then civil of *Emathian* wine,
> I sing (said he) and the *Pharsalian* Sign,
> Where the Historian of the Common-wealth
> In his own Bowels sheath'd the conquering health. (lines 21–4)

The lines ridicule May's pretensions as poet and historian, and make even his death seem foolish. Marvell's approach here is a good deal more subtle than the invective of 'The Character of Holland': rather than calling May a drunkard in half a dozen picturesque ways, he suggests, through the ironically inappropriate imagery, that May's last drink occasioned an unheroic and unintended suicide. 'Sheath'd the conquering health', with its literally impossible liquid sword, is a characteristically Marvellian detail; May choked to death while drunk, so the line is accurate as well as clever. The echo of May's own words (May's lines are 'Warres more than civill on Aemathian plaines / We sing; rage licensed; where great Rome distaines / In her owne bowels her victorious swords') accentuates the discrepancy between May's intentions and his achievements.[36]

A further passage in 'Tom May's Death' is not a direct line-by-line parody, but draws on May's *Pharsalia* in order to impale May once more on a sword of his own fashioning. The poem's central lines, the praise of the poet-hero resolute even at the worst of times, are in part based on Lucan's portrait of Cato (in May's words, 'Catos Legend') in Book ix of the *Pharsalia*. After Caesar's victory over Pompey, when Pompey's former supporters in great numbers desert the field, only Cato remains steadfast: 'His countrey wanting a protector then', he stands 'alone for liberty'. His troops appeal to fortune, to 'successe', to self-preservation as arguments for compliance with the victor:

> He whom wars fortunes make,
> Shall be our lord, no generall wee'll take.
> Unto the warre we followed thee alone;
> Wee'll follow fate, *Pompey*, now thou art gone.
> Nor have we cause to hope for good successe,
> Since *Caesars* fortune now doth all possesse.

Cato's answer is that 'bondage' is never acceptable, that excessive concern with one's own 'safety' is base, and that the service of truth and freedom does not depend upon the fortunes of war:

> To live in bondage you desire
> And for your slavish necks a yoake require...
> Oh servants lewd,
> When your first masters dead, his heir you'll serve.

'Danger' makes a good cause even better; a true Roman, Cato argues, will endure hardships courageously, aware that 'to know the way to dy is man's best fate'.[37] It is precisely these beliefs, Marvell argues by implication, that May violates in his surrender to expediency. The political circumstances of 'Tom May's Death' and of *The Rehearsal Transpros'd* differ, but the timeserver May is attacked on the same moral grounds as the timeserver Parker. The conviction that principles retain their validity even in the most daunting of circumstances, that 'successful Crimes' (line 70) do not cease being crimes by the verdict of fortune, lies at the heart of 'Tom May's Death', as of Marvell's later satiric writings. These lines, celebrating the true poet, defiant even 'though the World's disjointed Axel crack', express the ethical principles on which 'Tom May's Death' is based:

> When the Sword glitters ore the Judges head,
> And fear has Coward Churchmen silenced,
> Then is the Poets time, 'tis then he drawes,
> And single fights forsaken Vertues cause. (lines 63–6)

IV

From one point of view, *The Rehearsal Transpros'd* is the most successful of Marvell's satires, since contemporary comment indicates that Marvell triumphed easily over his adversary Parker. As Anthony à Wood, whose political and religious sympathies lay more on Parker's side, conceded:

It was generally thought, nay even by many of those who were otherwise favourers of Parker's cause, that he (Parker) thro' a too loose and unwary handling of the debate...laid himself too open to the severe strokes of his sneering adversary, and that the odds and victory lay on Marvell's side... Tho' Marvell in a second part replied upon our author's reproof, yet he judged it more prudent rather to lay down the cudgels than to enter the lists again.[38]

Here Marvell seems to have succeeded triumphantly in validating his standards; as with Dryden's re-creation of Shadwell as the son of Flecknoe, the historical Parker, even in his lifetime, disappeared into the image of 'pert *Bayes*, with Importance comfortable' about whom Rochester remarks dismissively in 'Tunbridge-Wells' (1674–5), '*Marvel* has enough expos'd his Folly.' Swift writes in *A Tale of a Tub*: 'We still read *Marvel*'s Answer to *Parker* with Pleasure, tho' the Book it answers be sunk long ago.'[39]

The success of *The Rehearsal Transpros'd* is largely due to Marvell's choice of persuasive strategy. In combining jest and earnest, Marvell is directing his arguments at two distinct audiences: those who were sympathetic toward the doctrines he espoused and those who, initially indifferent to these doctrines, could be brought to sympathize by an implicit appeal to common sense, geniality, and membership in a community of wits. Rhetorically, such an approach is effective because, as Ian Watt points out, it flatters the reader, appealing to a shared identity of attitude among all men of wit and judgment, who would not wish to associate with such fools as Parker.

The ironic posture, in fact, was both a formal expression of the qualitative division in the reading public, and a flattering reinforcement of the sense of superiority which animated one part of it.[40]

The distinction on which the ironic code depends is not primarily social, but intellectual and, in Marvell's view, moral. Though we need not take literally Marvell's claim that the general 'acceptance' of *The Rehearsal Transpros'd* was due to the cause he was defending rather than any abilities of his own, the moral sanctions he invokes clearly play a role in bringing about the reader's assent to an attack on 'unspeakable arrogance...a Vice so generally odious, that to repress it is no less grateful...there being scarce any spectacle more pleasing to God and Man than to see the proud humbled' (*RT*, II, p. 170). Still, much of the appeal of witty satire like *The Rehearsal Transpros'd* is aesthetic, and its persuasiveness is in large part a function of the method of raillery which Marvell has chosen to use.

The urbanity of Marvell's approach to prose controversy, looking forward to 'a more Augustan method of handling disputation', has often been pointed out.[41] Marvell anticipates Swift in preferring ironic insinuation to direct, bludgeoning assault, masking his indignation in a controlled, conversational tone. The effectiveness of 'fine raillery' comes in part from the illusion of unconcern: raillery is both a social and a stylistic ideal, associated with aristocratic nonchalance, and the rise of this new mode reflects a concern with form, in art as in social intercourse, characteristic of the Restoration and early eighteenth century. Dryden's remarks on his own practice in raillery, his desire to 'make a malefactor die sweetly', are full of the craftsman's pride in exercising his art. A similar quality is apparent in *The Rehearsal Transpros'd*.

This is the mystery of that noble trade, which yet no master can teach to his apprentice: he may give the rules, but the scholar is never the nearer in his practise. (*Essays*, II, 137)

The wit of *The Rehearsal Transpros'd*, like that of *Absalom and Achitophel* and *A Tale of a Tub*, though it is prompted by its occasion and never loses sight of its polemical end, nevertheless transcends its circumstances. But where in the greatest Augustan satires the central metaphors provide an organizing myth around which details can cohere, in *The Rehearsal Transpros'd* the element of fictionality is intermittent. This structural weakness is a serious flaw in the work, though individual episodes are brilliant displays of wit turned to satiric purposes.

The structural difficulties of *The Rehearsal Transpros'd* are in part the legacy of characteristic methods of disputation in the seventeenth century. In both *The Rehearsal Transpros'd* and *Mr. Smirke* (the subtitles of which are 'Animadversions Upon a late Book...' and 'Certain Annotations, upon the Animadversions on the Naked Truth'), the work's form is determined by what 'the nature of *Animadversions* requires' (*RT*, I, p. 49): both are detailed, point-by-point refutations of an opponent, quoting the words of the adversary as they fall, with appropriate satiric comment. Marvell's remark, 'I will take a walk in the Garden and gather some of Mr. *Bayes* his Flowers' (*RT*, I, p. 77), suggests the potential for satire in such an approach at the same time as it reveals its essential formlessness. There is no more effective way of convicting a man of folly than by turning his own words against him.

But therefore it was that I have before so particularly quoted and bound him up with his own Words as fast as such a *Proteus* could be pinion'd... Every change of Posture does either alter his opinion or vary the expression by which we should judg of it: and sitting he is of one mind, and standing of another. (*RT*, I, p. 92)

Milton, who employs a similar method in *Animadversions upon the Remonstrants Defence against Smectymnuus* and *An Apology against a Pamphlet*, like Marvell justifies 'this close and succinct manner of coping with the Adversary' for its polemical effectiveness in the war of truth against sophistry 'in the detecting, and convincing of any notorious enemie to truth and his Countries peace, especially that is conceited to have a voluble and

smart fluence of tongue'.[42] Milton's *Animadversions* observe the
conventions of debate scrupulously: the pamphlet is set out in the
form of statement and response, labelled 'Remonstrant' and
'Answer', and is divided into sections corresponding to those in the
work it is answering. Some of the 'Answers' are brief explosions of
scorn ('Ha, ha, ha', 'O pestilent imprecation!', or, their equivalents in Marvell, 'here is indeed material intellectual Puff-past';
'you foam again as in the Falling-Sickness'), others argue a contrary case in detail, and still others use the words of the Remonstrant as occasion for rhetorical displays. The subtler touches of
'fine raillery' have no place in Milton's conception of the proper
language of satire: his 'vehement vein throwing out indignation'
is conceived in religious terms as 'a sanctified bitternesse against
the enemies of truth'. The precedents he cites for his practice are
not the standard classical authors, but the words of Christ and the
Old Testament prophets: 'Christ himselfe speaking of unsavory
traditions, scruples not to name the Dunghill and the Jakes.'
Wit and indirection are not part of his arsenal; instead, he speaks
out, casting 'derision and scorne upon perverse and fraudulent
seducers', using such phrases as 'beggarly, and brutish', 'a sot, an
ideot', 'insatiate avarice, & ambition', 'the very garbage that
draws together all the fowles of prey and ravin in the land to
come, and gorge upon the Church'.[43] But if the style is different,
the form is the same, and this quotation-and-comment method
can be found in much of the controversial writing of the century –
e.g., in the exchanges of the rival Civil War newsletters, *Mercurius
Aulicus* and *Mercurius Britanicus*.[44]

Marvell's comments on the method of animadversions suggest
that he felt a certain uneasiness about the form. However brilliant
the local effects may be, the author of animadversions can only
respond to what his opponent has said:

Therefore I shall look to it as well as I can, that mine Arrows be well
pointed, and of mine own whetting; but for the Feathers, I must borrow
them out of his Wing. (*RT*, ii, p. 187)

The metaphor of pursuit, which Marvell employs in several
passages, presents the hunting down of a malefactor as both a
pleasure and a duty:

Yet I will not decline the pursuit, but plod on after him in his own way, thorow thick and thin, hill or dale, over hedge or ditch wherever he leads; till I have laid hand on him, and deliver'd him bound either to Reason or Laughter, to Justice or Pity. (*ibid.*)

A secondary implication of the hunt metaphor is that the satirist, as well as the quarry, is bound: where one goes, the other must follow, whether he wants to or not. The satirist, by reason of his greater self-knowledge and skill, is the master of the situation, controls the chase; May thus in 'Tom May's Death' is 'only Master of these Revels' when he provides the entertainment unwittingly by his own discomfiture, ending in a masque-like disappearance 'in a Cloud of pitch' (lines 98–9). But 'I will not decline the pursuit' implies 'I cannot decline the pursuit.' It is odd how often Marvell uses phrases suggesting that he himself is constrained by the rules of the game and has become a victim of necessity, if not a prisoner of his opponent's folly: 'Yet though I must follow his track now I am in, I hope I shall not write after his Copy' (*RT*, I, p. 49). To say as he does at one point, 'I have not committed any fault of stile, nor even this tediousness, but in his imitation' (II, p. 185), seems a curious abdication of artistic responsibility. 'Imitation' is not normally incompatible with an artist's shaping control, but here Marvell argues, quite fallaciously, that the corrective end of satire requires that the model to be scrutinized ('it being so necessary to represent him in his own likeness') must be followed exactly, even at the cost of 'tediousness'. When he comes to write *Mr. Smirke*, his impatience with the method of animadversion is plainly evident: it is a 'new Game' after the manner of academic disputation, redolent of 'the *Schools* and *Pew*' (p. 21) and suitable for pedants and ambitious 'Divines in Mode' (p. 33) who seek reputation by being 'received into the band of Answerers'. After almost fifty pages, he abandons the method entirely (with comments on the folly of 'endless disputing to no purpose') and turns instead to *A Short Historical Essay*, a clearly organized historical narrative and an entirely independent work. Here he no longer need submit to 'the Rules of . . . Play' whereby 'he always that hath writ the last Book' in a series establishes the terms of debate and awaits his turn 'until the other has done replying':

For I had intended to have gone Chapter by Chapter, affixing a distinct

Title, as he does to every one of them...But in good earnest, after having consider'd this last Chapter, so Brutal whether as to Force or Reason, I have changed my resolution. For he argues so despicably in the rest, that even I, who am none of the best *Disputers of this World*, have conceiv'd an utter contempt for him. He is a meer Kitchin-plunderer, and attacks but the Baggage...

But the Printer calls: the Press is in danger. I am weary of such stuffe, both mine own and his. I will rather give him the following Essay of mine own to busie him, and let him take his turn of being the *Popilius*. (*Mr. Smirke*, Sig. g3ᵛ)[45]

The most effective (and most characteristically Marvellian) passages in *The Rehearsal Transpros'd* are those in which he manages to break free of the constraints of the animadversion form. Even in quoting Parker and holding him to his own words, Marvell typically proceeds less by logical examination than by the free play of wit upon the materials Parker has inadvertently supplied. Parker is imprudent enough to apologize for any inadequacies in his book with the excuse that 'it must be ravish'd out of his hands before his thoughts can possibly be cool enough to review or correct the Indecencies either of its stile or contrivance' (*RT*, I, p. 6). The ineptness with which Parker uses a conventional apologetic formula provides Marvell an opening for a criticism both intellectual and moral, in which faults of language are shown to be faults of character: Parker can be convicted out of his own mouth of 'writing without thinking',[46] the distinguishing mark of a fool.

Some Man that has less right to be fastidious and confident, would, before he exposed himself in publick, both have cool'd his Thoughts, and corrected his Indecencies: or would have consider'd whether it were necessary or wholesom that he should write at all...But there was no holding him. Thus it must be, and no better, when a man's Phancy is up, and his Breeches are down; when the Mind and the Body make contrary assignations, and he hath both a Bookseller at once and a Mistris to satisfie: Like *Archimedes*, into the Street he runs out naked with his Invention. (*RT*, I, p. 7)

In the course of the passage, debate modulates into fiction: the historical Parker is melted down in an alembic and transformed into the comic character Bayes.

Marvell finds precedents for his method of dramatization in earlier English prose satire. As several recent critics have shown, the most effective satiric device employed in the Marprelate tracts is the transformation of 'Martin's' opponent John Bridges into a stage stage figure of a 'worshipful jester . . . whose writings and sermons tend to no other ende then to make men laugh'. By assuming the persona of a clever and bumptious country clown, creating miniature dramatic confrontations in which his opponents are addressed as though they were in the room with him ('But now alas brother Bridges I had forgotten you all this while. My brother London and I were so busie that wee scarce thought of you. Why coulde you not put me in minde that you staid al the whyle?'), Martin Marprelate gains the reader's approbation with his energy and inventiveness, while at the same time diminishing the authority of his opponents, defenders of the Anglican establishment who like Parker made much of their dignity.[47] But the quality of ironic detachment so characteristic of Marvell's verse and prose is absent from the Marprelate tracts, as it is from the prose polemic of the Civil War period. The element of fictionality is subordinate to the element of debate – indeed, of intense hand-to-hand combat. Pamphlet wars reflected literal wars, in which lives were at stake: 'Martin Marprelate' was hunted down mercilessly by the state, the press on which the tracts were printed was destroyed, and the probable author was hanged, while the editors of *Mercurius Aulicus* and *Mercurius Britanicus*, the royalist and parliamentary journals, treated their verbal exchanges as extensions by other means of the battles they wrote about. The humour of the Marprelate tracts and of the Civil War newsletters tends to be broad, aimed at inflicting pain on an adversary, and its primary modes are invective and burlesque. *Mercurius Aulicus* and *Mercurius Britanicus*, especially the latter, have moments of lively, entertaining writing (together with a good deal of crude caricature and name-calling), but the prose has none of Marvell's urbanity. The most vigorous passages are in the manner of medieval and Elizabethan flyting, the joy of insult:

But harke ye, thou mathematicall liar, that framest lies of all dimensions, long, broad and profound lies, and then playest the botcher, the quibling pricklouse every weeke in tacking and sticking them together; I tell thee (Berkenhead) thou art a knowne notorious odious forger: and though I will not say thou art (in thine owne language) the sonne of an Egyptian whore, yet all the world knowes thou art an underling pimpe to the whore of

Babylon, and thy conscience an arrant prostitute for the base ends. This is truth, not railing.[48]

Marvell's prose in *The Rehearsal Transpros'd*, on the other hand, has been accurately described as 'the prose version of the "metaphysical" style'.[49] As in his poems, a metaphor can provide a sudden illumination, remind us both of the variety of experience and of its unexpected connections. Marvell's wit can express itself in an aphorism, using homely allusions to point the lessons of common sense: 'A Prince that goes to the Top of his Power is like him that shall go to the Bottom of his Treasure' (*RT*, II, p. 235). Or, as in metaphysical poetry, conceits can be extended to a great length in a dazzling pyrotechnical display. Several conceits in the prose have close parallels in the poems, using geometrical, architectural, and scientific imagery in a manner reminiscent of such poems as 'The Definition of Love', 'A Dialogue between the Soul and Body', and 'Upon Appleton House'.

Bayes had at first built up such a stupendious Magistrate, as never was of God's making. He had put all Princes upon the Rack to stretch them to his dimension. And, as a streight line continued grows a Circle, he had given them so infinite a Power that it was extended unto Impotency. (*RT*, I, pp. 92–3)

And you would do well and wisely not to stretch, Gold-beat, and Wyerdrawe Humane Laws thus to Heaven: least they grow thereby too slender to hold, and lose in strength what they gain by extension and rarefaction. (II, p. 256)

Each of the metaphors, by a *reductio ad absurdum*, points out the buried implications of Parker's position, evoking an ideal of order by presenting grotesque and comic images of disorder. The wit here is an effective means of validation, since the reader, as he works out the conceit, tacitly allies himself with the author against Parker, who dreams of power and ends in 'Impotency'. One of Marvell's characteristic methods is a sudden and unexpected literalizing of a metaphor – seen, for example, in the following passage, in the course of which the conventional trope of the royal shepherd and his flock comes alive as a terrified herd of animals charging across the page:

The wealth of a Shepheard depends upon the multitude of his flock, the goodness of their Pasture, and the Quietness of their feeding: and Princes, whose dominion over mankind resembles in some measure that of man over other creatures, cannot expect any considerable increase to themselves, if by continual terrour they amaze, shatter, and hare their People, driving them into Woods, & running them upon Precipices. (*RT*, II, p. 234)

Rosalie Colie has described this technique in Marvell's poems as 'unfiguring' and 'refiguring', where the poet, alert to the implications of language, seeks to revitalize traditions, 'cleans them of their conventional metaphorical associations to begin anew'.[50] A similar literalizing of a metaphor occurs in Marvell's attack on Parker's claim that all earthly laws carry the obligation of Divine Law, to be obeyed at the peril of damnation:

Take heed of hooking things up to Heaven in this manner; for, though you look for some advantage from it, you may chance to raise them above your reach, and if you do not fasten and rivet them very well when you have them there, they will come down again with such a swinge, that if you stand not out of the way, they may bear you down further then you thought of. (*RT*, II, p. 255)

The irony in the last of these passages is typical of Marvell's conduct of his attack on Parker. Irony often involves *faux naiveté*: the pretence of offering friendly and wholesome advice, the patient, literal exposition of the logical consequences of a position which entirely undermines that position, allowing the reader to draw the necessary conclusions. An extended comic episode at the beginning of Part II of *The Rehearsal Transpros'd* builds a satiric fiction out of a few ill-chosen words by Parker: 'a dull and lazy distemper' which, Parker tells the readers of *A Reproof to the Rehearsal Transpros'd* (1673), prevented him from answering Marvell sooner. Marvell seizes on the phrase and mercilessly develops its full implications, until his opponent is reduced to a state of helplessness. For a dozen brilliant pages of sustained irony, he speculates on the nature, causes, and cure of Bayes's illness:

I am sorry if that should occasion a distemper, which I order'd as Physick; the *Rehearsal Transpros'd* being too only a particular prescription in his case, and not to be applyed to others without special direction. But some curious persons would be licking at it, and most Men finding it not distasteful to the Palate, it grew in a short time to be of common use in the Shops. (*RT*, II, p. 156)

His method here once again is to literalize the terms of the metaphor unexpectedly, giving the common terms 'taste' and 'marketplace' a direct physical reality. Metaphor becomes allegory, as he simultaneously makes the hapless Bayes appear a more and more ludicrous figure and, on another level, presents a defence of satire as a genre:

But it hath brought up such ulcerous stuff as never was seen; and whereas I intended it only for a *Diaphoretick* to cast him into a breathing sweat, it hath had upon him all the effects of a Vomit. Turnep-tops, Frogs, rotten Eggs, Brass-coppers, Grashoppers, Pins, Mushrooms &c. wrapt up together in such balls of Slime and Choler, that they would have burst the Dragon, and in good earnest seem to have something supernatural...But it is possible that after so notorious an evacuation he may do better for the future; and it is more then visible that either his Disease or his Nature cannot hold out much longer. (*RT*, II, pp. 158–9)[51]

In 'The Character of Holland' passages using comparable materials rarely rise above name-calling; here the materials have undergone imaginative transformation from polemic into fiction. The humour of the passage conveys a dual 'ethical argument' in the characterization of Bayes and the implied characterization of the satirist as scrupulous, impersonal anatomist, who knows that it is more important to lay open and diagnose the illness he has observed than to tell the patient what he wants to hear. His strong language, he suggests, is justified by its educative purpose: the foul matter released by purging the patient may be an object of revulsion, but it is far more harmful when festering within a diseased body than when it is evacuated.

A comparable passage in Part I is the extended character sketch of Bayes the mad priest. Here again the persuasive ends are ahieved less through explicit argument than through the creation of an imaginary world. The episode resembles Swift in its inventiveness and effective use of irony, as in the central assumption on which it is predicated – that the most damaging of diseases is self-delusion: 'Never Man certainly was so unacquainted with himself' (*RT*, I, p. 7).

With pretended sympathy, Marvell traces the course of the affliction by which Bayes, 'a man in the flower of his age, and the vigor of his studies', has fallen 'into such a distraction, That his head runs upon nothing but Romane Empire and Ecclesiastical Policy' (*RT*, I, pp. 28–9). The illness, he tells us, began with Bayes's early reading of *Don Quixote* and the Bible, which in combination 'have made such a medly in his brain-pan' (p. 29) that he became incurably mad. The description of Bayes's arrival in London after leaving university uses another of the mathematical conceits so characteristic of Marvell's poems; one is reminded of the attack on architectural ambition and scholarly folly in 'Upon Appleton House' ('Let others vainly strive t'immure / *The Circle* in the *Quadrature*!' lines 45–6).

But coming out of the confinement of the Square-cap and the Quadrangle into the open Air, the World began to turn round with him: which he imagined, though it were his own giddiness, to be nothing less then the *Quadrature* of the *Circle*. This accident concurring so happily to increase the good opinion which he naturally had of himself, he thenceforward apply'd to gain a-like reputation with others. (*RT*, i, pp. 29–30)

But his first severe attack, Marvell continues, came with his first wordly success. In the passage that follows, the ironic application of mechanistic terms to human behaviour resembles Swift's association of madness, pretended inspiration, and Cartesian mechanism in sections viii and ix of *A Tale of a Tub*. The wit lies partly in the surprisingly apposite details ('Precipice of his Stature', recalling 'mine own Precipice I go' in 'A Dialogue between the Soul and Body'), partly in the scientific neutrality with which the symptoms are narrated:

This thing alone [the praise he received] elevated him exceedingly in his own conceit, and raised his *Hypocondria* into the Region of the Brain: that his head swell'd like any Bladder with wind and vapour. But after he was stretch'd to such an height in his own fancy, that he could not look down from top to toe but his Eyes dazled at the Precipice of his Stature; there fell out, or in, another natural chance which push'd him headlong. (*RT*, i, p. 30)

Though he has a highly practical side, an eye for 'the main chance', any worldly achievements only serve as fuel for Bayes's madness; he may bask in the approbation of others, especially women, but his universe is essentially solipsistic. The conceit, familiar in Donne, of the lover's face reflected in the eye, emblematic of the shared universe the lovers inhabit, is here converted to satiric effect, suggesting Parker's grotesque, blind self-regard: 'For all this Courtship had no other operation than to make him stil more in love with himself: and if he frequented their company, it was only to speculate his own Baby in their Eyes' (*RT*, I, p. 31).

Throughout this extensive character portrait, the implicit standards of judgment are clear. The distorting mirrors of vanity and self-love are contrasted with the mirror of truth, madness with rationality. The ambitious, unprincipled man who frames his actions with regard only to what he believes 'would take' (*RT*, I, p. 30), who sees in others only what use he can make of them, violates nature in repudiating his common bond with all men. For a man to assume that he makes the world turn round, that he has, fulfilling Archimedes' prophecy, found a place outside common humanity from which 'he could now move and govern the whole Earth with the same facility', is simple madness. Such an affliction can only grow worse, since any accident the patient may meet with is likely to cause further deterioration:

He was transported now with the Sanctity of his Office, even to extasy: and like the Bishop over *Maudlin Colledge* Altar, or like *Maudlin de la Croix*, he was seen in his Prayers to be lifted up sometimes in the Air, and once particularly so high that he crack'd his Scul against the Chappel Ceiling...But being thus, without Competitor or Rival, the Darling of both Sexes in the Family and his own Minion; he grew beyond all measure elated, and that crack of his Scull, as in broken Looking-Glasses, multipli'd him in self-conceit and imagination. (*RT*, I, 31)

Once more the implicit metaphorical content of familiar phrases (rising in the world, the love of self, reflections seen in a mirror) is revitalized. The rhetorical technique in the narrative is akin to that in such poems as 'Mourning' or the meadow and forest sections of 'Upon Appleton House', where the writer presents phenomena and speculates on their possible cause: the ironist withholds his 'silent Judgment' ('Mourning', line 33), yet it is implied in the ordering of his materials. So the account remorselessly continues, describing the later stages of Bayes's illness, his rapid decline into total lunacy. Bayes decides 'he must be a madman in print' and the strain of writing causes new symptoms. When his book has been published and he can envision himself as a famous author, 'the Vain-Glory of this totally confounded him. He lost all the little remains of his understanding, and his Cerebellum was so dryed up that there was more brains in a Walnut and both their Shells were alike thin and brittle' (*RT*, I, pp. 31–2).

His further writings, 'all ... howling, yelling, and barking', are proof of total, irremediable insanity.

> And so in conclusion his Madness hath formed it self into a perfect *Lycanthropy*. He doth so verily believe himself to be a Wolf, that his speech is all turn'd into howling, yelling, and barking: and if there were any Sheep here, you should see him pull out their throats and suck the blood. Alas, that a sweet Gentleman, and so hopeful, should miscarry! (*RT*, I, p. 32)

The account of Bayes's madness, extending over several pages, is an example of the ironic dismantling of the pretensions of an opponent which in rhetorical skill, suavity, and an eye for the telling detail rivals Swift. Yet it is characteristic of *The Rehearsal Transpros'd* that the passage is an isolated episode rather than part of an integrated whole.

V

Marvell's later verse satires are all written with practical political ends in mind, and these at times make aesthetic considerations secondary. 'Clarindon's House-Warming' is intended to bring about Clarendon's downfall at the hands of Parliament, 'The Loyal Scot' to support a proposed act of union of England and Scotland, 'Upon his Majesties being made free of the Citty' and 'The Statue in Stocks-Market' to stir up feelings against the Duke of York and the King, warning, like Marvell's prose pamphlet of 1677, about the dangers of 'the growth of popery and arbitrary government in England'. The use of the metre and idiom of popular poetry in the last two poems and in 'The Statue at Charing Cross' indicates Marvell's concern in these works with immediate effectiveness. Such poems make use of language and arguments their intended audience of city merchants and tradesmen is likely to understand. It is quite wrong to think of these works as naive poetry: Marvell has deliberately assumed a particular voice, just as Swift does in the *Drapier's Letters*. The approach reflects the iconoclastic aesthetic of Marvell's satires. Though their language and imagery are shockingly indecorous according to superficial considerations of worldly greatness and court protocol, they observe a higher decorum of truth, revealing the reality behind the false facade: 'a king made of clouts' ('Statue in Stocks-Market', line 44), irresponsible, bankrupt, greedy, a source of sickness in the commonwealth. Despite occasional crudity and awkwardness in detail (perhaps in part the result of the uncertain state of the text, understandable in poems circulated anonymously in manuscript for some years after their composition), each is unified in conception. The historical occasion which prompted each poem is treated symbolically and at the same time realistically; thus, 'Upon his Majesties being made free of the Citty', which like the two statue poems is based on a particular incident recorded in Marvell's letters, develops a single metaphor throughout in portraying the King as an unruly apprentice and gives a lesson to its audience in applied politics, defining in immediate, homely terms the meaning of freedom and responsibility.

Other satires by Marvell carry the adoption of a particular tone of voice one step further, making their satiric point by the ironic manipulation of a persona. In 'The Kings Vowes' and the prose 'Mock Speech', wit once more is turned to a practical use. As the writings of Swift illustrate, the subtlest and most effective method of validation in satire is to place words in the victim's mouth which are entirely plausible and appropriate yet damn him irremediably. Both 'The Kings Vowes' and the 'Mock Speech' catch 'the accent of a living voice', present a believable character sketch of a man whose libertine beliefs and fecklessness might in other circumstances be attractive.[52] The words given to the monarch imply their own contrary norms, constituting a more effective argument against Hobbesian moral and political doctrines than any unironic equivalent could be:

> I will have a Religion then all of mine own
> Where *Papist* from *Protestant* shall not be known,
> But if it grow troublesome I will have none.   (lines 7–9)

> I will have a fine pond and a pretty Decoy
> Where the Ducks and the Drakes may their freedoms enjoy
> And quack in their language still, *Vive le Roy*.   (lines 49–51)

Though the central conceit is developed in 'The Kings Vowes' with considerable wit and subtlety, yet if we compare it to Swift's 'Argument against the Abolition of Christianity' or Rochester's 'The Maim'd Debauchee', the formal limitations of Marvell's poem become evident. Swift and Rochester not only parody a particular tone of voice with great accuracy, but construct an argument, with a clear forward progression, a beginning, middle, and end, a carefully worked-out plan to which each detail contributes. Marvell in contrast develops his initial conceit in an expandable series of discrete stanzas, subject to rearrangement and linked primarily by the repetition of a single rhetorical pattern ('I will'). Detailed commentary on the poem is hampered by the existence of varying manuscript and printed versions and the lack of a received text. But one cannot imagine another author tacking several additional pages at the end of 'A Modest Proposal', much less Swift writing several different versions, longer or shorter, of equal authority.

When we look at Marvell's other verse satires written during this period, we find a similar pattern: the poems possess a thematic unity, largely based on the development of conceits, and are alert to the decorum of occasion and audience, but only rarely does there appear to be any principle governing the order and inter-relationship of parts. Both 'The Loyal Scot' and 'Clarindon's House-Warming' suffer from occasional obscurity in details, but the shorter length of 'Clarindon's House-Warming', together with the artist's firmer control over the disposition of his materials, helps make it more coherent. 'The Loyal Scot', because of its piecemeal composition and its digressiveness, is the most miscellaneous and formless of Marvell's verse satires. Its various elements – the lines on the death of Douglas, the 'Cleveland' framework, the attack on the bishops, the epigram on Blood, the remarks on national unity – are loosely connected thematically, but except in the lines on the 'two nations' near the end there is little attempt to pull the disparate materials together. Whatever unity the poem possesses is entirely a response to its occasion; indeed, part of the problem, as the poem's several subtitles in different versions suggest, is that it has at least three separate occasions, the death of Douglas, the answer to Cleveland's 'The Rebel Scot' and the proposed act of union. The poem is lacking in structure and proportion: individual conceits and strings of conceits, as in Cleveland, run on at disproportionate length, and the separate parts could be rearranged without materially affecting the poem. As with 'The King's Vowes', there are several versions of the poem, of approximately equal authority, composed at different times.[53] 'Clarindon's House-Warming', in contrast, is more carefully organized, conceived as a whole rather than as an assemblage of disparate parts. Of all Marvell's satires, it is the closest to his lyrics in its structure and the conduct of its argument. The unity of 'Clarindon's House-Warming' is both thematic and rhetorical. The architectural, classical, and biblical imagery, prompted by its occasion, is developed consistently throughout the poem, beginning with the first stanza and reaching its climax in the dual image of the newly-built Clarendon House as the 'Temple of Warre and of Peace' (line 97) where the golden calf is worshipped and of Clarendon himself as a sacrificial beast to be 'roasted ... for publick good cheare' (lines 111–12) at the next session of Parliament. As in Marvell's lyrics, the argument is made explicit in the syntax (When ... But ... But then ... Thus daily ... But while ... Already ... And, henceforth ... To proceed ... They approv'd it thus far ... 'Twas then ... Or rather...).

'Last Instructions' is far too long a poem to be organized in a manner appropriate to a lyric, yet it is by no means as loose and digressive as 'The Loyal Scot'. Critics writing on 'Last Instructions' have generally recognized that the poem presents formal problems, but disagree in assessing the degree to which Marvell has solved the problems inherent in his materials and approach. Joseph Summers has stated the aesthetic question succinctly: 'How does one construct an admonitory picture of chaos?'[54] Or, in slightly different terms, how does one give structure to the imitation of a shapeless world, find significance in the undignified struggles of little men? The poem is tied to the facts of history, attempting like the *Growth of Popery* to provide an accurate historical narrative, revealing what might otherwise lie hidden. Many of the characters and events it records and presents a detailed commentary upon are obscure indeed; Legouis points out that eighty-four names of contemporaries are mentioned in slightly under one thousand lines.[55] The episodic action of the poem is in part dictated by its historical content: here as in *The Rehearsal Transpros'd*, Marvell defines imitation narrowly as following a literal model wherever it may lead. In this respect, Marvell differs strongly from his near-contemporary Dryden, who in both *MacFlecknoe* and *Absalom and Achitophel* imposes form on his historical materials by means of an epic action and a flexible heroic style. Though 'Last Instructions' contains epic elements, these are largely confined to particular episodes, and Marvell uses not one style but several. Passages vary enormously in their satiric approach as well as in the kind of language they employ, and the complex ironies found in the allusions to the world of epic and romance jostle with direct denigration, the iconoclastic portrait of the ugly features of a reality hostile to art.

Though several critics have made a case for the unity and coherence of 'Last Instructions', it seems to me a fruitless endeavour to seek for a structural pattern informing the details of the poem.[56] The recurrent addresses to a painter are too scattered to provide a principle of coherence; like the network of parallels with the epic tradition, they make up a series of thematic links, cross-references, and reminders, but cannot serve as a viable method of organizing a poem of this length and scope. As an annal or chronicle, the poem narrates the events of the year 1666–7 as the earlier 'Advices' had presented the events of the previous two years, and the narrative aims of inclusiveness and exposure of embarrassing truth ('Say, Muse, for nothing can escape thy sight, / And Painter, wanting other, draw this Fight', lines 147–8) necessarily lead to diffuseness. The unity of 'Last Instructions', such as it is, is thematic. The poem is consistent in its attitude toward the characters and events it depicts and it is consistent in its political purpose. In addressing itself to the King, to Parliament and to a more general readership, its aims are explicitly persuasive, and the patterns of imagery, together with the verbal skill and inventiveness in details, are meant to serve the end of persuasion.

'An Horatian Ode', 'Last Instructions', and *Absalom and Achitophel* represent three different methods of organizing a political poem, and from a formal point of view, 'Last Instructions' is the least successful of the three. The 'Horatian Ode' focuses on a particular moment identified in the title and the historical forces converging in it: the 'now' of the poem (the opening lines contain the words 'now' and ''tis time', to emphasize its concentration on the present) is that moment when Cromwell has returned from victories in Ireland and is poised to invade Scotland. The sense of immediacy is in part conveyed by Marvell's control of tense: lines 9–72, up to the death of Charles, are (except for statements of timeless philosophical and political truths) almost entirely in the past tense, while after the 'now' in line 73, the rest of the poem is primarily in the present and future tenses. Marvell's characteristic theme of the relationship between individual freedom and the external forces limiting choice finds expression in the poem's treatment of the present as that moment where the dead past and the unborn future meet, containing within it both the legacy of memory and the possibility of change. In the 'Horatian Ode', the present is explicitly a moment of revolutionary upheaval.[57] Any assumptions that past traditions automatically endure into a stable and predictable future have been destroyed by 'that memorable Hour' (line 65) of Charles's execution. The structure of the poem is carefully worked out, with its argument made clear by the syntax, and the changes in tense are directly expressive of content. Thus the extended simile comparing Cromwell to a lightning bolt, since it presents the relationship between the amoral, destructive hero and the institutions of the past, uses the past tense, where the falcon simile, which poses the problem of the relationship between the present and an uncertain future, uses verbs in the present tense as delicately balanced as the falcon itself. 'An Horatian Ode' differs from both 'Last Instructions' and *Absalom and Achitophel* in being analytical rather than persuasive; it seeks to capture the essence of a significant historical moment and to state a problem to which there is no certain solution. It ends as it begins, with cautionary imperatives: 'Still keep thy Sword erect' (line 116), for the uncertain future that lies in store.

'Last Instructions' and *Absalom and Achitophel* agree with the 'Horatian Ode' in seeking to apply a historian's understanding and an artist's imagination to give contemporary events a pattern. But as satires, they interpret events in such a way as to dispose the reader toward action. Both works display a fundamental moral concern, conceiving of satire's function as 'the amendment of Vices by correction.. harsh Remedies to an inveterate Disease'.[58] This militant attitude toward experience is entirely foreign to the 'Horatian Ode', but the division of mankind into the virtuous and vicious is central to both 'Last Instructions' and *Absalom and Achitophel*, however much the two poets may disagree in their definitions of what constitutes political vice and virtue. For our purposes, the aesthetic distinction between 'Last Instructions' and Dryden's poem as possible models for satire is far more important than their political differences; Marvell disagreed with Samuel Butler's political views no less than with Dryden's, but could say of Butler, 'His excellent Wit hath taken a flight far above these Whiflers: ... whoever dislikes the choice of his Subject, cannot commend his Performance' (*RT*, I, p. 22). Perhaps the central difference between 'Last Instructions' and *Absalom and Achitophel* is the way in which the two poems seek to organize the topical materials of which they are composed. Where Marvell's action in 'Last Instructions' is 'tied too severely to the laws of history', Dryden remakes history into allegory, so that each incident, while reflecting its historical origin, has meaning as a coherent part of an aesthetic whole. Marvell seeks to persuade by explicit argument and by recurrent patterns of imagery, Dryden by his controlling myth, embodied in a plot.[59]

The concentration on the immediate moment which characterizes Marvell's earlier poetry is not a method easily adapted to narrative satire. Marvell's is essentially a symbolic imagination which at the same time respects the exact contours of reality. His lyrics again and again begin with imperative verbs directly invoking the scene, more or less as in the 'composition of place' of formal meditation, usually with specific reference to the sense of sight: 'See how the Orient Dew', 'See with what Simplicity', '*Clora*, come view my Soul, and tell', 'See how the arched Earth does here', 'Heark how the Mower *Damon* Sung'. The poems then proceed to 'decipher' the meaning of the phenomena presented, speculate on what the 'prospect' suggests. Marvell's celebrated equipoise is in part a recognition of the instability of the moment: it is, Marvell suggests, only the constant awareness of the limits of man's power before the destructive forces of time ('But at my back I alwaies hear ...') that enables man to redeem the moment.[60] In 'Last Instructions' as in 'Upon Appleton House' the poet subjects himself to the flow of events, trying to extract their significance. But one does not feel the same imaginative control in 'Last Instructions', the ability to find a momentary harmony amid the welter of experience, a vision of a complete and satisfying 'lesser *World*...in more decent Order tame' ('Upon Appleton House' lines 765–6). If the conviction that the world is fallen informs both poems, the possibility of redemption through the imagination seems largely absent from 'Last Instructions'. The universe revealed there is not 'orderly and near' ('Upon Appleton House', line 26) but jagged and disharmonious, riddled with disease. Marvell's satiric intention in 'Last Instructions' is to suggest a diagnosis and a possible cure. The moral pattern implicit in the poem's recurrent imagery can thus adumbrate an ideal order in the terms by which the actual disorder is described:

> Not so does Rust insinuating wear,
> Nor Powder so the vaulted Bastion tear;
> Nor Earthquake so an hollow Isle overwhelm,
> As scratching *Courtiers* undermine a *Realm*:
> And through the Palace's Foundations bore,
> Burr'wing themselves to hoard their guilty Store. (lines 975–80)

But the imitation of a chaotic universe may simply appear chaotic, and the forces of disorder, once called forth, may appear to swamp the artist's ordering imagination.

Except in the two mock-heroic episodes, where Marvell allows his imagination more freedom, none of the characters in 'Last Instructions' become fictional figures as Bayes does in *The Rehearsal Transpros'd*. Instead, for most of the poem, Marvell's wit is set to the task of denigration, exposing a sordid reality:

> Blither than Hare that hath escap'd the Hounds,
> The *House* Prorogu'd, the *Chancellor* rebounds.
> Not so decrepid *Æson*, hash'd and stew'd
> With *Magic* Herbs, rose from the Pot renew'd:
> And with fresh Age felt his glad Limbs unite:
> His Gout (yet still he curst) had left him quite.
> What Frosts to Fruit, what Ars'nick to the Rat,
> What to fair *Denham* mortal *Chocolat*;
> What an Account to *Carteret*; that and more
> A *Parliament* is to the *Chancellor*.
> So the sad Tree shrinks from the Mornings Eye;
> But blooms all Night, and shoots its branches high.
> So, at the Suns recess, again returns,
> The Comet dread, and Earth and Heaven burns. (lines 335–48)

Here the string of metaphors and similes serve as running commentary on a basis of historical fact. The passage, describing

Clarendon's joy at a prorogation which temporarily frees him from the threat of Parliamentary inquiry, depends for its effects partly on casual allusions which its readers are expected to recognize: the poisoning of Lady Denham, the financial manipulations of Carteret. Yet the extended similes hint at a realm of universals which need no historical annotation. Validation here depends less on explicit topical commentary than on the cumulative force of the imagery of health and disease, life and death, a perverted and restored natural order. The incident is not singled out as more significant than any of a dozen others narrated in the poem, but its place in the poem's dominant moral pattern is clear and explicit: the last lines suggest a standard of order by which the disorder represented by Clarendon can be measured, hint that his moment of triumph will be only temporary, and implicitly argue the case for ministerial accountability to Parliament.

Reality could hardly appear more base than in the character sketches of the Earl of St Albans, the Duchess of York, and the Countess of Castlemaine near the beginning of the poem, but here too the depiction of disorder invokes by contrast the order which is being violated. St Albans' appointment as ambassador with no qualifications other than his sexual prowess (his 'Breeches were the Instrument of Peace' so that he, 'if the *French* dispute his Pow'r, from thence / Can straight produce them a Plenipotence', lines 42–4) indicates how far in Marvell's view the English court society depicted in the poem had sunk from normal standards of diplomacy as of morality. The aesthetic problem here is that the unrelenting concentration on evidence of degradation imposed on the poet by his aesthetic of truthful imitation 'thorow thick and thin, hill or dale, over hedge or ditch wherever he leads' may seem to foreclose the possibility of a viable alternative reality. The deliberately ugly, unpleasant parody of Milton's account of the birth of Sin and Death evokes a world which has soiled all artistic traditions:

> Her, of a female Harpy, in Dog Days:
> Black *Birch*, of all the Earth-born race most hot,
> And most rapacious, like himself begot.
> And, of his Brat enamour'd, as't increast,
> Bugger'd in Incest with the mungrel Beast.   (lines 142–6)

Yet even in this passage, the mythopoeic imagination is active.

For all the sordidness of the details, the passage illustrates the freedom of art, which can transform the historical figure of Colonel John Birch, M.P., into a creature of fiction, as in the lines immediately previous it has turned the Excise Bill into a Spenserian monster equipped with teeth, wings, jaws, and 'thousand Eyes' (line 134).

The most effective passages in 'Last Instructions', both as art and as persuasion, are the two extended mock-heroic episodes in which the imagination breaks free of the pressure of sordid fact, while at the same time respecting the historical reality from which it draws its materials. The imaginative energy displayed in these two sections of the poem, the element of sheer play prominent here and largely absent from the rest of 'Last Instructions', remind one of Marvell's lyrics and 'Upon Appleton House'. Each episode pays tribute to the power of the imagination to revivify and to create:

> The Sun much brighter, and the Skies more clear,
> He finds the Air, and all things, sweeter here.
> The sudden change, and such a tempting sight,
> Swells his old Veins with fresh Blood, fresh Delight.   (lines 529–32)

The Dutch invasion of the Medway is presented as a humiliation for the English, a violation of the natural order, and an index to the sickness of the court which allowed it to happen. The narration of this rape of the English countryside is given greater poignancy and force by Marvell's ironic employment of a pastoral-heroic idiom, with echoes of Enobarbus' description of Cleopatra on her barge. The lines adumbrate an alternative reality to which the imagination and senses can respond:

> His sporting Navy all about him swim,
> And witness their complaisence in their trim.
> Their streaming Silks play through the weather fair,
> And with inveigling Colours Court the Air.
> While the red Flags breath on their Top-masts high
> Terrour and War, but want an Enemy.
> Among the Shrowds the Seamen sit and sing,
> And wanton Boys on every Rope do cling.
> Old *Neptune* springs the Tydes, and Water lent:
> (The Gods themselves do help the provident.)   (lines 535–44)

In the last line quoted, Marvell draws a practical political moral similar to the lessons of history and physics about 'strong' and 'weak' men, 'emptiness' and 'penetration' in the 'Horatian Ode': fortune favours the provident and nature does not bend its laws to help the improvident. Here as throughout Marvell's writing, a hard Machiavellian common-sense realism is united with an awareness of the realm which lies beyond the apprehension of the senses.

A similar double awareness informs the details of the second mock-heroic episode, the battle of the excise:

> Of early Wittals first the Troop march'd in,
> For Diligence renown'd, and Discipline:
> In Loyal haste they left young Wives in Bed,
> And *Denham* these by one consent did head.   (lines 151–4)

In this episode, more than at any other time in 'Last Instructions', history has become fiction; the passage combines generality and specificity, in the manner of the satires of Dryden, Pope, and Swift. The extended conceit, like the allegory of *The Faerie Queene* and *Absalom and Achitophel*, functions on several levels simultaneously, as literal narrative and as moral and topical allegory. The terms in which the conceit of the roll-call of troops is developed have a vivid, comic, physical realism and yet consistently imply a moral judgment, suggesting in these lines that there are better uses for diligence and discipline than in blindly obeying a political paymaster and that a man who allows himself to be cuckolded in search of gain is both fool and knave. The episode contains a multitude of names: Ashburnham, head of the squadron of 'old Courtiers ... that sold their Master', '*Bronkard* Loves Squire', gentle lieutenant of the troop of Procurers, Apsley and Broderick, 'marching hand in hand' as equal commanders of the disorderly troop of Drinkers, and about twenty more (lines 155–6, 174–5, 212). But the mock-heroic fiction here would justify the claim that Pope, with comic exaggeration, makes of *The Dunciad*: the names of the characters are in a sense purely arbitrary, exist as historical examples of a general fictional truth.

But there may arise some obscurity in Chronology from the Names in the Poem, by the inevitable removal of some Authors, and insertion of others, in their Niches. For whoever will consider the Unity of the whole design, will be sensible, that the *Poem was not made for these Authors, but these Authors for the Poem*: And I should judge they were clapp'd in as they rose, fresh and fresh, and chang'd from day to day, in like manner as when the old boughs wither, we thrust new ones into a chimney. (*Dunciad Variorum, Poems*, Appendix I, p. 433)

The element of fiction in 'Last Instructions' as in *The Rehearsal Transpros'd* is intermittent. Marvell in his later satiric and polemical writings never manages the assured mastery of form that characterizes the best satires of the Augustans. There is little point in speculating on the reasons for his inability to arrive at a satisfactory structure for an extended satiric fiction: perhaps his preference for lyric forms associated with an earlier age, perhaps his increasing commitment during the 1660s and 1670s to direct political action, perhaps the Puritan suspicion of art which led him in his later writings to adopt an aesthetic of naked truth in some ways at variance with his natural gifts. Finally, his failures are less important than his successes, and his career provides an impressive and moving example of an artist's realism and courage in facing up to the problem of how to live in a fallen world. Whether or not the act of 'the wanton Troopers riding by' which provides the starting point of 'The Nymph complaining for the death of her Faun' has specific political connotations, it is entirely characteristic of the universe of Marvell's poems, in which wanton and indiscriminate slaughter makes up 'half the business in the world' (*RT*, II, p. 231). Marvell's recurrent subject in his political and non-political poems is the pressure of experience upon the vulnerable individual, the delicate equilibrium between historical necessity and individual choice. Even in the worst of circumstances, faced with a 'spectacle of Blood' ('Unfortunate Lover', line 42), the freedom of the soul remains unimpaired; since 'the Mind' is at all times 'in the hand of God', there is an inward realm which 'corporal punishments' cannot affect (*RT*, I, pp. 111–12). Art distils its perfume from the most unpromising materials, and the imagination, in recognizing the limits reality imposes on it, can defiantly assert its independence from the 'Tyrannick pow'r' ('Definition of Love', line 16) of circumstances. The ending of 'The Unfortunate Lover' can stand as Marvell's tribute to the power of the artistic imagination:

> Who though, by the Malignant Starrs,
> Forced to live in Storms and Warrs;
> Yet dying leaves a Perfume here,
> And Musick within every Ear. (lines 59–62)

APPENDIX. MANUSCRIPT
EVIDENCE FOR THE CANON OF
MARVELL'S POEMS

Lord argues that 'Tom May's Death', 'A Dialogue between Thyrsis and Dorinda', and 'On the Victory obtained by Blake over the Spaniards' are inauthentic because of their exclusion from Bodleian MS. Eng. poet. d. 49, the MS. on which his edition is largely based; see *Complete Poetry*, ed. Lord, p. xxxii. Bodleian MS. Eng. poet. d. 49 is a copy of *Miscellaneous Poems* (1681), with additional sheets bound in, containing seventeen verse satires of the Restoration period (all but one written in the same scribal hand used for the first half of the volume). The importance of the MS. stems from its apparent provenance and from the texts it provides for the three Cromwell poems, cancelled in all but two copies of the folio. There is no doubt that the exclusions are deliberate. Pages 35–8 (Sig. G2–G3), which in other copies of the folio contain the text of 'Tom May's Death', are missing; in their place a single blank sheet is bound in, containing a handwritten version of 'The Picture of Little T.C. in a Prospect of Flowers' (p. 35 of *Miscellaneous Poems*) and, on the verso, a handwritten version of 'The Match', stanzas I–V (p. 38 of *Miscellaneous Poems*). In similar fashion, pp. 103–10 (Sig. P4–Q1–3ᵛ), which in other copies of the folio contain 'On the Victory obtained by Blake over the Spaniards' and 'A Dialogue between Thyrsis and Dorinda', are replaced by a single blank sheet, on which the final three stanzas of 'Upon Appleton House' (p. 103 of *Miscellaneous Poems*) are written in the same hand.

MS. Eng. poet. d. 49 may have been compiled under the supervision of Marvell's nephew and close associate William Popple (1638–1708), and was evidently intended to form the basis of a second edition of Marvell's poems. But its authority is by no means as absolute and unquestionable as some recent scholars have claimed. The volume is a manuscript miscellany of the later seventeenth or early eighteenth century, differing from others of its kind primarily in combining emended printed text and manuscript poems. In the printed portion of the text it contains a large number of MS. emendations of the poems, many of which are attempts to provide greater metrical regularity, in the manner of Tottel's rewriting of Wyatt.[1] Moreover, its provenance is uncertain, since the sole authority for the widely accepted belief that it had been in Popple's possession is the credulous and unsystematic Edward Thompson in his 1776 edition of Marvell's *Works*. It can be shown without doubt that Thompson used the

MS. in his edition, but Thompson's assertion (*Works*, ed. Thompson, I, xxxvii) that the MS., presented to him by 'Mr. Matthias', was Popple's collection of his uncle's poems, may be in error. Matthias, whose wife was a lineal descendant of Popple, may have been misinformed in telling Thompson that the MS. had been among Popple's papers; after all, at least three quarters of a century had passed since the MS. was compiled (probably in the late 1690s, though the date cannot be fixed with any precision). The only direct internal evidence which may link the MS. to Popple is a four-line poem inserted in a hand which, as Hilton Kelliher points out (*Andrew Marvell*, p. 63), resembles that of Popple's son. If Wiliam Popple junior assembled the collection, he would of course have been less likely than his father to have first-hand knowledge of the canon of Marvell's writings; in any case, Popple senior can be ruled out for any date before 1688 (when he was living in France) and after 1696 (when he was in ill health and heavily burdened with his responsibilities as Secretary of the Board of Trade). Given the circumstances under which the folio was published – posthumously, under editorial supervision by the poet's house-keeper, masquerading as his widow – it is possible for poems not by Marvell to have been included erroneously in *Miscellaneous Poems*. But the exclusion alone is not sufficient reason to doubt the authenticity of 'Tom May's Death', 'Thyrsis and Dorinda', or 'Blake's Victory', without supporting evidence.

Such evidence exists for 'Thyrsis and Dorinda', but not for the other two poems. A version of 'Thyrsis and Dorinda' can be found in two MS. collections dating from the mid-1630s, British Library MS. Add. 31432, in the autograph of the composer William Lawes, and Bodleian MS. Rawl. poet. 199. The existence of these two MSS. argues against Marvell's authorship of the poem, on the grounds both of probable date and of attribution to another author. Add. 31432 is a collection of Cavalier lyrics and drinking songs set to music by Lawes. Evidence suggests that the MS. was transcribed in 1639 and that virtually all of Lawes's songs were written between 1634 and 1639.[2] The probable date of Rawl. poet. 199 is even earlier. According to Hilton Kelliher (*Andrew Marvell*, pp. 48–9), the latest datable poems in this MS. were writen in 1634 and 1635. Most of the poems can be identified as by Oxford authors or on Oxford subjects. The compiler was probably a member of Christ Church, of which many of the authors represented were alumni or still in residence in the mid-1630s. Contemporary poets who attended Cambridge, like Herrick, Waller, Suckling, or Thomas Randolph, are almost entirely unrepresented in the collection. If Kelliher's date of 1635 is correct, it effectively rules out Marvell's authorship, since Marvell was fourteen years old at the time (and attended Cambridge, not Oxford).

The attribution to H. Ramsay in Rawl. poet. 199 is further evidence against Marvell's authorship. Henry Ramsay, listed in *Alumni Oxoniensis* as having been a student at Christ Church, Oxford, between 1635 and 1639, is credited with the authorship of a second poem in Rawl. poet. 199, 'To his Mistress feigning to conceale love'. He is also the author of three English and two Latin poems in Oxford volumes published on various occasions between 1635 and 1638, as well as the author of a poem in *Jonsonus Virbius* (1638), a commemorative volume on Ben Jonson.[3] I therefore would conclude that 'A Dialogue between Thyrsis and Dorinda' was written by Ramsay c. 1635–6, was set to music by Lawes a year or two later, remained popular during the next forty-odd years because of two later musical settings by John Gamble and Matthew Locke, and was erroneously included in the 1681 folio edition of Marvell.

The evidence which the second part of Eng. poet. d. 49, headed 'Satyres', provides for the canon of Marvell's poems has generally been misinterpreted. Indeed, inclusion of a poem in this part of the volume cannot even count as 'attribution' to Marvell, since aside from notes by Thompson no explicit statements of attribution to Marvell appear in the collection. Lord places great emphasis on a series of crosses, in ink, placed next to the titles of ten of the poems, which he interprets as authenticating marks by which someone other than the scribe sought to distinguish poems by Marvell, poems probably not by Marvell, and poems by other authors. Poems distinguished by crosses are 'Second Advice to a Painter', 'Third Advice to a Painter', 'Clarindon's House-Warming', 'Last Instructions to a Painter', 'The Kings Vowes', 'The Loyal Scot', the epigram 'Upon Blood's Attempt to Steale the Crown', 'Upon his Majesties being made free of the Citty', 'The Statue in Stocks-Market', and 'The Statue at Charing Cross'. A more likely explanation for the crosses, however, is that, rather than authenticating marks, they are attempts to distinguish those poems which were published in an early edition of *POAS* from those which remained unpublished or were published in later editions. The ten poems with crosses next to their titles all were published in *POAS* 1689, 1697, or 1698. Four of the five poems without crosses were included in none of these editions. Though the fifth, 'On the Monument', is included in *POAS* 1689, it bears no attribution, is in a different part of the collection from most of the poems attributed to Marvell, and was not reprinted in any subsequent edition. It is possible, therefore, that the person making the crosses may have overlooked this printing.

The position of the crosses and other marks on Eng. poet. d. 49 provides additional evidence that the crosses represent an attempt to distinguish published from unpublished poems (or parts of poems). In addition to crosses next to titles and dates, there are cross-marks next to the heading 'To the King', which in 'Second Advice', 'Third Advice', and 'Last Instructions' separates the concluding envoi from the rest of the poem. In *POAS* 1689 and 1697, each 'To the King' is printed as a separate poem and listed as such in the table of contents. Moreover, the crosses and check-marks scattered through the text of three of the poems, 'Second Advice', 'The Loyal Scot', and 'Upon his Majesties being made free of the Citty', indicate passages in which the text published in *POAS* 1689 and 1697 differs from the text of the manuscript at hand. Though Lord uses the 'textual authority' of these marks to eliminate lines 115–236 of 'The Loyal Scot' from his edition entirely, the marks simply indicate the absence of these lines from *POAS* 1697. Crosses next to thirteen other lines in 'The Loyal Scot' indicate further discrepancies from the text of *POAS* 1697, and in all these cases the text of Thompson, volume III (already printed when he wrote his preface to volume I), follows *POAS* 1697 exactly.

The conclusion is inevitable: the marks were made by someone who checked the MS. against one or more editions of *POAS*, and that person was Thompson. The first four of the poems not marked with crosses are printed in the preface to Thompson's edition, along with the Latin version of 'Upon Blood's Attempt to Steale the Crown'; in the Bodleian MS., there is a cross next to the English version of the epigram and none next to the Latin version. Thompson's having singled out precisely those poems not marked with a cross in Eng. poet. d. 49 strongly suggests that he was responsible for marking some poems and not others. A note on the two 'Advices' in Thompson's preface and further notes to 'The Chequer Inn' and 'Upon the Cutting of Sir John Coventry's Nose' show that he compared the text of these four satires with the text as printed in two separate editions of *POAS*, 1697 and 1704. I would therefore conclude that when Thompson received the manuscript, after the body of his edition was 'finished in the press', he hastily marked the MS. to indicate which poems had already been published and included in his preface texts of poems 'never before published' or not previously identified as Marvell's. The general atmosphere of confusion which surrounds Thompson's editing – for example, he attributed several eighteenth-century poems to Marvell and accepted all attributions, either in *POAS* or in manuscripts, without question – is a sufficient explanation of any anomalies which may exist.

If my interpretation of the cross-marks is correct, the authority of Bodleian MS. Eng. poet. d. 49 in fixing the canon of Marvell's satires is greatly lessened. The presence or absence of cross-marks has no bearing on the question of authenticity, and the only distinction the MS. makes between 'The Doctor Turn'd Justice' (for which there is not a scrap of supporting evidence) and 'Last Instructions' (for which there is considerable supporting evidence) is that one was printed in *POAS* and one was not. If the compiler, whether Popple or an anonymous Whig of 1697–1704, was sometimes right in assigning poems to Marvell and sometimes demonstrably wrong (as with 'Upon the Cutting of Sir John Coventry's Nose', 'The Doctor Turn'd Justice', and 'On the Monument'), then he cannot be relied upon to any greater degree than the compilers of any of the dozens of extant manuscript miscellanies of the period.

This revaluation of the physical evidence of Eng. poet. d. 49 has immediate bearing on the authorship of the following poems: 'Scaevola Scoto-Britannus', 'The Loyal Scot', 'Second Advice', 'Third Advice', 'Further Advice', and the epigrams 'Upon his House' and 'Upon his Grand-Children'. Lord's doubts about the first two are unjustified, while the case for the second two is materially weakened once we accept that the crosses are not authenticating marks. As for the last three, which Lord rejects because they are not included in Eng. poet. d. 49, their authenticity is indeed doubtful, but not for the reasons Lord suggests.

'Scaevola Scoto-Britannus', challenged by Lord because it lacks the distinguishing cross, is unquestionably authentic: it is attributed to Marvell in British Library MS. Add. 34362 and it bears close stylistic and thematic parallels to his other poems, Latin and English. 'Scaevola Scoto-Britannus', like eleven of Marvell's fifteen other Latin poems, is composed in elegiac couplets, full of puns and verbal antitheses. Like *The Rehearsal Transpros'd* and the epigram on Blood, the poem is an attack on politically ambitious bishops, presenting rebellion as the 'unavoidable' (*RT*, ii, p. 240) consequence of pride and oppression. The conceits in which the rebellious Scot James Mitchell, undergoing torture, is presented as calm and unmoved, a spectator at the drama of his own dismemberment, offering his foot to the torturer as to a shoemaker (lines 15–22), are reminiscent of the lines in the 'Horatian Ode' describing the behaviour of Charles I on the '*Tragick Scaffold*'.

There is no question about Marvell's authorship of some version of 'The Loyal Scot', since the poem is attributed to him in several independent sources, listed in Margoliouth, and large parts of it are based on a passage in the undoubtedly authentic 'Last Instructions'; thus, unless another author plagiarized Marvell's work, the two poems must have a single author. The problem here concerns a portion of the poem, a lengthy attack on the Anglican hierarchy, missing from the two earliest published versions, *Chorus Poetarum* 1694 and *POAS* 1697. Though the anti-prelatical additions found in four MSS. and one printed text may be digressive, an element of anti-clerical satire is essential to the shorter versions as well: lines 115–236 simply expand an earlier twenty-two lines attacking the worldliness of the 'state divines' (lines 146) with some spirited invective in the manner of Cleveland's 'The Rebel Scot'. Transitional passages explicitly link the anti-clerical passages in both versions with the beginning and end of the poem, stressing the contrast of national unity and divisiveness. The initial occasion of the poem was a proposed act of union between England and Scotland, under debate in Parliament in 1670. Internal evidence suggests a date of 1674 for the expanded version, after Marvell's satire on clerical pride and ambition in *The Rehearsal Transpros'd* (1672 and 1673) and before he returned to the same theme in *Mr. Smirke* and *A Short Historical Essay* (1676). Though both Margoliouth and Lord have expressed doubts about the additions, the strong probability is that both the shorter and the longer versions are authentic.

The evidence for Marvell's authorship of 'Second Advice' and 'Third Advice', both claimed for him by Lord, is inconclusive. Alleged parallels in style and imagery, as Ephim Fogel points out in his rejoinder to Lord, are commonplaces familiar to any schoolboy of the period, and the similarities in political position and objects of attack can be explained in terms of Country Party politics. Of the four contemporary attributions of these poems to Marvell, the one carrying most conviction, because of its early date and because of the general reliability of its annotations and textual corrections, is that on the title-page of Bodleian MS. Gough London 14, a copy of *Directions to a Painter*, a volume containing the four 'Advices' published in 1667. But neither it nor any of the other three specifically singles out 'Second Advice' and 'Third Advice', distinguishing them from the later poems in the series, 'Fourth Advice' and 'Fifth Advice', which Margoliouth has shown convincingly not to be Marvell's. The authorship of 'Second Advice' and 'Third Advice' must still be considered uncertain.[4]

'Upon his House' and 'Upon his Grand-Children', two epigrams attacking Clarendon printed as Marvell's by Margoliouth, can be confidently rejected as inauthentic, while the authorship of 'Further Advice', also included in Margoliouth's edition, is uncertain. 'Upon his House' (found in one MS. and in *POAS* 1697, with no indication of authorship) was first printed as Marvell's in Cooke's edition of 1726 and 'Upon his Grand-Children' (found in four MSS, unattributed, but not in *POAS*) first assigned to Marvell in Grosart's edition of 1872; neither editor cites any authority for the attribution, other than the inclusion of the poems in the *Directions* volume (1667), where they follow 'Clarindon's House-Warming'. The accusations against Clarendon in 'Upon his House' are commonplace, occurring in such contemporary verse satires as 'Vox & Lachrymae Anglorum', numerous pamphlets, and speeches delivered in Parliament during impeachment proceedings. Indeed, two of the charges in 'Upon his House', that Clarendon failed sufficiently to reward the Old Cavaliers and that he made an inglorious peace with Holland, are inconsistent with Marvell's known views as expressed elsewhere. Since there is neither external nor internal evidence supporting Marvell's authorship, both poems can be excluded from the canon.

In the case of 'Further Advice', there is no reliable direct evidence that Marvell wrote the poem, since the attributions to him in *POAS* 1697 and National Library of Scotland MS. Advocate 19.1.12 can both be discounted. Advocate 19.1.12, described by Lord as 'generally unreliable' (*POAS*, ed. Lord, p. 214), attributes three 'painter' poems to Marvell; since two of them, 'Fourth Advice' and 'Advice to a Painter to Draw the Duke by' are definitely inauthentic, the third attribution must be treated with suspicion.

Margoliouth points out one parallel: the attack in the last eighteen lines of the poem on 'the five recanters of the Hous' (line 49), who in the words of Marvell's letter to Popple of 28 November 1670 'openly took leave of their former Party, and fell to head the King's Busyness' (*Poems and Letters*, ed. Margoliouth, I, 376–8; II, 318). But despite the naming of Sir Edward Seymour, Sir Robert Howard, and Sir Richard Temple as turn-coats in both poem and letter, I would still consider Marvell's authorship doubtful. The apostasy of Seymour and the others was after all public knowledge and would be likely to come under attack from any of Marvell's allies in the Country Party opposition. There is another argument, admit-tedly subjective, against Marvell's authorship: where each of Marvell's satires which can be shown to be authentic is characterized by a unity of conception, a use of rhetorical and metaphorical patterning, 'Further Advice', in contrast, can be described as a fragment of sixty-odd lines, with no overall form and no dimension beyond the immediate.

Like 'The Loyal Scot', 'The Kings Vowes' exists in several different versions, and one needs to ask which versions, if any, Marvell is responsible for. Margoliouth includes several stanzas which can be shown to be by an author other than Marvell, and the version printed in *POAS* 1697 is demonstrably inauthentic. An early complete text, found in British Library MS. Add. 18220, contains eleven stanzas and a six-line introduction. Essentially the same text appears in two other MSS., Add. 29497 and Yale MS. Osborn f.b. 140, and in an early printed edition, *A Prophetick Lampoon (PL)*. Topical references and annotations in two of the MSS. confirm a date of 1669–70 for this eleven-stanza version: Add. 18220 is dated 20 May 1670, and a copy of *PL* cited by Margoliouth bears the date 2 February 1668/9. There are three shorter texts of the poem among the Yale MSS: Osborn b. 54, in six stanzas, dated 1667, and two separate versions included in Osborn b. 52/1, one in nine and one in ten stanzas. Except for the additions, the order of stanzas is the same in the nine, ten, and eleven-stanza versions. The nine and ten-stanza texts evidently repre-sent earlier states of the poem, written between 1667 and 1669; stanza VII ('I will have a fine son'), missing in the nine-stanza version, refers to events of September 1668, while stanza VI, missing in both, refers to the rebuilding of London after 1667. It is uncertain whether Osborn b. 54 represents the earliest version of the poem or an incomplete, defective text; its many inferior readings (e.g., in the penultimate line, 'Where the Drake shall the Duke with freedome enjoy', obscuring the line's political point) suggest the latter.

An expanded version of the poem, with four additional stanzas and some rearrangement of the order of the other stanzas, appears in Eng. poet. d. 49 and in a second 'Nettleton' MS., now no longer extant but known to be of eighteenth-century origin, quoted by Thompson in his edition (*Works*, ed. Thompson, I, vi–vii). The reference to the Dutch War in stanza v suggests a date of 1672 or after. Three passages were then added to the poem later. A stanza on the attack by the King's Life Guards on Sir John Coventry was added sometime after December 1670, when the assault took place. Three further stanzas concerning the Earl of Danby and a fourth stanza on Nell Gwynne were added in 1675; every text I have seen which includes the Coventry stanza – Add. 34362, *POAS* 1697, and several MSS. deriving from *POAS* 1697 – also contain these stanzas, but they are evidently of a later date, after the attempt to impeach Danby in 1675. Finally, *POAS* 1697 and the related MSS. include a variant of stanza IV rewritten to refer to the Duke of York rather than Clarendon. This stanza explicitly treats the Exclusion Bill crisis of 1679–81 and thus must have been written after Marvell's death.[5]

Attributions to Marvell in *POAS* 1697 and to the Duke of Buckingham in *PL* and Add. 29497 can be discounted. Both title and date of *PL* are fictitious: *A Prophetick Lampoon, Made Anno 1659, By his Grace George Duke of Buckingham: Relating to what would happen to the Government under King Charles II.* The prophecy is obviously *ex post facto*, and Buckingham's authorship is made more improbable by the attack on him in stanza XIII ('Of my Pimp, I will make my *Ministre premier*'). In 1668–70, Buckingham was a prominent member of the Cabal government and did not go into opposition until several years later. An attribution to Charles Sackville, Lord Buckhurst (later the Earl of Dorset) in Osborn b. 54, the six-stanza version, is more plausible, especially since the compiler of this manuscript, a commonplace book of 1677, attempts to date works and assign authorship with some care ('though not always accurately: 'mannerly obscene', line 61 in Rochester's 'An Allusion to Horace', becomes a reference to a poet named Mannerly). During the period 1667–70 Buckhurst was very much in royal favour, and indeed he is attacked in *Flagellum Parliamentarium* (1672) as a corrupt court pensioner. While the attitude toward politics generally expressed in Buckhurst's verse is an aristocratic disdain, 'The Kings Vowes', in contrast, is a partisan political satire attacking authoritarian principles of government, expressing views similar to those in Marvell's letters to Popple and his other poems written during this period.

The many variant versions of the poem suggest that it grew by accretion, with additions by several different authors. But in its early form, in nine, ten, or eleven stanzas, the poem is clearly organized and coherent: the first six stanzas survey the political institutions of England, all according to the poet rendered ineffective, where the last three stanzas associate the unbridled pursuit of sexual pleasure with arbitrary government.[6] As in Marvell's 'Mock Speech' (1675), which similarly adopts the persona of the King, the author makes his points by witty indirection, allowing the speaker to convict himself out of his own mouth. The repeated 'I will' not only serves as refrain, but suggests that the weakness in a system of arbitrary monarchy is precisely its reliance on the unrestrained 'will' of the monarch: all institutions which might otherwise provide 'a controll' (Parliament, the clerical hierarchy, the Privy Council, the Exchequer) are perverted to serve the monarch's desires, all 'consciences' of those who seek their own advancement are 'flexible to my commands' (lines 14, 34). The note of petulance in the repetition of 'I will' perfectly catches the character of a monarch who has learned nothing from his exile other than that once his 'Stomach' were no longer 'empty' (line 3), none of his desires should ever be frustrated. Though the poem never states the principles of responsible government against which Charles's imagined words are measured, they are implicit throughout.

There is thus no inherent improbability in Marvell's authorship of an early version of 'The Kings Vowes' written in 1668–70: the verdict must be 'authorship unknown; possibly Marvell's'. The later additions, on the other hand, are unlikely to be Marvell's work, and some of them are definitely inauthentic. Of the four stanzas added in 1672, two are irregular metrically and unclear in their wording: the questionable scansion of such lines as 'Miss and I will both learn to live on exhibition' (line 44) might suggest a different author. In general, however, the stanzas added in Eng. poet. d. 49 are compatible with the earlier poem, both in style and in political attitude, though they accuse Charles II of weakness and incompetence rather than tyranny. The stanza on Sir John Coventry, unlike these stanzas, differs sharply from the earlier version in tone, eschewing irony for direct attack. There is no reason to assign this stanza to Marvell: the incident described was a *cause célèbre*, commonly cited by contemporaries as an example of royal misrule. The lines on Danby and Nell Gwynne exist in two versions, and are inauthentic in both. Stylistic considerations rule out Marvell's authorship for the lines as they appear in Add. 34362. The metre is a a clumsy iambic pentameter, where the rest of the poem is in anapaestic tetrameter:

> Some one I will advance from mean descent,
> So high that he shall brave the Parliament,
> And all their bills for publike good prevent.

These lines are as anomalous politically and aesthetically as they are metrically: they direct their attack primarily on a person other than the King and they ignore the decorum of speaker, putting a Country Party oration in Charles's mouth. In *POAS* 1697, the four stanzas are rewritten to accord better with the prevailing metre of the rest of the poem:

> Some one I'll advance from a common Descent,
> So high, that he shall hector the Parliament,
> And all wholsom Laws for the Publick prevent.

But the late date of the *POAS* version of 'The Kings Vowes' and its many dubious emendations throughout the poem suggest that the rewritten passage is no less inauthentic; without exception, the *POAS* variants in other passages are inferior readings to the text as found in the earlier MSS.

NOTES

1. 'An Horatian Ode upon Cromwel's Return from Ireland', in *The Poems and Letters of Andrew Marvell*, ed. H. M. Margoliouth, rev. Pierre Legouis and E. E. Duncan-Jones, 3rd edn (2 vols., Oxford, 1972). Marvell's satires have been edited by George de F. Lord in *Andrew Marvell, Complete Poetry* (New York, 1968), and in *Poems on Affairs of State: Augustan Satirical Verse, 1660–1714*, 1: *1660–1678* (New Haven and London, 1963). I have consulted Lord's texts for the satires, sometimes adopting his readings in preference to those of Margoliouth.

2. *The Reason of Church-Government*, in *Complete Prose Works of John Milton* ed. D. M. Wolfe *et al.* (8 vols., New Haven and London, 1953–), 1, 821–2; subsequent references will be to *CPW*.

3. *CPW*, 1, 822: Sonnet vii ('How soon hath time'), line 14, in *Poetical Works of John Milton*, ed. Helen Darbishire (2 vols., Oxford, 1965).

4. See Zera S. Fink, *The Classical Republicans* (Evanston, Ill., 1945), p. 85; and Norman Mailer, *The Armies of the Night* (New York, 1968).

5. *The First Anniversary of the Government Under His Highness The Lord Protector*, lines 131–42 (title from *Complete Poetry*, ed. Lord).

6. There is some doubt about the authenticity of 'Tom May's Death'. Lord classifies the poem as 'of doubtful authorship' because of its exclusion from Bodleian MS. Eng. poet. d. 49; see the introduction to his edition, p. xxxii. My own view is that the poem is demonstrably Marvell's; for further discussion, see chapter 5 and the Appendix.

7. Andrew Marvell, *The Rehearsal Transpros'd* and *The Rehearsal Transpros'd; The Second Part*, ed. D. I. B. Smith (Oxford, 1971), p. 231; subsequent references will be to *RT*, 1, and *RT*, 11.

8. See, e.g., M. C. Bradbrook and M. G. Lloyd Thomas, *Andrew Marvell*, 2nd edn (Cambridge, 1961), pp. 84–5, 89; and Patrick Cruttwell, *The Shakespearean Moment* (New York, 1960), pp. 185–207. Essays by Barbara Everett and Joseph Summers have challenged the conventional assumption that Marvell's lyrics date from the years before the Restoration; as they point out, few of his poems can be dated with any precision, and those poems, mostly occasional, which can be assigned dates do not suggest a simple bifurcation of 'early' and 'late' Marvell.

See 'The shooting of the bears: poetry and politics in Andrew Marvell', in *Andrew Marvell: Essays on the tercentenary of his death*, ed. R. L. Brett (Hull and Oxford, 1979), pp. 63–4; and 'Andrew Marvell: private taste and public judgement', in *Metaphysical Poetry*, ed. D. J. Palmer and Malcolm Bradbury (Stratford-upon-Avon Studies, 11, 1970), pp. 185–6. Yet Marvell speaks of his own career as changing direction after 1657 (*RT*, II, p. 203); recently discovered letters show him 'to have been continuously employed in the service of the state from his appointment as Thurloe's secretary to his death as M.P. for Hull thirty-one years later' (Hilton Kelliher, 'Some uncollected letters of Andrew Marvell', *British Library Journal*, 5 (1979), 149).

9. J. M. Wallace, *Destiny His Choice: The Loyalism of Andrew Marvell* (Cambridge, 1968). Several critics have attempted an overall, synoptic view of Marvell's career: I would single out as particularly useful George de F. Lord, 'From contemplation to action: Marvell's poetical career', in *Andrew Marvell: A Collection of Critical Essays*, ed. George de F. Lord (Englewood Cliffs, N.J., 1968), pp. 55–73; Christopher Hill, 'Society and Andrew Marvell', in *Puritanism and Revolution* (London, 1958); and Isabel Rivers, *The Poetry of Conservatism, 1608–1745: A Study of Poets and Public Affairs from Jonson to Pope*, (London, 1973). Annabel M. Patterson, *Marvell and the Civic Crown* (Princeton, 1978), provides a valuable corrective to Wallace, though she is more concerned with rhetorical traditions than with the political context of the poems.

10. Wallace, *Destiny*, pp. 74–5, 81, and chapters two and three *passim*.

11. *Ibid.*, pp. 146, 182–3, 230. Donal Smith, in 'The political beliefs of Andrew Marvell', *University of Toronto Quarterly*, 36 (1966), 55–67, seems to me similarly to distort Marvell's views. By wrenching passages from Marvell's prose out of context, Smith purports to prove that Marvell believed in royal prerogative, disapproved of rebellion in any form, and believed that 'an independent and impartial monarch was the first essential for the real functioning of government' (p. 66). Smith's thesis that Marvell was essentially an independent Trimmer rather than a Whig seems to me an oversimplification, which does not pay sufficient attention to the complexities of late seventeenth-century politics and the individual circumstances of Marvell's works.

12. Caroline Robbins, *The Eighteenth-Century Commonwealthsman* (Cambridge, Mass., 1959), p. 52. See also the account of Marvell's *Growth of Popery* in David Ogg, *England in the Reign of Charles II*, 2nd edn (2 vols., London, 1956), II, pp. 541–2.

13. Wallace, *Destiny*, p. 146.

14. Milton, *Of Education*, *CPW*, II, 405.

15. John S. Coolidge, in 'Martin Marprelate, Marvell, and *Decorum Personae* as a satirical theme', *PMLA*, 74 (1959), 526–32, points out a

source for Marvell's satiric strategy and concept of decorum in the Marprelate pamphlets; see also Thomas Kranidas, *The Fierce Equation* (The Hague, 1965), pp. 49–82, for a full discussion of the contrast between 'inner' and 'outward' decorum in Milton's prose writings.

16. Cf. Dryden, 'Discourse concerning satire', *Of Dramatic Poesy and other Critical Essays*, ed. George Watson (2 vols., London, 1962), II, 125–6 (subsequent references will be to *Essays*); and Pope, *The First Satire of the Second Book of Horace*, lines 69–76; *An Epistle to Dr. Arbuthnot*, lines 151–6; both in *The Poems of Alexander Pope*, ed. John Butt, one-volume edn (New Haven, 1963); (subsequent references will be to *Poems*).

17. Dryden, 'Discourse concerning satire', pp. 126–7.

18. Pope, *Epilogue to the Satire: Dialogue II*, lines 197–204, in *Poems*.

19. John Locke, *Two Treatises of Government*, II, ch. xix, par. 224, ed. Peter Laslett (Cambridge, 1960, 2nd edn 1967).

20. 'Tom May's Death', line 30; 'A Dialogue between the Resolved Soul, and Created Pleasure', line 47 (hereafter referred to as 'Resolved Soul'). Roman Catholic doctrine is parodied wittily throughout 'Fleckno' and attacked directly in *The Growth of Popery* as 'a compound of...absurdityes...compiled of Terrours to the Phansy, Contradictions to Sense, and Impositions on the Understanding' (pp. 5–7).

21. Andrew Marvell, *A Short Historical Essay touching General Councils, Creeds, and Impositions in Matters of Religion* (London, 1680), p. 19.

22. Milton, *Animadversions*, *CPW*, I, 663–4.

23. 'Upon Appleton House', line 561; 'The Garden', lines 12, 16; 'Tom May's Death', line 66; letter to William Popple, 15 July 1676, quoting Marvell's letter to Herbert Croft, *Poems and Letters*, ed. Margoliouth, II, 347.

2. POWER AND CONSCIENCE:
MARVELL AND THE ENGLISH REVOLUTION

1. Joseph Mazzeo, 'Cromwell as Machiavellian Prince in Marvell's "An Horatian Ode"', *Renaissance and Seventeenth-Century Studies* (New York and London, 1964), pp. 166–82.

2. In this respect, Machiavelli is at one with Hobbes, for whom 'power' is a central term both in his ethics and in his political theory. The attitude of Marchamont Nedham's tract, *The Case of the Commonwealth of England, Stated* (London, 1650), differs from that of Marvell in that it expresses a Machiavellian realism unmixed with regret. Nedham's arguments for acceptance of Cromwell's rule are entirely prudential: 'It is a more current way of perswasion, by telling men

what will be *profitable* and *convenient* for them to do, than what they ought to doe' (Sig. A 3ᵛ). Cromwell may rule by naked power alone, but, Nedham argues, 'the Power of the *Sword* is, and ever hath been, the Foundation of all Titles to Government' (chapter heading, part I, chapter 2).

3. Yeats, 'The Gyres', line 12, in *The Collected Poems of W. B. Yeats* (New York, 1951).

4. Milton, Sonnet VII ('How soon hath Time'), lines 9–10.

5. W. H. Auden, 'Spain', lines 103–4, in *Poetry of the Thirties*, ed. Robin Skelton (Harmondsworth, 1964).

6. See John S. Coolidge, 'Marvell and Horace', in *Andrew Marvell: A Collection of Critical Essays*, ed. Lord, p. 98; R. H. Syfret, 'Marvell's "Horatian Ode"', *Review of English Studies*, 12 (1961), 160, 168; and Cleanth Brooks, 'Marvell's "Horatian Ode"', in *Andrew Marvell*, ed. John Carey (Harmondsworth, 1969), pp. 191–2.

7. For a clear exposition of the theory of the mixed state and an account of its popularity in seventeenth-century England, see Fink, *The Classical Republicans*, esp. pp. 1–27.

8. Thomas Hobbes, *Leviathan*, XIII, ed. Michael Oakeshott (Oxford and New York, 1960), p. 81.

9. Several earlier studies emphasize the thematic unity of Marvell's major poems. John Creaser, in 'Marvell's effortless superiority', *Essays in Criticism*, 20 (1970), 403–23, finds as a recurrent theme in Marvell's poems 'the myth of the Fall...mortality and alienation'; see also Ann E. Berthoff, *The Resolved Soul* (Princeton, 1970), pp. 3–6; the essay by the editor in *Approaches to Marvell*, ed. C. A. Patrides (London, 1978), p. 41; and, with particular attention to 'The Nymph complaining', Ruth Nevo, 'Marvell's "Songs of Innocence and Experience"', *Studies in English Literature*, 5 (1965), 1–21.

10. 'The Mower's Song', lines 1–2; 'The Mower to the Glo-Worms', 15–16; 'The Mower's Song', line 15; 'Damon the Mower', line 74; 'The Mower's Song', line 22; 'The Garden', lines 63–4.

11. *Paradise Lost*, XI, lines 814–17; Seneca, *De Otio, Moral Essays*, tr. John W. Basore (London and Cambridge, Mass., 1935), II, 186–7: 'Si res publica corruptior est quam ut adiuvari possit, si occupata est malis, non nitetur sapiens in supervacuum nec se nigil profuturus impendet.'

12. Barbara Lewalski argues for a tradition of Protestant meditation in which 'application to the self' is explicit, but the formula should not be applied too literally; see *Donne's Anniversaries and the Poetry of Praise: The Creation of a Symbolic Mode* (Princeton, 1973); and 'Marvell as religious poet', in *Approaches to Marvell*, ed. Patrides, p. 262.

13. Joseph Hall, *Occasional Meditations*, 3rd edn (London, 1633), Proem,

Sig. A7–A7ᵛ. For the view in Renaissance Platonism of the imagination as 'intermediate' between sense and reason, see Gianfrancesco Pico della Mirandola, *De Imaginatione*, tr. H. Caplan (New Haven, 1930), p. 41; and Ralph Cudworth, *A Treatise concerning Eternal and Immutable Morality*, appended to *The True Intellectual System of the Universe* (3 vols., London, 1845), III, 614–15.

14. Cudworth, *Treatise*, III, 564, 566. There are interesting discussions of Cudworth's epistemology in Noam Chomsky, *Cartesian Linguistics* (New York, 1966), pp. 67–70; and J. A. Passmore, *Ralph Cudworth, An Interpretation* (Cambridge, 1951), pp. 19–39.

15. St Ignatius of Loyola, *Spiritual Exercises*, quoted in Louis L. Martz, *The Poetry of Meditation* (New Haven, 1954), p. 27.

16. I am not counting five first-person-singular pronouns in the speech of the nun in section two, since there the nun is speaking, not the poem's narrator. For an excellent commentary on this section of the poem, see Rosalie L. Colie, *My Ecchoing Song: Andrew Marvell's Poetry of Criticism* (Princeton, 1970).

17. 'Rom. Cap. 9. ver. 19' ('And do they so'), lines 11ff., in *The Works of Henry Vaughan*, ed. L. C. Martin (Oxford, 1967); cf. Herbert, 'Affliction', (I), lines 57–60 in *The Works of George Herbert*, ed. F. E. Hutchinson (Oxford, 1941).

18. See Maren-Sofie Røstvig, *The Happy Man: Studies in the Metamorphoses of a Classical Ideal*, vol. I: *1600–1700*, 2nd edn (Oslo, 1962), pp. 153–4, 183–5. Røstvig seems to me to overestimate the Hermetic element in 'Upon Appleton House', interpreting the poem almost exclusively in esoteric terms, but Fairfax's interest in Hermetism is well documented.

19. 'Spring and Fall: to a young child' (lines 10–11), in *The Poems of Gerard Manley Hopkins*, ed. W. H. Gardner and N. H. Mackenzie, 4th edn (London, 1967).

20. 'Horatian Ode', lines 24, 34; Henry Fielding, Preface to *Miscellanies*, ed. Henry Knight Miller (2 vols., Oxford, 1972), I, 10–13. For a useful discusion of differing contemporary views of 'the problem of Cromwell', see Ruth Nevo, *The Dial of Virtue* (Princeton, 1963), pp. 74–137.

21. Anthony Ascham, *Of the Confusions and Revolutions of Governments* (London, 1649), p. 102. This and other tracts are discussed in Wallace, *Destiny*, pp. 30ff.; and Quentin Skinner, 'The ideological context of Hobbes's political thought', *Historical Journal*, 9 (1966), 303–17.

22. Rivers, *The Poetry of Conservatism*, pp. 109–16. Other critics who treat the poem's religious dimensions in some depth include Mazzeo, 'Cromwell as Davidic King', *Renaissance and Seventeenth-Century Studies*, pp. 183–208; and Steven Zwicker, 'Models of governance in Marvell's "The First Anniversary"', *Criticism*, 16 (1974), 1–12.

23. 'Tantis incoeptis, tantis vertutibus, non adfuisse perseverantiam dolebit;

ingentem gloriae segetem, & maximarum rerum gerendarum materiam praebitam videbit, sed materiae defuisse viros...Qui liberi igitur vultis permanere, aut sapite imprimis, aut quamprimum resipiscite: si servire durum est, atque nolitis, rectae rationi obtemperare discite, vestrum esse compotes.' Latin text of *Defensio Secunda* from *The Works of John Milton* ed. F. A. Paterson, *et al.* (18 vols., New York, 1931–8), viii, 250, 254; tr. Helen North, in *CPW*, iv, part i, 684–5.

24. See *Writings and Speeches of Oliver Cromwell*, ed. W. C. Abbott (4 vols. Cambridge, Mass., 1937–47), iii, 437–8; and A. S. P. Woodhouse, ed., *Puritanism and Liberty*, 2nd edn (London, 1951).

25. 'Libertatis verae ac solidae...quae non foris, sed intus quaerenda' – *Defensio Secunda*, *Works*, viii, 130, tr., *CPW*, iv, part i, 624; Sonnet xii ('I did but prompt the age'), lines 8–12.

26. J. P. Kenyon, *The Stuart Constitution 1608–1687: Documents and Commentary* (Cambridge, 1966), p. 332.

27. Cromwell, *Writings and Speeches*, iii, 455.

28. Instrument of Government, par. 1, in Kenyon, *The Stuart Constitution*, p. 342.

29. Cromwell, *Writings and Speeches*, iii, 455.

30. 'Deserimur Cromuelle; tu solus superes, ad te rerum summa nostrarum rediit; in te solo consistit; insuperabili tuae virtuti cedimus cuncti, nemini vel obloquente, nisi qui aut aequales inaequalis ipse honores sibi quaerit, aut digniori concessos invidet, aut non intelligit nihil esse in societate hominum magis vel Deo gratum, vel rationi consentaneum, esse in civitate nihil aequius, nihil utilius, quam potiri rerum dignissimum' (*Works*, viii 222; tr. *CPW* iv, part i, 671–2).

31. *A True State of the Case of the Commonwealth* (London, 1654), p. 30. The probable author of this pamphlet is Marchamont Nedham.

32. Wallace, *Destiny*, pp. 106–44. A view of the poem as 'propaganda' for the Protectorate constitutional settlement is argued in Rivers, *The Poetry of Conservatism*, pp. 110–11; and A. J. N. Wilson, 'Andrew Marvell's "The First Anniversary of the Government under Oliver Cromwell": the poem and its frame of reference', *Modern Language Review*, 69 (1974), 254–5.

33. On Marvell's use of Old Testament analogies to argue the case against kingship, see Zwicker, 'Models of Governance', pp. 2–5; and Patterson, *Marvell and the Civic Crown*, pp. 81–8.

34. James Harrington, *The Commonwealth of Oceana* (London, 1656), p. 190; cf. Fink, *The Classical Republicans*, pp. 68–71.

35. I have used the translation of William A. McQueen and Kiffin A. Rockwell, *The Latin Poetry of Andrew Marvell* (Chapel Hill, 1964), with my own revised version of lines 2 and 101.

36. Lines 143–4, an obscure couplet whose text may be corrupt, seems to warn the parliament not to refuse an advantageous offer of peace from

the Dutch: 'Unless our Senate, lest their Youth disuse, / The War, (but who would) Peace if begg'd refuse.' The army evidently favoured a peace settlement, if one on favourable terms could be obtained, and the ill-feeling between Parliament and the army was in part due to their differing views on the war; see Samuel R. Gardiner, *History of the Commonwealth and Protectorate 1649–1656* (4 vols., London, 1894–1901), II, 142–4, 164.

37. Christopher Hill, *The Century of Revolution 1603–1714* (New York, 1966), p. 136; cf. Kenyon, *The Stuart Constitution*, pp. 334–5.

38. Title and text of 'Poem upon the Death' are from *Complete Poetry*, ed. Lord.

3. IN THE ARENA

1. They were actually published 'with no other than a mercenary View' by Marvell's former landlady and two of his friends, as part of a somewhat unsavoury plot to regain £500 which had been deposited in Marvell's name before his death. See *The Works of Andrew Marvell, Esq.*, ed. Thomas Cooke (2 vols., London, 1726), I, 36; and Bradbrook and Lloyd Thomas, *Andrew Marvell*, pp. 145–8.

2. *Works*, ed. Cooke, I, 3, 15, Cf. *The Works of Andrew Marvell, Esq. Poetical, Controversial, and Political*, ed. Edward Thompson (3 vols., London, 1776), II, 5.

3. The 1697 edition of *Poems on Affairs of State* (*POAS*) contains twelve satires attributed to 'A. Marvell, Esq.', making up a self-contained unit of roughly seventy pages. The *POAS* attributions are notoriously unreliable but they attest to Marvell's contemporary reputation as a satirist.

4. *Poems on Affairs of State: From The Time of Oliver Cromwell, to the Abdication of K. James the Second* (London, 1697), Sig. A3–A5.

5. The poem, which initially appeared in *POAS* (1697), is printed in *Poems on Affairs of State: Augustan Satirical Verse, 1660–1714*, I: *1660–1678*, ed. Lord, pp. 436–7; subsequent references will be to *POAS*, ed. Lord.

6. See Caroline Robbins, 'A critical study of the political activities of Andrew Marvell', unpublished Ph.D. thesis, University of London, 1926, p. 4; and K. D. H. Haley, *The First Earl of Shaftesbury* (Oxford, 1968), p. 185. Miss Robbins's study remains the best account of Marvell's political career, and I am indebted to it throughout this chapter.

7. In addition to 'Last Instructions' and 'Clarindon's House-Warming', both accepted by Margoliouth, four other poems attacking Clarendon have been attributed to Marvell, but these may be inauthentic. Lord presents arguments (which I do not find convincing) in favour of Marvell's authorship of 'Second Advice to a Painter' and 'Third

Advice to a Painter', two anti-Clarendon satires, in 'Two New Poems by Marvell?', *Evidence for Authorship*, ed. David V. Erdman and Ephim G. Fogel (Ithaca, 1966), pp. 25–44; and Marvell, *Complete Poetry*, ed. Lord, p. xxxii.

8. Letters to William Popple, 21 March 1670 and 14 April 1670, in *Poems and Letters*, ed. Margoliouth, II, 315, 317.

9. 'The Kings Vowes', lines 46–51 (text from *Complete Poetry*, ed. Lord); 'A Dialogue between the two Horses', lines 157–8 (text from *Poems and Letters*, ed. Margoliouth). Lord has shown 'A Dialogue between the two Horses' to be inauthentic (*POAS*, ed. Lord, 274–5), pointing out that the only ascription to Marvell occurs in *POAS* 1697 and its successors (which contain such wild and muddled guesses as 'said to be written by Sir John Denham, but believed to be writ by Mr. Milton' for all four 'Advices to a Painter' or the attribution of 'Oceana and Britannia' (1681) to Marvell, who had died three years earlier). We can state as a general rule that attribution to Marvell in early editions of *POAS* constitutes no evidence whatever that Marvell wrote a particular poem. The case of 'The Kings Vowes' is more complex. The poem appears to have grown by accretion, with stanzas added at different times by different authors. But it is likely that the earliest versions of the poem, in nine, ten, or eleven stanzas, are by Marvell. (For further discussion, see the Appendix.)

10. 'Upon his Majesties being made free of the Citty', lines 24, 100–2, 60 (text from *Complete Poetry*, ed. Lord; title from *Poems and Letters*, ed. Margoliouth); letter of 24 January 1671, *Poems and Letters*, ed. Margoliouth, II, 322; 'Upon his Majesties being made free of the Citty', lines 7–9, 130–2.

11. See, e.g., 'A Charge to the Grand Inquest of England' (line 10) (1674), in *POAS* ed. Lord; 'The Duke of Buckingham's Litany', stanza XVII, in *POAS* (1704), III, 93; *A Common-place Book Out of the Rehearsal Transpros'd* (London, 1673), p. 12; 'A Letter from Amsterdam to a Friend in England', in *Calendar of State Papers, Domestic* (1678), p. 122; and Roger L'Estrange, *An Account of the Growth of Knavery, under the Pretended Fears of Arbitrary Government and Popery*, 2nd edn (London, 1681), pp. 3–5.

12. Marvell, *Remarks upon a late Disingenuous Discourse* (London, 1678), p. 40; 'Third Advice', lines 439–40 (text from *Complete Poetry*, ed. Lord).

13. Preface to *Absalom and Achitophel*, in *Poems of John Dryden*, ed. J. Kinsley (4 vols., Oxford, 1958), I, 216. (Subsequent references will be to *Poems*.)

14. Baldassare Castiglione, *The Courtyer*, tr. Sir Thomas Hoby (London, 1561), Sig. Zz2ᵛ. Cf. Patterson, *Marvell and the Civic Crown*, p. 117.

15. For a discussion of the constitutional issues involved, see Clayton

Roberts, *The Growth of Responsible Government in Stuart England* (Cambridge, 1966), pp. viii, 151–4.

16. 'Clarindon's House-Warming', lines 111–12 (text from *Complete Poetry*, ed. Lord).

17. See *POAS*, ed. Lord, pp. xxxii–xxxvii; and Pierre Legouis, *Andrew Marvell: Poet, Puritan, Patriot* (Oxford, 1965), pp. 160–2.

18. The 'Mock Speech', of which there are several MS versions, is printed in *POAS* (1704), III, 84–8. The text here (British Library MS Add. 34362), which differs in some details from the *POAS* version, is taken from Bradbrook and Lloyd Thomas, *Andrew Marvell*, pp. 125–7.

19. 'The Statue at Charing Cross', lines 39, 55–6 (text from *Complete Poetry*, ed. Lord). 'The Statue at Charing Cross', 'The Statue in Stocks-Market', and 'Upon his Majesties being made free of the Citty' are accepted as authentic by Margoliouth and Lord, and there is no reason to doubt their authenticity. 'The Statue at Charing Cross' is so close to Marvell's letter to Popple of 24 January 1675 in its details and in its analysis of Danby's policies that it can be considered a reworking of that letter: see *Poems and Letters*, ed. Margoliouth, II, 341–2; and 'The Statue at Charing Cross', lines 1–8, 17–24.

20. Caroline Robbins has pointed out that in *The Growth of Popery* Marvell showed political writers of later generations that parliamentary reporting could be used effectively as propaganda; see *The Eighteenth-Century Commonwealthsman* (Cambridge, Mass., 1959), p. 54; and see 'Political activities of Marvell', p. 2.

22. Nevo, *The Dial of Virtue*, p. 7.

23. 'The Loyal Scot', lines 239–44 (text from *Andrew Marvell, The Complete Poems*, ed. Elizabeth Story Donno, Harmondsworth, 1972).

24. Andrew Marvell, *Mr. Smirke; or, The Divine in Mode* (London, 1676), Sig. g3.

25. *Poems and Letters*, ed. Margoliouth, II, pp. 324–5. On the systematic use of bribery and influence, see Ogg, *England in the Reign of Charles II*, II, 529; and Andrew Browning, *Thomas Osborne, Earl of Danby and Duke of Leeds, 1632–1712* (Glasgow, 1951), *passim*. Several of the men Marvell praises as patriots in 'Last Instructions' accepted office or received large bribes a few years later, and became supporters of the government. The most celebrated anecdote about Marvell concerns his refusal of a bribe offered to him personally by Danby; see Legouis, *Andrew Marvell*, p. 120.

26. 'A Lampoon', line 6, in *The Penguin Book of Restoration Verse*, ed. Harold Love (Harmondsworth, 1968), p. 112. The term 'cheat' and references to marked cards, loaded dice, and other methods of cheating are ubiquitous in Marvell's treatment of 'the publick game' by Charles II's ministers: see, e.g., 'Last Instructions', lines 105–22, 179, 307–14, 367–8; *RT*, I, p. 126; and *Growth of Popery*, pp. 6, 11, 81, 155.

27. On the idea of a natural aristocracy in the political theory of Milton, James Harrington, and others, see Fink, *The Classical Republicans*, pp. 58–9, 96–7. C. B. Macpherson, *The Political Theory of Possessive Individualism* (Oxford, 1962), argues that seventeenth-century liberal political theory in England reflects the class bias of its authors in identifying freedom with the ownership of tangible property.

28. *RT*, Editor's introduction, p. xvii.

29. George Savile, Marquess of Halifax, 'A character of King Charles the Second', *Complete Works*, ed. J. P. Kenyon (Harmondsworth, 1969), p. 252.

30. *Halifax, Complete Works*, ed. Kenyon, p. 262; 'The History of Insipids', line 151, in *POAS*, ed. Lord, p. 251; 'A Satyr on Charles II', line 11 in *The Complete Poems of John Wilmot, Earl of Rochester*, ed. David M. Vieth (New Haven and London, 1968). 'Britannia and Raleigh', by Marvell's associate John Ayloffe, reaches republican conclusions which go beyond anything Marvell ever expresses ('Tyrants, like lep'rous kings, for public weal / Must be immur'd'), but its view of the dangers of absolutist counsels by the King's advisers ('I'th' sacred ear tyrannic arts they croak, / Pervert his mind, his good intentions choke') resembles that in 'Last Instructions' (lines 29–30, 148–9, in *POAS*, ed. Lord). On its authorship see *ibid.*, p. 228.

31. On the 'ethical proof', cf. *Mr. Smirke*, Sig. g2ᵛ: 'A great Skill of whatsover Orator is, to persuade the Auditory first that he himself is an honest and a fair man.'

32. Letter to William Popple, 24 July 1675, in *Poems and Letters*, ed. Margoliouth, II, 341. On Marvell's use of pictorial conventions in his satires, see Earl Miner, 'The "poetic picture, painted poetry" of *The Last Instructions to a Painter*', in *Andrew Marvell: A Collection*, ed. Lord, pp. 165–74; and Patterson, *Marvell and the Civic Crown*, pp. 111–74.

33. *RT*, I, p. 145. The source of the anecdote about Protogenes is Pliny, *Natural History*, XXXV, 10.

34. See Aristotle, *Poetics*, I, IV, V; and *Rhetoric*, I, 9. For a statement roughly contemporaneous with Marvell, cf. Dryden, Preface to *Annus Mirabilis*, *Essays*, I, 101.

35. Cf. Karl Marx, *Theses on Feuerbach*, XI.

36. 'The Statue at Charing Cross' and 'Upon his Majesties being made free of the Citty' are written in a similar 'low' style, with jog-trot metres imitating those of broadsheet ballads. Several other satires of the period which have been attributed to Marvell, 'A Ballad call'd the Chequer Inn', 'On the Cutting of Sir John Coventry's Nose', and 'The History of Insipids', resemble these Marvell poems in deliberately adopting a popular style, as well as in their attitude toward Charles II and toward parliamentary corruption. The first of these is probably and

the other two certainly by one of Marvell's political allies rather than by the poet himself. Though one MS. attributes 'The Chequer Inn' to Marvell, four attribute it to Henry Savile, whose political views accord with those expressed in the poem. There is no solid evidence linking Marvell to the poem on Coventry, and 'The History of Insipids' is by the Shaftesburian Whig John Freke: see Frank H. Ellis, 'John Freke and the History of Insipids', *Philological Quarterly*, 44 (1965), 472–83.

37. Smith, 'The political beliefs of Andrew Marvell', p. 63; Wallace, *Destiny*, p. 227 *et passim*; Robbins, 'Political activities of Marvell', p. 259. In a letter to me Miss Robbins has qualified her earlier statement, placing Marvell 'consistently in opposition' after 1666, but not earlier in the reign of Charles II; 'like nearly everyone else he at first distinguished Charles from the Cavaliers'.

38. *RT*, I, p. 44. See Maurice Lee, Jr, *The Cabal* (Urbana, 1965), pp. 186–7.

39. K. D. H. Haley, *William of Orange and the English Opposition 1672–1674* (Oxford, 1953), p. 106; *Poems and Letters*, ed. Margoliouth, II, 325; *Growth of Popery*, p. 16.

40. *Growth of Popery*, pp. 29, 35–6. Cf. 'The Statue in Stocks-Market', lines 25–6: 'This statue is surely more scandalous far / Than all the Dutch pictures that caused the war.'

41. Samuel Parker, *A Discourse of Ecclesiastical Politie* (London, 1669), p. 300.

42. Romans 13: 1–2. Cf. Michael Walzer, *The Revolution of the Saints* (London, 1966), pp. 76–86.

43. *State Tracts* (London, 1689), p. 2.

44. Haley, *William of Orange*, pp. 106, 166; *A Relation of the most material Matters handled in Parliament*, in *State Tracts*, pp. 26, 34. Marvell's connection with Du Moulin and his clandestine network was first revealed in Haley, *William of Orange*, pp. 57–63. Haley (p. 166) has argued that *A Relation* 'might conceivably have been [Marvell's] work'. The resemblance is striking to *The Growth of Popery*, which it anticipates in its documentary method, but there is no positive evidence that Marvell wrote the pamphlet; collaborative authorship is more likely.

45. Haley, *William of Orange*, p. 139. 'Advice to a Painter to Draw the Duke by', an attack on the Duke of York as the leader of the Catholic absolutist faction, is not by Marvell, but by Henry Savile; see *Poems and Letters*, ed. Margoliouth, I, p. 421. Lines 85–126 of 'Upon his Majesties being made free of the Citty' attack the Duke of York as seeking to 'advance / The government of *France*' and the Roman Catholic religion.

46. See Roberts, *Growth of Responsible Government*, p. 196; and Ogg, *England in the Reign of Charles II*, I, 369, 385-6.

47. Letter by Sir William Temple quoted in Haley, *William of Orange*, p. 135; cf. *Poems and Letters*, ed. Margoliouth, II, 341. The suppositious poems 'A Ballad call'd the Chequer Inn' and 'A Dialogue between the Two Horses' (the first possibly by Marvell, the second almost certainly not) attack Danby's wholesale bribery of Parliament members.

48. The passage quoted refers to Buckingham; for a similar passage on Shaftesbury, see *Growth of Popery*, p. 44, and cf. also *ibid.*, p. 72.

49. 'Fire-side' in this passage is a witty, tactful allusion to Charles II, and suggests the chief of the 'disadvantages' the Parliamentary opposition faced.

50. Roger L'Estrange, *The Parallel* (London, 1679), preface 'To the Reader' (not paginated).

51. J. G. A. Pocock, 'Machiavelli, Harrington, and English political ideologies in the eighteenth century', *William and Mary Quarterly*, ser. 3, 22 (1965), 558-67.

52. L'Estrange, *An Account of the Growth of Knavery*, p. 4. Shaftesbury and his allies organized pamphlet campaigns during the Exclusion Bill controversy; see J. R. Jones, *The First Whigs* (London, 1961), pp. 94-6, 159-61, 168-74.

53. Robbins, 'Political Activities of Marvell', pp. 240-1, 249-54.

54. *Growth of Popery*, p. 155; L'Estrange, *An Account of the Growth of Knavery*, p. 5.

55. *A Seasonable Argument*, in Andrew Browning, ed., *English Historical Documents, 1660-1714* (London, 1953), p. 240. *A Seasonable Argument* is a reworking of an earlier unpublished list, composed in 1672 and published in the nineteenth century under the title *Flagellum Parliamentarium* (Aungervyle Society Reprints, 1881). Arguments which strongly suggest that Marvell is the author of both *A Seasonable Argument* and *Flagellum Parliamentarium* are presented in Robbins, 'Political activities of Marvell', pp. 313-15; and George de F. Lord, 'Comments on the canonical caveat', in *Evidence for Authorship*, ed. D. V. Erdman and E. G. Fogel (New York, 1967), pp. 108-9.

56. Haley, *Shaftesbury*, pp. 401-2, 412-19, makes the important point that the dissolution of Parliament was not the agreed policy of the Country Party in general but the policy of Shaftesbury and his closest allies; many of the leading members of the opposition in the House of Commons distrusted Shaftesbury and opposed dissolution. Cf. also Robbins, 'Political activities of Marvell', pp. 214-19, 407.

57. For an interesting discussion of the ideology of *The Growth of Popery*, especially its stress on independence, see Pocock, 'Machiavelli, Harrington, and English political ideologies in the eighteenth century', pp. 564-6. On several occasions the opposition introduced place bills,

disabling all holders of governmental 'office or place of profit' from membership in Parliament; see J. H. Plumb, *The Origins of Political Stability, England 1675–1725* (London, 1967), p. 58.

58. Sonnet xv ('Great men have been among us'), lines 3–4, in *The Poetical Works of William Wordsworth*, ed. Thomas Hutchinson and Ernest De Selincourt (London, 1950); John Adams, *Thoughts on Government* (Philadelphia, 1776), p. 7, quoted in Bernard Bailyn, *The Ideological Origins of the American Revolution* (Cambridge, Mass., 1967), p. 45. The political writings of these figures and their influence on radical and republican thought in the eighteenth century are discussed in Robbins, *The Eighteenth-Century Commonwealthsman*, pp. 22–67, and in Fink, *The Classical Republicans*, pp. 52–169.

59. Wallace, *Destiny*, pp. 6–7, 67.

60. *Ibid.*, p. 68.

4. CHRISTIAN LIBERTY

1. Roger Manwaring, *Religion and Allegiance* (London, 1627), p. 10.

2. 'Of Reformation in England', *CPW*, I, 520. Marvell's accusations against Parker and the Laudian clergy in *The Rehearsal Transpros'd* and *Mr. Smirke* are close in tone and substance to those found in Milton's anti-prelatical pamphlets of 1641–2.

3. *CPW*, III, 198–9. Locke is notoriously inconsistent in his treatment of the state of nature, but he never identifies the state with the biblical story of Adam and Eve. John Dunn, in *The Political Thought of John Locke* (Cambridge, 1969), argues that Locke's political theory implicitly depends upon a theological position essentially similar to that of Milton; but even if we grant Dunn's thesis that unstated religious premises lie behind much of Locke's thought, the terms of Locke's argument remain almost entirely secular (in Dunn's terms 'dechristianized') and the fall received little emphasis in his writing.

4. Robert Frost, 'The Oven Bird', line 14, in *Complete Poems of Robert Frost* (New York, 1949).

5. *RT*, II, p. 226. Marvell is quoting Parker's *Discourse of Ecclesiastical Politie* (London, 1669), p. 317.

6. *RT*, editor's introduction, p. xvii.

7. Cf. *Paradise Lost*, IX, lines 1127–31; Sidney, in *A Defence of Poetry*, writes that one consequence of 'that first accursed fall of Adam' is that 'our erected wit maketh us know what perfection is, and yet our infected will keepeth us from reaching unto it' (*Miscellaneous Prose*, ed. Katherine Duncan-Jones and Jan Van Dorsten (Oxford, 1973), p. 79).

8. See 'Upon his Majesties being made free of the Citty', lines 35, 44–8.

9. 'His Majesty's Most Gracious Speech to both Houses of Parliament',

in Bradbrook and Lloyd Thomas, *Andrew Marvell*, p. 125. In a later passage, the monarch is represented as praising his own 'Zeal' in converting his 'Natural Sons from Popery': 'It was my owne Worke, and so much the more peculiar than the begetting of them. It would do Your Heart good to hear how prettily little George can read in the Psalter. They are all fine Children, God bless 'em, and so like me in their Understandings' (*ibid.*, pp. 126–7).

10. Locke, *Two Treatises of Government*, II, ch. vi, par. 61; vii, par. 90, 93. Locke expresses a similar view of a child as potentially a rational creature yet needing to 'grow up to the Use of Reason' in *Some Thoughts Concerning Education* (London, 1693), pp. 37–43: 'The Difference lies not in the having or not having Appetites, but in the Power to govern and deny our selves in them.'

11. The identification of Louis XIV with Hobbesian absolutist doctrine is common in Country Party satires, e.g., 'Britannia and Raleigh', lines 25–118. The Latin epigrams in praise of Louis XIV which Marvell submitted in a competition in 1671 do not of course reflect his opinion of the monarch.

12. Cf. *Leviathan*, XXIV, pp. 161–2.

13. *Leviathan*, XXI, p. 143; Parker, *Discourse of Ecclesiastical Politie*, p. 27.

14. Sir Robert Filmer, *Patriarcha* (London, 1680), p. 100; Locke, *Two Treatises of Government*, II, ch. xviii, par. 199. 202. Cf. Hobbes, *Leviathan*, XXIX, p. 212.

15. Marchamont Nedham, *The Case of the Common-Wealth of England, Stated* (London, 1650), p. 43; *The Excellencie of a Free-State* (London, 1656), pp. 45–6. A similar view of 'ambition and lust of power above the law' as 'predominant passions in the breasts of most men' is common in political writing of the seventeenth and eighteenth centuries; see Bailyn, *Ideological Origins of the American Revolution*, pp. 60–1.

16. James Harrington, *The Commonwealth of Oceana*, p. 11; for parallel statements, cf. Halifax, *Complete Works*, pp. 54, 56; and Aristotle, *Politics*, III, 16.

17. Milton, *Tenure of Kings and Magistrates*, CPW, III, 199–200.

18. Parker, *Discourse*, p. 145. According to Hobbes, 'the virtue of a subject is comprehended solely in obedience to the laws of the commonwealth...In sum, all actions and habits are to be esteemed good or evil by their...usefulness in reference to the commonwealth' (*Behemoth*, ed. Ferdinand Tönnies (London, 1889), pp. 44–5).

19. Parker, *Discourse*, pp. 14, 33–4, 141.

20. *Ibid.*, pp. 4, 5, 7, 300. Hobbes makes a similar case against conscience in *Leviathan*, singling out the belief in the sanctity of conscience as one of the false doctrines which weaken the commonwealth or tend to its dissolution; cf. *Leviathan*, XXIX, p. 211.

21. Parker, like Filmer, rejects the Hobbesian idea of a social contract and sees the origin of government as patriarchal (*Discourse*, pp. 29-31). But the differing theoretical accounts of the origins of authority do not affect their basic agreement as to the need for absolute authority in the state. Cf. Filmer, Preface to 'Observations Concerning the Original of Government, Upon Mr. Hobs his Leviathan', in *Political Discourses* (London, 1680), Sig. N2: 'With no small Content I read Mr. Hob's Book *De Cive*, and his *Leviathan*, about the Rights of Sovereignty, which no man, that I know, hath so amply and judiciously handled: I consent with him about the Rights of *exercising* Government, but I cannot agree to his means of *acquiring* it.'

22. *RT*, II, p. 227: 'Some, for the attainment of [Publick Peace and Tranquillity], hold it to be Necessary that Subjects should have no Arms, others that they should have no Wealth, no Propriety, and a third that they should have no Understanding, no Learning, nor Letters.' Cf. also *RT*, II, pp. 229-31.

23. *Areopagitica*, in Milton, *CPW*, II, 514-15; 'Resolved Soul', lines 23-4.

24. Parker, *Discourse*, p. 71; *RT*, I, p. 23; 'Resolved Soul', lines 55-6. Cf. *Discourse*, pp. 71, 75-6: 'All Religion must of necessity be resolv'd into Enthusiasm or Morality. The former is meer Imposture, and therefore all that is true must be reduced to the latter...But when we have set aside all manner of Vertue, let them tell me what remains to be call'd Grace, and give me any Notion of it distinct from all Morality,'

25. Parker, like Filmer, argued from patriarchal authority that 'no man could be born into the World without being subject to some Superiour: every Father being by Nature Vested with a Right to govern his Children' (*Discourse*, p. 29; cf. Filmer, *Patriarcha*, p. 12; and *Directions for Obedience to Government in Dangerous or Doubtful Times*, in *Political Discourses*, pp. 65-8, Sig. M3-M4^v). In Hobbes's view, men born into society are bound by the terms of a social contract entered into by their ancestors, and no man can be free of these bonds unless the commonwealth of which he is a member is dissolved (*Leviathan*, XVII, pp. 113-14; XXIX, p. 218).

26. Norman Cohn, *The Pursuit of the Millennium* (London, 1957), pp. 187-8. For a more sympathetic view of the doctrines of the seventeenth-century Ranters, see Christopher Hill, *The World Turned Upside Down* (Harmondsworth, 1975), pp. 197-230.

27. Parker accepts the 'Hobbist' view that the usefulness of religion in keeping the common people in place is independent of its truth or falsity: 'If our Religion were nothing else but...the Belief of Tales publickly allowed, and the Priesthood only a Succession of Cheats and Juglers; yet after all this, they are and must be allowed necessary Instruments in the State to awe the common People into fear and

Obedience, because nothing else can so effectually enslave them as the dread of invisible Powers, and the dismal Apprehension of the World to come' (*Bishop Bramhall's Vindication* (London, 1672), Sig. e2ᵛ–e3).

28. *RT*, I, p. 49. On censorship and the sedition laws, see Christopher Hill's review of Wallace's '*Destiny His Choice*', in *English Historical Review*, 84 (1969), 613; and Hugh Macdonald, 'The law and defamatory biographies in the seventeenth century', *Review of English Studies*, 20 (1944), 177–98.

29. On the hostility of the Puritan left to the clergy as a separate entity, see Hill, *The World Turned Upside Down*, pp. 102–6, 298–9.

30. Dryden, *Poems*, I, 215–16.

31. *A Supplement to Burnet's History of my Own Time*, ed. H. C. Foxcroft (Oxford, 1902), p. 216; cf. Legouis, *Andrew Marvell*, p. 201.

32. *A Common-place Book Out of the Rehearsal Transpros'd* (London, 1673), pp. 12, 48; [Richard Leigh], *The Transproser Rehears'd* (Oxford, 1673), pp. 34, 46–7. See also Edmund Hickeringill, *Gregory, Father-Greybread, With his Vizard off* (London, 1673), pp. 17, 38, 275; and Samuel Parker, *A Reproof to the Rehearsal Transpros'd* (London, 1673), pp. 1–2, 250–2, 274–5. Elsie Duncan-Jones has pointed out to me that Richard Leigh's accusations of sodomy in *The Transproser Rehears'd* take a hint from a couplet in *RT*, I, p. 121, which, if obscene, is characteristically witty rather than brutal.

33. See Douglas R. Lacey, *Dissent and Parliamentary Politics in England, 1661–1689* (New Brunswick, 1969), pp. 59, 287, 307; see also *The Diary of John Milward*, ed. Caroline Robbins (Cambridge, 1938), pp. 225, 238, 282.

34. *RT*, I, pp. 79, 83; see also *RT*, II, pp. 295–6, 303–5, 325; and *Mr. Smirke*, p. 41.

35. Thomas Birch, 'The life of Dr. John Tillotson', in *John Tillotson, Works* (3 vols., London, 1752), I, cxvii.

36. *Poems and Letters*, ed. Margoliouth, II, 347; [Edward Pearse], *The Conformist's Plea for the Nonconformists*, 3rd edn (London, 1683), p. 2; Louis G. Locke, *Tillotson, Anglistica* IV (1954), 79.

37. John Davenant, *An Exhortation to Brotherly Communion betwixt the Protestant Churches* (London, 1641), p. 12; William Chillingworth, *The Religion of Protestants a Safe Way to Salvation*, 3rd edn (London, 1664), ch. iv, par. 81, p. 161.

38. Hales, *A Tract Concerning Schism, Works* (3 vols., Glasgow, 1768), I, 114–15. Marvell quotes the passage in part in *RT*, I, p. 79.

39. Hales, *A Tract, Works*, I, 118. Cf. Herbert Croft, *The Naked Truth* (London, 1675), Preface, Sig. A3ʳ–A3ᵛ; and Pearse, *The Conformist's Plea for the Nonconformists*, pp. 52–5.

40. Locke, *Two Treatises of Government*, II, ch. xix, par. 226.

41. See, e.g., among Anglicans, Jeremy Taylor, *A Discourse of the Liberty*

of Prophesying (London, 1647), pp. 199–200; and Croft, *The Naked Truth*, pp. 2–3; and among Puritans, William Walwyn, *The Compassionate Samaritane* (1644), and Henry Robinson, *Liberty of Conscience* (1644).

42. Hales, 'Of Enquiry and Private Judgment in Religion', *Works*, III, pp. 156, 162.

43. Chillingworth, *Religion of Protestants*, ch. ii, par. 113, pp. 85–6. Cf. Milton, *Areopagitica*, *CPW*, II, 543.

44. Pierre Des Maizeaux, *An Historical and Critical Account of the Life and Writings of William Chillingworth* (London, 1725), p. 372.

45. Joseph Glanvill, *Essays on Several Important Subjects in Philosophy and Religion* (London, 1676), p. 17.

46. Lucius Cary, Viscount Falkland, *Discourse of Infallibility, with an Answer to it: And his Lordships Reply* (London, 1651), p. 119. Chillingworth, *Religion of Protestants*, Preface, par. 12, Sig. B4ᵛ.

47. Glanvill, 'Anti-fanatical religion and free philosophy', *Essays*, pp. 17–19.

48. Samuel Parker, *A Free and Impartial Censure of the Platonick Philosophie* (Oxford, 1666), pp. 73–4; *Discourse*, pp. 74–6.

49. For the latitudinarian attitude toward good works and toward election, see Hales, 'Of Dealing with Erring Christians', *Golden Remains, of the Ever Memorable Mr. John Hales*, 2nd edn (London, 1673), p. 37; Des Maizeaux, *Historical Account of Chillingworth*, p. 81; Louis G. Locke, *Tillotson*, pp. 95–8.

50. *Remarks upon a late Disingenuous Discourse* (London, 1678), p. 3. Owen in his answer to Parker argued similarly that to speak of religion 'since the fall of Adam without respect unto sin, is to build Castles in the air. All the religion that God now requires, prescribes, accepts, that is or can be, is the Religion of *Sinners*' (*Truth and Innocence Vindicated* (London, 1669), p. 208).

51. Croft, *The Naked Truth*, pp. 15–16. The latitudinarian argument that ceremonies were 'things indifferent' suggests how distinct the latitudinarian and Puritan positions on Christian liberty were, since the heart of the authoritarian case was that 'indifferent' matters, not specifically mentioned in Scripture, could safely be left to the discretion of the central state or church authority. For an excellent guide through the thickets of Puritan and 'Arminian' theology, see John S. Coolidge, *The Pauline Renaissance in England: Puritanism and the Bible* (Oxford, 1970).

52. For a similar attack on Roman Catholic ceremonies, cf. *Growth of Popery*, p. 6.

53. Croft, *The Naked Truth*, p. 16. Hales's ecumenical instincts extended to Roman Catholics, who could in his view 'joyn with us in those *Prayers* and holy *Ceremonies*, which are common to them and us'

('Of dealing with Erring Christians', *Golden Remains*, p. 53). Marvell's opposition to any schemes of 'reconciling all the Churches to one Doctrine and Communion', especially to any theoretical reunion with Rome, is evident in *RT*, I, p. 15.

54. Tillotson, *Works*, I, 175. The basic conservatism of the latitudinarian policy of comprehension finds striking expression in the writings of Edward Stillingfleet, who in *Irenicum* (London, 1661) can urge a comprehensive church settlement uniting Anglicans and Presbyterians in a single communion, while at the same time attacking 'a liberty of all opinions' as leading inevitably to 'the subverting a Nations peace', and two decades later, in *The Mischief of Separation* (London, 1680), inveighs against conscientious dissent no less violently than Parker. The disagreements between advocates of comprehension and toleration are discussed in Norman Sykes, *From Sheldon to Secker* (Cambridge, 1959), pp. 78–82.

55. John Locke, *A Letter Concerning Toleration*, tr. William Popple (London, 1689), 'To the Reader', Sig. A3ᵛ, A4ʳ.

56. Roger Williams, *The Bloudy Tenent, of Persecution, for cause of Conscience, discussed* (London, 1644), Sig. a2ᵛ–a3ʳ; Locke, *Letter Concerning Toleration*, p. 47. Cf. Milton, *Treatise of Civil Power*, in *CPW*, VII, 256. For Marvell's position, see *Growth of Popery*, pp. 5–14.

57. Thomas Belford, *An Examination of the Chief Points of Antinomianism* (London, 1647), p. 77.

58. *Anti-Toleration, or a Modest Defence of the Letter of the London Ministers to the Reverend Assembly of Divines* (London, 1646), pp. 11–12, 14, 19, 27, 29. Cf. Woodhouse, ed., *Puritanism and Liberty*, introduction, pp. 51–3, 59–70.

59. 'On the new forcers of Conscience under the Long Parliament', line 6.

60. *Treatise of Civil Power*, *CPW*, VII, 271; *Anti-Toleration*, p. 27; Joshua Sprigge, in Whitehall Debates, 14 December 1648, in Woodhouse, ed., *Puritanism and Liberty*, p. 145.

61. *Areopagitica*, *CPW*, II, 514, 563; Robinson, *Liberty of Conscience*, in William Haller, ed., *Tracts on Liberty in The Puritan Revolution* (3 vols., New York, 1934), III, 172, 175.

62. Owen, *Sermon...With a Discourse upon Toleration* (London, 1649), p. 70. The commonplace that kings should be 'nursing fathers' to religion derives from Isaiah 49: 23.

63. Woodhouse, ed., *Puritanism and Liberty*, introduction, p. 58; cf. Woodhouse, 'The argument of Milton's *Comus*', *University of Toronto Quarterly*, 11 (1941), 46–71.

64. Williams, *The Bloudy Tenent*, p. 105.

65. Williams, *The Bloudy Tenent*, p. 70.

66. *CPW*, VII, 257, 258, 270.

67. Robinson, *Liberty of Conscience*, in Haller, ed., *Tracts on Liberty*, III, 119, 143; Walwyn, *The Power of Love*, ibid., II, 277.
68. Marvell was a layman, like many writers of the Puritan left – Robinson, Walwyn, Milton, and others.
69. Woodhouse, ed., *Puritanism and Liberty*, p. 168; further relevant passages may be found in *ibid.*, pp. 152–69. See Woodhouse's excellent discussion of the points at issue in *ibid.*, introduction, pp. 65–7.
70. *Treatise of Civil Power, CPW*, VII, p. 260; John Goodwin in Whitehall debates, Woodhouse, ed., *Puritanism and Liberty*, p. 157.
71. *Walwyn's Just Defense*, in William Haller and Godfrey Davies, eds., *The Leveller Tracts 1647–1653* (New York, 1944), p. 372.
72. Robinson, *Liberty of Conscience*, in Haller, ed., *Tracts on Liberty*, III, 177; Walwyn, *The Compassionate Samaritane, ibid.*, III, 81, Williams, *The Bloudy Tenent*, p. 201.
73. Williams, *The Bloudy Tenent*, p. 201.
74. A similar position is upheld by Walwyn in *A Whisper in the Eare of Mr. Thomas Edwards*: 'I do conceive it more safe for them, and more for the quiet of the people, that they be freed from all other employments, except preaching and administering the publick worship of God' (Haller, ed., *Tracts on Liberty*, III, 327).
75. Milton, *Of Education, CPW*, II, 366–7.
76. Milton, *De Doctrina Christiana*, I, viii, ed. Maurice Kelley, tr. John Carey, in *CPW*, VI, 326. For the tendency in advanced radical circles in the 1640s to reject 'orthodox and traditional dogmas of original-sin', see Hill, *The World Turned Upside Down*, pp. 162–9.
77. Cf. Milton, *De Doctrina Christiana*, I, iii and iv, in *CPW*, VI, 163–5, 182–3; and *Paradise Lost*, III, lines 111–25.
78. Milton and Goodwin redefine predestination in non-Calvinist terms as general and conditional rather than particular: the elect are those who by the grace of God believe and persevere in their faith. Cf. *Paradise Lost*, III, lines 185–202; and *De Doctrina Christiana*, I, iv, in *CPW*, VI, 176–7, 189. As Goodwin says, this position is in accordance with Lutheran rather than Calvinist doctrine, and emphasizes God's love and mercy, instead of His arbitrary will: see *Truths Conflict with Error* (London, 1650), pp. 110, 113; and *Redemption Redeemed* (London, 1651), pp. 68–9.
79. John Creaser, 'Marvell's Effortless Superiority', *Essays in Criticism*, 20 (1970), 408.
80. Some of the tensions implicit in the Puritan doctrine of conscience are explored in Hill, *The World Turned Upside Down*, esp. pp. 152–5, 171–3, 190–2, 370–3.
81. Milton's emphasis on the temptation of despair in *Samson Agonistes* is often interpreted as a direct response to the failure of the Puritan revolution; see, e.g., James H. Hanford, '*Samson Agonistes* and Milton

in old age', *Studies in Shakespeare, Milton, and Donne* (New York, 1925), pp. 167–89; and M. A. N. Radzinowicz, '*Samson Agonistes* and Milton the politician in defeat', *Philological Quarterly*, 44 (1965), 454–71.

82. *Poems and Letters*, ed. Margoliouth, II, pp. 315, 317.

83. *Poems and Letters*, ed. Margoliouth, II, p. 312.

5. MARVELL'S SATIRES: THE SEARCH FOR FORM

1. All quotations from 'The Loyal Scot' are from *Andrew Marvell, The Complete Poems*, ed. Donno.

2. Samuel Parker, *A Free and Impartial Censure of the Platonick Philosophie* (Oxford, 1666), p. 75. Parker's attacks on 'rampant Metaphors, and Pompous Allegories, and other splendid but empty Schemes of speech...frenzies of a bold and ungovern'd Imagination' (p. 73) have often been cited to illustrate the influence of Baconian ideals of science and rationality on seventeenth-century prose style, e.g., in R. F. Jones, 'Science and English prose style in the third quarter of the seventeenth century'. *The Seventeenth Century* (Stanford, 1951), pp. 101–2.

3. See T. S. Eliot, *Selected Essays* (New York, 1950), pp. 251–2.

4. 'Mixt Wit', according to Addison, is particularly characteristic of 'Epigram, or those little occasional Poems that in their own Nature are nothing else but a Tissue of Epigrams', *Spectator*, no. 62, in *The Spectator*, ed. Donald F. Bond (5 vols., Oxford, 1965).

5. J. B. Leishman, *The Art of Marvell's Poetry* (London, 1966), pp. 86–91; cf. Hugh Richmond, 'The fate of Edmund Waller', *South Atlantic Quarterly*, 60 (1961), 230–8. The titles quoted are from poems by Lovelace and Carew.

6. Legouis, *Andrew Marvell*, p. 168.

7. See Joseph Hall, *The Arte of Divine Meditation* (London, 1607), pp. 10–11. Contemporary theories of occasional meditation emphasize the variousness of nature more than any readily recognizable pattern: 'God hath not straited us for matter, having given us the scope of the whole world; so that there is no creature, event, action, speech, which may not afford us new matter of Meditation. And that which we are wont to say of fine wittes, we may as truly affirme of the Christian hart; that it can make use of any thing' (*ibid.*, pp. 19–20).

8. Edward W. Rosenheim, Jr, *Swift and the Satirist's Art* (Chicago, 1963), p. 13.

9. Accounts of the psychology of laughter by Hobbes and Freud suggest that satire gains its reader's assent through the assertion of power implicit in inflicting pain or disgrace on another. 'Wit permits us to make our enemy ridiculous through that which we could not utter

loudly or consciously on account of existing hindrances; in other words, *wit affords us the means of surmounting restrictions and of opening up otherwise inaccessible pleasure sources*. Moreover, the listener will be induced by the gain in pleasure to take our part, even if he is not altogether convinced', *Wit and Its Relation to the Unconscious, The Basic Writings of Sigmund Freud*, tr. A. A. Brill (New York, 1938), p. 698. See also Hobbes, *Leviathan*, VI, p. 36. '*Sudden glory*, is the passion which maketh those *grimaces* called LAUGHTER; and is caused either by some sudden act of their own, that pleaseth them; or by the apprehension of some deformed thing in another, by comparison whereof they suddenly applaud themselves.'

10. Dryden, 'Discourse concerning satire', *Essays*, II, p. 122.

11. Pope, *The First Satire of the Second Book of Horace*, line 121.

12. Juvenal, Satire I, line 30.

13. For a similar statement by Milton, see *An Apology against a Pamphlet*, *CPW*, I, 871.

14. Jonathan Swift, *Tale of a Tub*, ed. A. C. Guthkelch and D. Nichol Smith, 2nd edn (Oxford, 1958), p. 52; *Battle of the Books*, in *ibid.*, p. 215.

15. John Cleveland, *A Character of a Diurnal-Maker* (London, 1654), pp. 6–8; 'Smectymnuus, or the Club-Divines', lines 49–58, in *Poems of John Cleveland*, ed. Brian Morris and Eleanor Withington (Oxford, 1967).

16. Richard Aldington, ed., *A Book of Characters* (London, [1924]), p. 167.

17. Cf. 'Upon Appleton House', lines 21–4; *RT*, II, p. 239.

18. See Aristotle, *Rhetoric*, I, 9, tr. W. Rhys Roberts, in *The Basic Works of Aristotle*, ed. Richard McKeon (New York, 1941), pp. 1356–7, 1359.

19. Aristotle, *Rhetoric*, I, 2, p. 1329.

20. Pope, 'A Letter to the Publisher', *Poems*, p. 322. Cf. 'Martinus Scriblerus, of the Poem' (*Dunciad Variorum*, 1729), *ibid.*, pp. 344–5; and Swift, 'Verses on the Death of Dr. Swift', in *Poetical Works*, ed. Herbert Davis (London, 1967), lines 463–70.

21. Milton, *Areopagitica*, *CPW*, II, 514–16; Pope, notes to *Dunciad Variorum*, p. 381.

22. E. E. Duncan-Jones, 'A great master of words', Warton Lecture on English Poetry (1975), pp. 11–13.

23. 'Satyre IV', lines 1–8, in *John Donne, The Satires, Epigrams and Verse Letters*, ed. W. Milgate (Oxford, 1967).

24. Mary Claire Randolph, 'The structural design of the formal verse satire', *Philological Quarterly*, 21 (1942), 368–84. Cf. Dryden, *Essays*, II, 144.

25. See Alvin P. Kernan, *The Cankered Muse* (New Haven, 1959), pp. 30–4; and *The Plot of Satire* (New Haven, 1966), pp. 99–104; and Patricia Meyer Spacks, 'Some reflections on satire', *Genre*, I (1968),

13-20. According to Spacks, the essence of satire is the feeling of uneasiness it creates in its audience; it works by raising emotions and leaving them unpurged – a process which she compares to the Brechtian alienation-effect.

26. Dryden, *Essays*, II, 145-6. Randolph's conception of formal satire as bipartite' is indebted to Dryden, who in turn draws on Isaac Casaubon's *De Satyrica Graecorum Poesi et Romanorum Satira* (1605); see Randolph, 'Structural design', pp. 369, 380-3.

27. Dryden, *Essays*, II, 126; Pope, *The First Satire of the Second Book of Horace*, line 117; R. A. Brower, *Alexander Pope: The Poetry of Allusion* (London, 1959), p. 11. Brower, who does not discuss 'Tom May's Death' or 'Fleckno', contrasts Dryden and Marvell in this respect, characterizing Marvell's post-Restoration satires as 'parochial', lacking in the 'breadth of vision' of Dryden's satires.

28. 'Apologeticall Dialogue, To the Reader', lines 101-7, *Poetaster*, in *Ben Jonson*, ed. C. H. Herford, Percy and E. M. Simpson (11 vols., Oxford, 1925-52), IV, 320; 'Tom May's Death', line 44. Lines 33-6 of 'Tom May's Death' may specifically allude to the action of *Poetaster*, in which the figure of Horace was generally taken to represent Jonson himself. The best discussion of the role of Jonson in 'Tom May's Death', though it makes no mention of *Poetaster*, is Christine Rees, ' "Tom May's Death" and Ben Jonson's Ghost: a study of Marvell's satiric method', *Modern Language Review*, 71 (July 1976), 481-8.

29. Rees cites Jonson's Preface to *Volpone* as stating the ethical position on which 'Tom May's Death' is based: 'the impossibility of any mans being the good Poet, without first being a good man' (Rees, ' "Tom May's Death" ', p. 484; *Ben Jonson*, ed. Herford and Simpson, V, 17). Cf. Milton, *An Apology against a Pamphlet*, CPW, I, 874: 'How he should be truly eloquent who is not withall a good man, I see not.'

30. *The History of the Parliament* (London, 1647), Preface, Sig. A3.

31. The arguments of Lord (*Complete Poems*, pp. xxx-ii) that 'Tom May's Death' is inauthentic are discussed in the Appendix.

32. Cf. Legouis, *Andrew Marvell*, p. 91; Margoliouth, I, 303-4; and Rees, ' "Tom May's Death" ', p. 485. The elegy on Villiers is indeed royalist – a fire-eating, abusive statement by a violent partisan, eager to go into battle and kill roundheads – but the evidence linking it to Marvell is extremely slim, an unsubstantiated MS. attribution dating from at least forty years after the poem's anonymous publication. Though George Clarke (1660-1736), who attributed the poem to Marvell, was a reliable witness to poems by authors personally known to him (see *Poems and Letters*, ed. Margoliouth, I, 432-5), he is not likely to have privileged information about a poem written twelve years before his birth. The poem claims to be written by a member of the royalist army; it begins with a contemptuous attack on noncombatants (such as

Marvell himself, who spent the years 1642–6 travelling on the continent) and ends with a call to stack up a 'Pyramid / Of Vulgar bodies' in 'just vengeance' (lines 116–17, 127). Marvell's authorship is thus highly improbable.

33. Attempts to reconcile 'Tom May's Death' with the 'Horatian Ode' include Duncan-Jones, 'A great master of words', pp. 20–1; and John S. Coolidge, 'Marvell and Horace', *Modern Philology*, 63 (1965), 111–20.

34. This position is argued in Rees, ' "Tom May's Death" ', pp. 487–8; cf. *RT*, I, pp. 124–35.

35. *History of the Parliament*, pp. 30–1. Brutus is presented in similar terms in the *Pharsalia*; in the dedication to Book II, May characterizes that book as 'the deathlesse Monument / Of *Brutus* worth, and sacred *Catoes* praise', remarking on the need for 'such an one, / Free from ambition, free from faction', in 'our age'. See *Lucan's Pharsalia... Englished by Thomas May, Esquire* (London, 1627), Sig. B6.

36. Margoliouth points out the parallel in *Poems and Letters*, I, 305.

37. *Lucan's Pharsalia*, Book IX, Sig. Q3^v, Q6^v–Q7^v.

38. *Athenae Oxoniensis*, quoted in *RT*, editor's introduction, p. xiv. Cf. Gilbert Burnet's tribute to Marvell's success with 'all the men of wit... from the King down to the tradesman', *History of My Own Times*, ed. O. Airy (2 vols., Oxford, 1897), I, 467–8; cf. *Supplement to Burnet's History*, ed. Foxcroft, p. 216.

39. 'Tunbridge-Wells', lines 64–9, in *Poems by John Wilmot, Earl of Rochester*, ed. Vivian de Sola Pinto (Cambridge, Mass., 1953); *A Tale of a Tub*, p. 10.

40. 'The ironic tradition in Augustan poetry from Swift to Johnson', in *Focus: Swift*, ed. C. J. Rawson (London, 1971), p. 218.

41. Bradbrook and Lloyd Thomas, *Andrew Marvell*, p. 93. See also Hugh Macdonald, 'Banter in English controversial prose after the Restoration', *Essays and Studies by Members of the English Association*, 32 (1946), 21–34; and Ronald Paulson, *Theme and Structure in Swift's Tale of a Tub* (New Haven, 1960).

42. *Animadversions*, *CPW*, I, 662–4; *An Apology against a Pamphlet*, *CPW*, I, 872.

43. *Animadversions*, *CPW*, I, 718, 720, 726; *An Apology against a Pamphlet*, *CPW*, I, 895, 899–901; *RT*, II, pp. 263, 309.

44. Quotation and refutation, with satiric comments, make up the last section of the royalist *Mercurius Aulicus* and nearly all the contents of the parliamentary *Mercurius Britanicus* in each issue. Both claim to be written in the service of truth, and accuse the other of deliberate falsehood. There is a good detailed account of the pamphlet warfare of *Aulicus* and *Britanicus*, with numerous quotations, in Joseph Frank, *The Beginnings of the English Newspaper 1620–1660* (Cambridge,

Mass., 1961); see also P. W. Thomas, *Sir John Berkenhead 1617–1679: A Royalist Career in Politics and Polemics* (Oxford, 1969).

45. 'Popilius' refers to the method of formal debate, with 'Antiochus' and 'Popilius' as first speaker and respondent; see *ibid.*, p. 20.

46. Charles Sackville, Lord Buckhurst, 'On Mr. Edward Howard upon his British Princes', line 23, in *POAS*, ed. Lord, p. 339.

47. *An Epitome*, Sig. a 1, Sig. E 3, in *The Marprelate Tracts* (Scholar Press, 1970). See John S. Coolidge, 'Martin Marprelate, Marvell, and *Decorum Personae* as a satirical theme', *PMLA*, 74 (1959), 526–32.

48. *Mercurius Britanicus*, 69 (3–10 February, 1645), quoted in Frank, *The Beginnings of the English Newspaper*, p. 76. The general method of *Mercurius Aulicus* and *Mercurius Britanicus* is to assault the credibility and dignity of the opposing side in fairly direct and simple terms, as, e.g., in the tale of the flight of the roundhead Captain Fule in *Mercurius Aulicus*, 39 (25 Sept. 1643): 'The bold Captain leapt nimbly out of his bed, wrapt his red Coate about him, and in his Pantoffles (without a doublet) ran a full mile from the Towne, and as he ran over hedge and ditch, his Coate was pluckt from his shoulders by a Thorne (the Captaine thinking a Cavalier was at his back) and so held on his chace in his shirt, till he found a ditch (almost as deep as the *Saw-pit*) where he lay from seven in the morning till twelve at noone…We hope he may recover, else this melancholy kingdome will lose a great deale of laughing.'

49. Bradbrook and Lloyd Thomas, *Andrew Marvell*, p. 109. Cf. Isabel G. MacCaffrey, 'Some notes on Marvell's poetry, suggested by a reading of his prose', *Modern Philology*, 61 (1963), 261–9.

50. Colie, *My Ecchoing Song*, pp. 79, 101.

51. Cf. *Faerie Queene*, I. i. stanzas 20–6. On the role of medical imagery in the English satiric tradition, see Mary Claire Randolph, 'The medical concept in English Renaissance satiric theory: its possible relationships and implications', *Studies in Philology*, 38 (1941), 125–57; and Kranidas, *The Fierce Equation*, pp. 49–71.

52. Bradbrook and Lloyd Thomas, *Andrew Marvell*, p. 124.

53. For substantiation, see the more detailed discussion of 'The Loyal Scot' and 'The Kings Vowes' in the Appendix.

54. Joseph H. Summers, 'Andrew Marvell: private taste and public judgement', *Metaphysical Poetry*, ed. Palmer and Bradbury, p. 203.

55. Legouis, *Andrew Marvell*, p. 169.

56. See Earl Miner, 'The "Poetic Picture, Painted Poetry" of *The Last Instructions to a Painter*', in *Andrew Marvell: A Collection*, ed. Lord, pp. 165–74; Michael Gearin-Tosh, 'The structure of Marvell's "Last Instructions to a Painter"', *Essays in Criticism*, 22 (1972), 48–57; and David Farley-Hills, *The Benevolence of Laughter: Comic Poetry of the Commonwealth and Restoration* (London, 1974), pp. 72–98.

57. This is the central point of Christopher Hill's interesting interpretation of the poem in 'Society and Andrew Marvell', *Puritanism and Revolution*, pp. 337–66.
58. Dryden, Preface to *Absalom and Achitophel, Poems*, I, 216.
59. Dryden, Preface to *Annus Mirabilis, Essays*, I, 95. According to the Aristotelian criteria which Dryden recognizes in his prefatory remarks to *Annus Mirabilis*, both that poem and 'Last Instructions' are to be classified as 'historical poems': where the historian writing in prose or verse must attempt to record as accurately as possible what actually happened, the imaginative artist is ruled by the demands of probability and necessity within the work of art itself. See Aristotle, *Poetics*, IX.
60. 'On a Drop of Dew', line 1; 'The Picture of little T.C. in a Prospect of Flowers', line 1; 'The Gallery', line 1; 'Upon the Hill and Grove at Bill-borow', line 1; 'Damon the Mower', line 1; 'To his Coy Mistress', line 21; see also 'Mourning', lines 1–4.

APPENDIX.

MANUSCRIPT EVIDENCE FOR THE CANON OF MARVELL'S POEMS

1. Several of the emendations appear to have some authorial or other basis (stemming from MSS. in the compiler's possession, now lost), where others seem wholly arbitrary. For further discussion, see Hilton Kelliher, *Andrew Marvell Poet & Politician* (London, 1978), p. 63. The many corrections which eliminate elisions and modify spelling are unlikely to have any authorial warrant, and several variant readings introduced by the emendations (in 'Eyes and Tears', 'Fleckno', and 'To his Coy Mistress') are manifestly inferior to those in the uncorrected folio. No editor of Marvell is likely to follow Eng. poet. d. 49 in excising the last four lines of 'A Dialogue between the Soul and Body' and asserting the poem to be unfinished (*desunt multa*).
2. See Murray Lefkowitz, *William Lawes* (London, 1966), pp. 11, 203.
3. *Jonsonus Virbius* (London, 1638), pp. 60–1; *Coronae Carolinae Quadratura* (Oxford, 1636), Sig. b2–2ᵛ; *Musarum Oxoniensis Charisteria* (Oxford, 1638), Sig. Cl; *Flos Britannicus* (Oxford, 1638), unpaged; *Death Repeal'd by a Thankfull Memoriall Sent from Christ-Church in Oxford* (Oxford, 1638), pp. 39–40. Nothing is known of Ramsay after he left Oxford in 1639.
4. See George de F. Lord, 'Two new poems by Marvell?', and E. G. Fogel, 'Salmons in both', both in *Evidence for Authorship*, ed. Erdman and Fogel; *Poems and Letters*, ed. Margoliouth, I, 349; and Annabel Patterson, 'The second and third advices-to-the-painter', *Papers of the Bibliographical Society of America*, 71 (1977), 473–86.
5. The four MSS. which derive from *POAS* 1697 all contain fourteen

stanzas, arranged in the same order, and present a corrupt or heavily emended text; for a discussion of these MSS. and their common origin, see William J. Cameron, 'A late seventeenth-century scriptorium', *Renaissance and Modern Studies*, 7 (1963), 25–52.

6. In the 1669–70 version, the stanzas are in the following order (Margoliouth's numbering): 1, 2, 3, 4, 10, 9, 6, 7, 11, 13, 16. The order of these stanzas is changed in Eng. poet. d. 49 to accommodate the four additional stanzas: 1, 2, 3, 4, 5, 6, 7, 8, 10, 9, 11, 13, 14, 15, 16. Add. 34362 retains this order, except that 10 and 9 are reversed and 12 (the stanza on Coventry) is inserted; the four stanzas of 1675 are added as stanzas 17–20.

INDEX

Abbreviation used: M for Marvell

authoritarian theories of, 108–19;
as contractual in origin, 104, 118;
Commonwealth and Protectorate,
21–2, 49–55, 57–8, 59–60; M's
ideal of, 57, 62, 80–1, 106, 141;
a product of the fall of man, 104–5
Green Ribbon Club: 96
Grosart, A. B., editor of M: 63, 211

Hales, John: 123, 124, 125–6, 127,
128, 131, 230–2; quoted by M,
123, 126
Haley, K. D. H.: 93, 225, 226
Halifax, George Savile, 1st Marquess
of: 81–2, 95, 228
Hall, Joseph, Bishop of Exeter: 32,
123, 218–19, 234
Harrington, James: 2, 18, 53, 100–1,
109
Herbert, George: 35, 84
Hermetism: 38, 219
Hill, Christopher: 216, 221, 229,
230, 233
history, Renaissance theories of: 175
Hobbes, Thomas: 21, 80, 143, 195,
217; and authoritarian theory,
101, 104, 108–9, 110–12, 114–15,
116–19, 228–9; on laughter, 234–
5
Hoby, Sir Thomas: 68–9
Holland: Cromwell's policy towards,
56–7, 164–5, 220–1; M on Third
Dutch War (1672–4), 91–4, 225;
see also 'Character of Holland',
under Marvell, works of
Hopkins, Gerard Manley: 39
Horace: 154, 158, 166, 170–2, 236
Howe, John: 144
Hull, M as M.P. for: 63
Hyde, Anne, Duchess of York: 76,
202

iconoclasm: in M, 10–11, 83–6;
satire and, 11
Ignatius of Loyola, St: 33, 219
imagination (fancy): 24, 32–9, 58,
146, 152, 201–5, 219
Instrument of Government: 50, 52,
54, 59
Ireton, Henry: 49, 139
irony, in M: 18–19, 41, 141–3, 190–
4

James II (Duke of York): 65–6, 72,
91, 93, 95, 194, 225

Jonson, Ben: 3, 11, 175, 179–80, 236
Juvenal: 158, 159, 166, 179

Kelliher, Hilton: 207, 216, 239
Kenyon, J. P.: 49, 220, 221
Kermode, Frank: 154
Kranidas, Thomas: 217, 238

Lacey, D. R.: 230
latitudinarians: cited by M, 123,
230; M's agreement with, 124–6;
M's differences from, 129–32,
231–2
Laud, William, Archbishop of
Canterbury: 124, 130
Lauderdale, John Maitland, 1st Duke
of: 90
law: and reason, 109, 119; and will
of sovereign, 106–7, 108–9, 118,
213–14, 228; liberty only possible
under the rule of (M), 49, 109,
115, 116–17; Mosaic, abrogated by
the coming of Jesus (M), 139, 233;
separation of human and divine,
135–6; supremacy of, under
limited monarchy, 109–10
Legouis, Pierre: 155, 197, 223
Leishman, J. B.: 154, 155
L'Estrange, Roger: 96, 97, 226
Levellers: 48, 133, 138
Lewalski, Barbara: 218
libertarian (liberal) political theory:
100–1, 106–10, 115–19, 227, 228
libertarians, Puritan: 128, 129, 132–
41, 144–5, 233
liberty: 102–50; and order, 51, 59,
92, 105, 113, 132–5, 232; absolute
and limited, 20–1, 49, 52–3, 59,
106–10, 115–17; authoritarians
on, 218–19, 229; of conscience, see
under conscience; M reputation as
proponent of, 64, 221; and
Providential direction, 17, 18–19,
141–50
Locke, John: compared with M, 9–
10, 88, 101, 104, 113, 116–17,
126, 128, 227; on education, 228;
on reason and law, 107, 115, 117,
119, 228; on toleration, 132–3;
writings directed at absolutists,
101, 108, 113
Lord, George de F.: 206–11, 215,
216, 221–2, 226, 239
Louis XIV: 90–1, 93, 108, 228

15573

CHARTERHOUSE LIBRARY

015573